MY
BIG
FAT
QUEER
LIFE

The Best of

MICHAEL THOMAS FORD

Manufactured in the United States of America.

This trade paperback original is published by Alyson Publications,
P.O. Box 4371, Los Angeles, California 90078-4371.
Distribution in the United Kingdom by
Turnaround Publisher Services Ltd.,
Unit 3, Olympia Trading Estate, Coburg Road, Wood Green,
London N22 6TZ England.

First edition: September 2003

03 04 05 06 07 a 10 9 8 7 6 5 4 3 2 1

ISBN 1-55583-574-0

Library of Congress Cataloging-in-Publication Data
Ford, Michael Thomas
My big fat queer life : the best of Michael Thomas Ford.—1st ed.
ISBN 1-55583-574-0
1. Homosexuality—Humor. 2. Gay men—Humor. 3. Gay wit and humor. I. Title.
PN6231.H57F678 2003
814'.54—dc21 2003052479

Credits
Cover photography by Chaloner Woods.
Cover design by Matt Sams.

Contents

Introduction

I'm sitting at my desk surrounded by a pile of greatest hits CDs. I've always found music to be inspiring, and these are supposed to be giving me some help. Unfortunately, they're having the opposite effect of what I'd hoped for. The idea was that in looking at other people's best-of collections I'd be given some direction for how to put my own together. Instead, I'm reminded of how much I generally don't like best-of collections.

The problem is that, too often, greatest hits collections disappoint. Sometimes it's because along with old favorites they contain a lot of material that really isn't all that great. Take *Timespace: The Best of Stevie Nicks.* I could listen to "Stand Back" over and over. But why does she persist on trying to convince us that "Whole Lotta Trouble" is a good song?

Just as frustrating as the inclusion of tepid material is the omission of material that deserves to be there. How could Cyndi Lauper be so cruel as to leave her brilliant and impossible-to-find ditty "Hole in My Heart (All the Way to China)" from the *Vibes* soundtrack off her *12 Deadly Cyns* collection? Why, oh why, isn't "Say You Don't Know Me" on any of the numerous Kim Carnes collections? And worst of all, why did I have to buy the otherwise wretched *Come Upstairs* because no one has been smart enough to put Carly

Simon's "Jesse" on a best-of collection? It's just not right.

Even worse are best-of collections that make you realize that bands you always thought were so great really only had a handful of songs worth hearing. The first concert I ever went to was by the Go-Go's, and I hold a special place in my heart for the dysfunctional, over-mascaraed quintet. But take a listen to their best-of CD and you realize that apart from "We Got the Beat," "Vacation," "Head Over Heels," and "Our Lips Are Sealed," you pretty much hit the skip button a lot. The same goes for other bands I once thought churned out unforgettable hit after unforgettable hit: Missing Persons, Bananarama, the Thompson Twins. Perhaps I should have known better, but I'm still let down.

Some artists try to break the traditional best-of mold by presenting their material in unusual ways. The charming Mary Chapin Carpenter, for example, on *Party Doll and Other Favorites*, delivers a number of her best songs in live versions. Indeed, Chapin is extraordinary when heard live, and this is a nice thought. But that's what live albums are for. As it is, this mix of original versions and live offerings falls flat because it tries to be two things at once.

Then again, some best-of discs are pure magic, collections of shimmering stars that light up the night play after play. As I write this I'm listening to Joan Armatrading's best-of CD, a perfect constellation of well-written songs that never fails to make me happy. And there are others: the punk-to-New Wave joy of the Motels' *No Vacancy*, Joni Mitchell's *Misses* (better, ironically, than its partner, *Hits*), the Pretenders' *Singles*, Jann Arden's *Greatest Hurts*, Matraca Berg's *Lying to the Moon and Other Stories*, the Rolling Stones' *40 Licks*, and Cris Williamson's absolutely brilliant best-of. If you don't own any of these, shame on you.

With music, choosing the best of an artist's repertoire is

more or less a straightforward affair—you take all the chart toppers and, if you're a few songs short, throw in the less successful numbers that are still crowd favorites to fill up the disc. With books, things are a little harder. It's not as if there's a Top 40 for essays. I know which pieces have received the most mail and which ones have gone over best at readings, but other than that it's a fairly subjective business.

Frankly, it feels weird doing a best-of collection at all. I can still visualize, as if it were yesterday, the office in which I wrote the first of the pieces that became the "My Queer Life" column, which in turn became the first collection, *Alec Baldwin Doesn't Love Me.* I remember the thrill of the first book tour, the excitement of winning my first Lambda Literary Award, as if these things occurred weeks, not years, ago. But the reality is that it's been five years, four collections, three tours, two cross-country moves, and thousands of letters and E-mails since I began all of this.

So here we are. In selecting the pieces for this book I've tried to pick essays that represent both the most popular of the four collections from which they're taken, as well as work that illustrates the progression I think has taken place in my writing with each new book. Some essays I chose because they received the most mail, or because they've been audience favorites. Others I've elected to include because they represent various issues or topics I think are representative of the central theme of my work—the joys and challenges of living as a queer person today. And still others are here simply because they make me laugh when I read them, and I hope they'll make you laugh as well. And to help you justify putting out money for pieces of books you may already have, I've written some brand new material that only appears in this collection. In addition, each essay in the book begins with some brief personal comments and/or reflections from me.

Undoubtedly some readers will be unhappy with my selections. Favorites will have been left out, while some of my choices will be questioned. Some of you are sure to complain that several of the essays contradict each other. (Hey, I never claimed to be consistent.) Like any best-of, the worth of this one is subject to the opinions of the buyer. But hopefully you'll find something here that you like.

—Michael Thomas Ford

My Life as a Dwarf, Part 1: Sleepy

Some people wake up in the morning thinking about food, or sex, or perhaps what they're going to do that day. I wake up and think about how long it is until I can go to bed again.

It's not that there's anything particularly distressing about the idea of getting up. I actually enjoy the morning. It's when I get to go for a long walk with the dogs. It's when I do most of my writing. It's pleasant in a cheerful, nonthreatening, have-some-sugary-breakfast-cereal-and-toast kind of way.

But there's something especially appealing about going to bed. And for me bedtime means 10 o'clock. For as long as I can remember I have been in bed and ready for sleep as soon as that second hour of prime-time television is over. I have never seen a single episode of shows such as *E.R., NYPD Blue*, or *The West Wing*. I wouldn't know these shows if, as my friend Robrt likes to say, they entered me from behind. As far as I'm concerned, as soon as the end credits on *Malcolm in the Middle* roll, the world shuts down for the night.

It's true that I have, on occasion, stayed up past my bedtime. I have several times forced myself to remain awake to see which film won the Best Picture Oscar, or perhaps to finish reading a particularly engrossing book. I have even, once or twice, actually been outside of the house past 10.

This is especially dangerous, however, as I become a different person once that magic hour arrives. Like one of those weird little gremlins who turn evil when fed after midnight, something about the hour of 10 o'clock affects my psyche in an unpleasant way. I suddenly want to be home, in bed, with the lights out. I don't want to be chatting, or eating, or watching the dancing waters at the Bellagio in Las Vegas. I want to be asleep, and I resent deeply being kept from it.

When Patrick and I were first dating I managed for quite some time to always be home by 10. Like Cinderella, I made sure to be far away from my prince when the clock struck and the curtain of illusion was ripped away, revealing weary, reddened eyes and an unpleasant disposition. But inevitably the time came when I failed to make my exit on time. Then the glass slipper came off and I turned back into the tired pumpkin I truly am.

"Are you OK?" Patrick asked me. "You're not saying much."

"Grr," I said, trying to keep my eyes from closing.

"Did I do something wrong?" he tried.

"Mph," I answered reassuringly, thinking of how soft and warm my bed was.

Eventually I had to tell him about my affliction. He was understanding, if a bit unnerved. This is a man who used to bartend until 2 or 3 in the morning. He likes being out. He thinks nighttime activity is amusing. He wasn't quite sure what to do with a man who turns into a grumpy little bat just when most people are ready for the fun to begin. I worried for a while that this would be a problem. But several months later we were sitting in a theater watching *Shrek.* At the point in the movie where we discover the princess's secret—that she turns into an ogre at nightfall—Patrick turned to me and whispered kindly, "That's just like you."

The analogy is apt, but slightly flawed, for I don't see my sleepiness as a curse. My fondness for bedtime is due not to any physical need, but solely to the fact that I am hopelessly in love with sleep. It is, to me, the most magical state you can inhabit.

Have you ever watched dogs or children sleep? It's amazing. They throw their entire beings into it, surrendering totally to the embrace of unconsciousness. Sometimes I lie on the floor and just watch Roger, my 10-year-old Labrador, sleep. His chest rises and falls rhythmically as thunderous snores roll from his nose. Occasionally his great paws will twitch and he'll give a little bark, chasing rabbits. Sometimes he even rolls onto his back and balances there, front paws dangling and hind legs stretched out, his lip curled back in a smile. I watch him and wonder what he dreams, envious. He sleeps the same way he eats, as if nothing else in the world matters.

Children too seem to fall easily and fully into sleep. I always marvel when I see a baby in a stroller, head lolling to one side as Mom or Dad chauffeurs her through the world. Even better are the children on planes, chattering excitedly one minute and then suddenly slumped in sleep the next, as if a switch somewhere has been thrown that cuts off all power to the part of the brain that needs to be experiencing the world.

This is an art most of us lose as adults. It's almost as if we develop a fear of sleep, a distrust of not being fully conscious and in control, even for a moment. In sleep we are vulnerable, exposed physically to anything and everything that can creep into our rooms and stand over us thinking murderous thoughts. Even the insects hold sway over us, capable of scampering across our slumbering bodies without fear of being crushed or brushed away, tickling us with their four, eight, 300 feet, perhaps even biting us in revenge for the times we swatted a cousin or flushed an auntie down the toilet.

I am rather famous among my friends for being able to sleep almost anywhere and through almost anything. I have slept through earthquakes and hurricanes, on airplanes as they bounced wildly through storms, and even once through the last half of an Amy Grant concert (this was not, I should point out, Amy's fault). I have even attempted, much to the annoyance of my dive buddies, to go to sleep underwater while scuba diving. There, suspended in water, I feel as if I come the closest I ever will to dreaming while awake, like an unborn child floating in the universe of its mother's belly. In all other respects I may appear to be fully grown, but when it comes to sleep I am still five years old.

Children do, of course, have their own night terrors: the monster under the bed, the thing in the closet, the creature lurking in the shadows. But our adult fears of sleep are far more insidious. As grown-ups we recoil from the idea of being temporarily out of the loop not because we think the bogeyman is finally going to get us but because we fear what our minds, uncontrolled, will get up to.

Children dream of flying; adults dream of crashing. At 5 or 6 I dreamed often of running along a street and suddenly finding my feet lifting from the ground. Rising into the sky I flew up and up, dipping and soaring. It seemed virtually effortless, and when I woke in the morning I was always convinced, despite repeated failed experiments suggesting the contrary, that if I just tried hard enough it would happen.

I no longer dream of flying, at least not very often. Now I dream of people I knew a long time ago, of places I've been and things I've done. Sometimes these are real people and places and events, but often they're complete creations of my imagination. I'm not sure which I prefer. There's something wonderful but a little disturbing about having my head inhabited by people who just seem to show up, uninvited, and use my dreams as the stage for their lives. I'm almost more comfortable being visited by familiar friends, and even enemies.

I went through a period where every morning I took time to write down my dreams from the night before. I was sure these were important and needed to be preserved. I think at the time I'd been reading a lot of New Agey books about how to harness creativity. Or perhaps I was just bored. Either way, I still have the diaries. Here is a typical example, from October 21, 1998:

> I was staying at my father's house. It was the middle of the night, and I was up reading. I heard a noise outside and went to the window. Outside I saw a huge cornfield filled with tall cornstalks. There was someone running around in the field. It was a man, and he was carrying huge, living salmon in his arms. Their tails were thrashing around as he hauled them away. He was stealing them from our land, but I don't know where from. There were also some big black dogs out there, barking at the man. He was kicking them. That made me angry, and I ran outside. I tackled the man. Then I didn't know what to do with him. I ended up throwing him on his back, shoving a hose into his mouth, and filling him with water.

Now, there are all kinds of ways you could interpret this dream. (Note: Please do *not* send them to me.) But why? I am not a big proponent of interpreting dreams, preferring to leave them to themselves. Trying to "figure things out" almost always results in unpleasantness, like modern art or experimental theater. The point is, this is really not something I would be likely to come up with while awake. It was only possible in sleep. Only there, in the realm of infinite possibilities, would a man carrying salmon be running through the cornfield behind my father's house, pursued by big black dogs and myself. And this is why I close my eyes every night and wait to see what will happen.

I remember as a third or fourth grader being told about Harriet Tubman, famous for helping hundreds of slaves escape to the North during slavery. I am ashamed to admit that it wasn't Tubman's bravery that impressed me so much as it was her narcolepsy. She reportedly could fall asleep at any moment, even while leading her charges across rivers or through forests. Often those she was aiding had to wait, fearfully, for her to wake up and resume the journey.

I'm sure narcolepsy was deeply inconvenient to Tubman, as it is to all those who are afflicted with it. But I can't help see something wondrous in it. Imagine being at the mercy of sleep, never knowing when it's going to come over you and sweep you away in its dark arms. It's a kind of wild magic, out of control and dangerous, beautiful in its mystery and its equal potential for either disaster or enchantment.

When, years ago, I saw the first of the *Alien* movies, I was less taken with the monster than I was with the notion that Ripley and the rest of her crew had been kept for many years in a state of suspended animation while they traveled through space. This artificial sleep meant they could shut their eyes on one world and open them again on another, perhaps one, five, or 50 years later. What, I thought, could be more perfect?

Even my computer has a sleep mode, a dormant state between full functionality and complete shutdown. It's set to enter sleep whenever I don't use it for a specified period of time. Then, with a touch of a button, it springs to life again, ready to send its little series of 1's and 0's spinning around in the constellations and nebulae out of which documents and files and directories are created. Whenever I see this happen I imagine the tiny unseeable gods who inhabit my hard drive being shaken from their naps so they can resume their work, yawning and stretching and rubbing the sleep from their eyes.

I think a lot of us fear sleep because it's the closest we get to death on a regular basis. Removed from the physical world, from the touch of lovers and the familiar sights and sounds of home, we're thrust into a sort of netherworld where nothing is certain. Then too we talk of putting animals "to sleep" when really we're offering them up to death. Perhaps the two have become conjoined in our minds. Maybe those of us who find sleep difficult or even impossible to accept are simply fighting to stay alive, afraid that this time when we slip out of consciousness we won't come back. Instead we roam our houses, eyes bleary and stomachs sloshing with too many cups of coffee, because we aren't yet ready to go gently into that dark night.

When it's my time, I very much want to die in my sleep, not so much because it seems far easier than any other alternative, but because I imagine staying forever in whatever dream I'm having at the time. I just hope it's one in which I'm flying.

Packing for the Second Coming

When I tour to support a book, I generally don't like to read the same pieces at every appearance. On the tour for Alec Baldwin Doesn't Love Me, *however, I found people requesting that I read this piece night after night. This was particularly true in the South, where I discovered that, like myself, a whole lot of people had experienced childhoods dominated by the anxious anticipation of the Second Coming. Unlike in Yankee cities, where I was frequently asked whether or not this story is true (it is), in the South readings of the piece were greeted with hoots of recognition and howls of laughter over a shared experience. While I was overjoyed that people liked the story, I was even more relieved to discover that what I had assumed to be my own particular childhood trauma was not as unusual as it had always seemed to me to be. Almost inevitably, reading this story began a swapping of anecdotes concerning other Baptist-oriented memories such as the dreaded flannel-graph board, Bible "sword drills," and peeing in the baptism tank.*

When I was 7 years old, I packed for the Second Coming of Jesus Christ Our Savior. I did it in shoeboxes—17 of them—filled to near bursting with everything I thought I might need in the great hereafter. I even labeled them: PHOTOS, ART SUPPLIES, STAR WARS FIGURES. After watching my mother organize numerous moves, I knew how it was done, and I was a model of efficiency. When I got to heaven, I would know exactly which box my toothbrush was in.

The hardest part was choosing which of my cherished items to leave behind. I knew from what my mother had told me about the streets being paved with gold that money was no good in heaven, so I left out my piggy bank. But being a veteran of school lunch-hour sandwich swaps, I had a vague suspicion that some form of barter was sure to exist behind the Pearly Gates, just as it did in the cafeteria of Westgate Elementary School. So in went the chrome-plated Collector's Series Hot Wheels cars my friend Mickey and I jealously collected. They were the rarest thing I owned, next to the shark tooth my grandmother had sent me from Florida, and I was sure they would come in handy.

Clothes were not a problem, since it had been made abundantly clear to me early on that everyone Up There wore only shining gowns of whitest silk. Despite this fact, it was with some reluctance that I left my favorite item of clothing—my *Hee-Haw* overalls—folded in the drawer. I assumed also that accessories would be thoughtfully provided, so I left my Cap'n Crunch Decoder Ring in its box, albeit wistfully. Since my mother had never been completely clear as to the status of pets in the Afterlife, I threw in a stack of photos of the hamsters, the dogs, and the cat. Of these, the cat and one of the hamsters had already preceded me into the Beyond, and I half believed I would find them waiting when I arrived. But being a sensible child, I figured it couldn't hurt to prepare for the worst. Photos of my family remained behind, as I innocently expected them all to be there with me.

The remainder of the boxes housed my extensive collection of *Charlie's Angels* trading cards. I didn't honestly know what I would do with them once I arrived in my Lord's bosom, but I had put more effort into collecting and organizing them than I had into anything else I'd ever done in my short life, and I wasn't leaving them behind. Secretly, I hoped that one of the rewards awaiting me was the hard-to-find card featuring Kelly in hot pants, which had long eluded me.

Two things were responsible for this frenzy of packing. One was the approaching American bicentennial celebration of 1976. For months I'd heard about this wondrous event, and although I had no idea what it actually was, I figured anything that could inspire both a newly minted quarter and a series of McDonald's commemorative jelly glasses must be of some significance. The only thing I could conceive of being worthy of such honors was the return of Jesus, which both the pastor of our church and my mother insisted would happen soon but, when pressed, could not put an exact date on. Putting two and two together, I thought myself very clever indeed for unraveling the mystery that had puzzled biblical scholars for centuries.

The second, and probably most influential, thing was a charming little song called "I Wish We'd All Been Ready," which I'd recently heard one of my sisters playing on her stereo. It was sung by a Christian rock singer named Larry Norman, and it was all about the unbelievers who were left behind when Jesus came to sweep up His chosen people before the world was burned up in the End Times. For whatever reason, it had gained some amount of popularity among the teenage Christian set that summer, and was quickly replacing Ocean's "Put Your Hand in the Hand" as the anthem of socially conscious American youth.

It says something about the nature of Norman's cheery ditty that I can still remember most of it today. It isn't hard, really, because essentially each verse was a mini horror movie about another unfortunate soul shocked into awareness of his or her sinful existence by the sudden disappearance of a more pious friend or loved one during the Rapture. Take, for instance, my personal favorite line: "A man and wife asleep in bed / She hears a noise and turns her head [dramatic pause] / He's gone." Just in case the message was somehow lost, the chorus nailed it home. "I wish we'd all been ready. There's no time to change your mind / The Son has come and you've been left behind."

Children, they say, are visual creatures to begin with. In my little, and admittedly overactive, mind, I saw a woman rolling over in bed, only to find it empty because her husband (who of course had begged her for years to accept Christ in preparation for just this kind of thing) had flown up to heaven, leaving her to face the tortures of Armageddon, not to mention the bills and hungry pets, all by herself. From there it was but a small leap to picturing myself waking up one sunny morning and going in search of my family, only to find the house empty and Satan himself knocking at the front door.

I decided that the Fourth of July would be The Day. I was certain Jesus would want to make a big entrance, and it made sense that he would surprise everyone by showing up in time for the fireworks and picnics I was told were in the planning. Having determined that the time was upon us, I prepared accordingly. When I'd packed everything and sealed it tightly with tape, I arranged the boxes in a pile. Then I attended to my traveling wardrobe. According to my mother, what one wore for a trip was of utmost importance, especially if traveling long distances. I had no idea how far heaven was from

Virginia, but since John Denver swore that West Virginia was "almost heaven," I assumed it was probably somewhere above Route 19, perhaps near Gaithersburg. I'd been there once, and I recalled that the ride back featured only one pit stop at Dairy Queen, which meant it wasn't too far.

Opening my closet, I thought about what outfit would be most fetching in the eyes of the Lord, Our God. While I knew that shortly after arrival I would be shedding my earthly clothes for those of heavenly design, I wanted to make a good first impression. After pausing briefly at my green polyester three-piece suit purchased especially for Easter, I decided instead on an ensemble of shorts and a shirt, which the attached raccoon Garanimal tags assured me were perfectly suited for one another in both color and form. They were lightweight—which I was certain would be an advantage when being lifted up to God—and sporty.

After dressing, I sat on my bed and waited. I wasn't entirely sure what I was waiting for, but I did it patiently and expectantly. No one had ever explained to me exactly what would happen when the Rapture occurred, but I had some ideas. Drawing from a variety of sources, I had determined that there would probably not be much warning, and that it would all be over rather quickly. Those who were left on Earth would suddenly discover themselves riding in cars without drivers, talking to companions who were no longer there, and becoming tangled in jump ropes as the turners on either side were whisked away to the Great Reward.

I confess I was secretly thrilled by the idea of unmanned cars skidding around the roads while the sinners inside screamed, and I hoped I'd get to see it. I also allowed myself to wonder, momentarily and a little guiltily, if all of my family members would really be joining me on the trip. It strikes me odd now that I didn't tell any of them of my plans. I like to think that I was just preoccupied with the preparations, and that there was no malice of forethought in my secrecy.

As for myself, I suppose I expected the heavens to open up and to feel myself being raised gently into the skies like a kite, or like the revolving swing ride at the annual State Fair, giving me a good view of all the doubters below crying out for forgiveness as I hovered, saved, above their heads. I wondered if it would feel like being in an airplane. I hoped someone would present me with a plastic pin commemorating the event, as a friendly pilot had once done on a Pan American flight my family took from Africa back to America.

And so I sat and waited. After a few minutes, when everything seemed to be going on just as it had before I'd packed, I started to wonder if maybe something was a little off in my timing. I tried to remember whether Norman had specified precisely *what time* the Son was coming. I thought about going downstairs and getting my sister's record of the song and checking the liner notes for clues, but I feared that being separated from my belongings when the Blessed Event occurred would be a tactical error similar to attempting to check through nine pieces of luggage and two pets at Heathrow while changing planes for Venice. My father had done this once, and we'd arrived in Italy with three cats and six bags, none of which were our own, while our two Irish setters and my favorite shirt made their way to Rome. While I knew it was not a charitable thought, I didn't want another Christian to arrive in the Lord's presence with my trading cards.

After an hour had gone by with not the slightest hint of a Rapture, I decided that I'd been had. Jesus wasn't coming. I got up and looked out the window. Outside, kids were running up and down the street playing kick the can in the afternoon light. None of them seemed worried in the slightest about missing Act 2 of the Earth's destruction (Act 1 being the flood Noah escaped from). They were laughing and having a good time while I sat inside waiting for someone who clearly had no intention of keeping our date.

Suddenly, the skies clouded over with angry gray. There was a rumble of thunder, followed by a crack of lighting, and it began to pour. The kids scattered as the rain descended in sheets and darkness fell over the neighborhood. The whole world seemed to be surrounded by the storm. It certainly wasn't what I'd expected the Rapture to look like. I'd thought it would be more like *The Sonny and Cher Comedy Hour*, with bright lights and maybe some lively music.

Then a horrible thought entered my mind: What if this wasn't the Rapture, but the beginning of Armageddon? Every good Baptist child knew that after the beauty of the Rapture was the horror of Armageddon, the final battle in which Satan's demons warred with the troops of heaven. It was, we were told, a terrible time, filled with death and fire and long lines at the supermarkets, where only those whose foreheads were branded with 666—the Mark of the Beast—would be allowed to purchase food. The branding itself might not be so bad, but the trade-off was that, once marked as Satan's plaything, a person would never be allowed into heaven. Being faced with the choice of either starvation or eternal damnation was not something I was keen to have happen.

What if Jesus had already come while I was packing, and now the storm was heralding the imminent arrival of the Seven-headed Beast with the Whore of Babylon astride it's back? Oblivious to the departure of the saved, I could have missed the whole thing, and now the Apocalypse was upon me. I reeled at the thought that somewhere along the line,

I'd skipped a step in the process of salvation, and now I was doomed to burn with all the other sinners. Maybe Jesus had sensed my earlier gleeful musings on viewing the punishment of the wicked and decided to leave me behind.

Filled with terror, I ran from my room screaming. I half expected the halls of my house to be overrun with lurching demons reaching out to drag me into hell. Holding my arms in front of my face as protection, I dashed into the living room, wailing, "No, Jesus! I didn't mean it! Please, come back! Whatever I did, I'm sorry!"

Sitting on the couch were two women I had never seen before. They looked at me, pieces of cake paused in midair in front of their open mouths. I stopped, gasping in huge breaths, and stared at their anxious faces. They didn't look like demons to me, but I couldn't be sure. I knew the Devil and his ways well enough to know his minions appeared in many forms, even as cake-eating middle-aged ladies. "Be gone!" I shouted forcefully, dragging up from my subconscious the words our pastor claimed Jesus used to vanquish the evil ones. I pointed my finger at them defiantly. "In the name of Jesus Christ, go back to hell!"

The ladies looked at me, panting and wild-eyed before them. Then they screamed. Then I screamed. Then I fainted.

The next thing I knew, I was lying in my bed with my mother looking down at me worriedly. "Is this heaven?" I asked hopefully, thinking maybe Jesus, impressed by my stand against the demons, had decided to come back for me after all.

"What?" she said.

"Where are the demons?" I asked.

"What demons?" she said. "What are you talking about? And why did you interrupt my garden club meeting? You scared Mrs. Whitley and Mrs. Hogan half to death."

Garden club? Then it wasn't really the Apocalypse after all. I breathed a sigh of relief. I started to get out of bed.

"Oh, no, you don't," my mother said. "You stay right there and take a nap. I think you have a fever."

She left, shutting the door behind her. I looked out the window. It was still raining, but the world wasn't ending. Larry Norman was a big, fat liar. I wasn't sure at first if I was comforted or saddened by this thought. On the one hand, it would have been fun to have seen heaven and found out once and for all what it was really like. Never having met anyone who'd been there, all I had to go one was second-hand descriptions. I wanted to see it for myself. And I had done such a nice job of packing. It was a shame to see it all go to waste.

Then again, there were a few things to look forward to right here on Earth. It was summer. I'd just gotten a skateboard and new sneakers I hadn't even worn yet. My father had promised to take me and my friend Stephanie to *Star Wars* for the ninth time. My birthday was coming up, and I'd been hinting around for a bike. Besides, it was the Fourth of July, and I knew there were sparklers in my future when the rain stopped. There was a lot left to do; maybe heaven could wait a while. Satisfied that I wasn't quite ready for Jesus to come back after all, I settled into the pillows and closed my eyes.

Before I drifted off, I looked at the stack of boxes next to the bed. Half asleep, I picked up the box with my favorite *Charlie's Angels* cards in it and tucked it behind my pillow. Just in case.

Cheaper by the Dozen

Recently, while avoiding a deadline, I happened to catch an episode of a talk show dedicated to the subject of teenagers who wanted to have babies. To give the kids a taste of what parenthood is like, they were each given a realistic baby doll that somehow or other cried when it was hungry or left alone, "woke up" at random times during the night, and participated in every type of bodily function enjoyed by real infants. The challenge given to the kids was to live with their babies for three days. They did, and when they came back to the show after their parenting experiences they happily threw their charges back into the arms of the producers and declared that they would never, under any circumstances, be producing children of their own. Thinking back on my own experiences with child-rearing, I nodded in solidarity. While the trial babies of today may be more high-tech than they were when I was a teenage parent, the message is the same: Having kids isn't always as easy as it's cracked up to be.

Twice in the last month I have been asked if I would like to become a father. All of my lesbian friends are going baby-mad, and two different couples put out feelers to see if I might be interested in helping them produce additions to their families.

Michael Thomas Ford

I'm honored to be asked, of course. It's nice to know that someone might want to take a chance on my DNA. And all it involves is a small jar, good aim, and the right moment. But I don't know. The last time I did this, it almost gave me a nervous breakdown.

I was 13. I know, that's a little young to be a dad. But it wasn't like I had a choice in the matter. It was either that or take a failing grade, and I figured having a kid would be easier to explain to my parents than an F on my report card.

It was eighth grade. Health class. We were discussing the responsibilities of parenting, which was a fairly relevant issue in my little country school where every year at least a handful of girls waddled down the aisle at commencement in maternity gowns. Our teacher, Mr. Travis, decided that we were taking the whole thing far too lightly and needed a lesson in the difficulties of having young ones to care for. So we all became parents for a week.

Our children were eggs. Mr. Travis set a couple of cartons of them on his desk and, one by one, we went up and claimed our babies. Returning to our seats, we held them anxiously while Mr. Travis explained what his little exercise entailed.

We were to keep our baby eggs for one week, naming them and decorating them in any way we saw fit. We could carry them around in any kind of conveyance we came up with, but we had to have them with us at all times. They couldn't sit in our lockers. And if we had to be involved in some activity that took us away from our charges—like gym class—we had to find a baby-sitter. At night, of course, we were allowed to refrigerate our charges, lest they become spoiled.

If we managed to make it through the week without any harm coming to our child, we would receive an A on the assignment. But if Friday dawned and our little one had become scramble or cracked, we would get an F. It was that simple: pass or fail. There were no in-between grades. And because we had to decorate our eggs in some distinctive way, Mr. Travis would know if we cheated and substituted another one for a deceased child.

We took to the challenge with mixed emotions. Most of the girls thought it was great fun, while the boys looked at the fragile eggs cradled in their clumsy hands and immediately considered hard boiling them to make them sturdier. This, however, was one of the many options forbidden to us. So we did the best we could, constructing all kinds of clever carrying cases for our progeny that would survive any catastrophe.

What we hadn't counted on, however, was the almost irresistible appeal of infanticide. What started out as a well-intentioned exercise in parenting soon turned into a bloodbath as we discovered that finding ways to bring about the demise of the eggs of our friends and enemies was much more entertaining than minding our wards. By the end of third period we had our first casualty; Jason Pritchard tripped Louis Sutton on the way to algebra and little Louis Jr. fell headlong to the cold hallway floor, his yellow insides splattering the tile. We stared at the fragments of eggshell, and instead of feeling sorrow for Louis's loss, we immediately hatched evil plans of our own.

Like some kind of primal instinct, destroying other students' children became our foremost goal. Each of us wanted to be the last one standing come Friday. We lurked on stairs, pushed chairs into the paths of rival parents, and bumped into one another in the lunch line. The sound of an egg hitting the floor while a bereaved parent howled in anguish became music to our ears, and we chortled horribly whenever someone else bit the dust and our own eggs were still safe and sound.

My egg was named Rupert. He had a cheerful little painted-on face, and he lived in a carriage made of Styrofoam egg carton pieces, cotton, and lots of tape to hold him in place. While I confess I was concerned for his well-being more out of a desire to maintain a high grade point average than from any sense of paternal duty, I did care for him in my own way. I was careful to keep him with me at all times, eyeing anyone who came near me with suspicion. I even walked home with him every night, lest some bully on the bus kidnap him and pitch him out the window, as had happened to Anne Chattam one afternoon when she refused to hand over five bucks to free her precious Charlotte from the clutches of a tenth grader.

By Wednesday, fully half the class had lost their egg babies to neglect, accident, or murder. There had even been one case of a hired nanny shaking an egg in her charge so badly that it cracked. She claimed it was the fault of a one-armed intruder, but none of us believed her.

On Thursday, the pressure intensified. Those without eggs decided the rest of us would join them in failure. It was an all-out slaughter. Eggs were ripped from their parents' arms and hurled against walls. Gangs of eggless thugs roamed the halls, descending on anyone foolish enough to get in their way. Some anxious kids tried to protect their offspring by sending them to live with younger siblings in the lower grades for the day. But that proved their undoing, as day care was strictly forbidden and Mr. Travis pronounced them unfit parents.

By Friday morning, there were only two of us remaining. I had managed to keep Rupert unharmed largely because I'd asked my friend John Reynolds, a senior with a lot of muscles and a bad attitude, to be Rupert's godfather in exchange for doing his English homework. My friend Carolyn also still had her egg, Mellicent, whom she had kept intact by threatening to report anyone who came near her to the principal, who also happened to be the egg's grandfather.

It was down to the two of us. This wouldn't have been a problem under normal circumstances, but Carolyn and I were always vying for the top spot in our class, and at that moment we were in a dead heat. Whichever of us was the best parent would be victorious. But when we both walked into class with our little ones in tow, it seemed we would have to settle for a draw.

When the moment came to present our healthy bouncing babies to Mr. Travis, Carolyn went first. She carried Mellicent to the front of the class and held her up. Mellicent had beautiful yellow glued-on hair, and she was the picture of health. Mr. Travis beamed and wrote an A next to Carolyn's name.

Carolyn started to return to her seat. But before she got there, she stumbled (I swear it was an accident) and Mellicent went flying. We all watched as the unfortunate Mellicent turned in the air, her glorious hair flapping about her, and fell to the floor.

But instead of the usual smacking sound, there was just a gentle cracking as Mellicent shattered into a hundred tiny pieces. There was no yolk, no gore. Nothing at all. Mr. Travis walked over, bent down, and examined the remains of Carolyn's egg.

"Well," he said. "It seems someone tried to get away with blowing out her egg. Would you like to explain this, Miss Pratt?"

Carolyn turned red. She'd been caught. She was an egg-blower. It was a trick none of the rest of us had thought of. We were impressed. But Carolyn had still cheated, and even being the principal's daughter couldn't save her this time.

"I guess that makes Mr. Ford the only responsible parent in the class," Mr. Travis said. He picked up Rupert and shook him, making sure he was still intact. "Good work," he said. "A."

I took Rupert home that afternoon triumphant. I was a good dad, and I had the grade to prove it. But now that the week was over, I had no idea what to do with my boy. Being a father had been a good experience, but I wasn't sure I wanted to spend the next 18 years carting Rupert around and tucking him into the refrigerator every night.

My mother was in the kitchen, making a cake. A bowl of eggs sat near her. Sensing my opportunity to be rid of my responsibilities once and for all, I slipped Rupert in next to the plain old eggs and held my breath. When my mother reached into the bowl, I watched as Rupert was lifted out, cracked against the side of a bowl, and mixed into the batter. My mother, too busy reading her recipe, hadn't even noticed his little face as she ended his life. That night, as I ate my piece of chocolate cake, I had pangs of remorse. But that cream cheese frosting was really good, and by the second piece I'd gotten over it.

Now that I'm older and wiser, I watch my gay male friends who have adopted children or acquired them in the usual way, and I think it might be fun to have a kid around. And sometimes when my lesbian friends try to lure me back into fatherhood I'm tempted to give it another try. But then I remember little Rupert, and how good he tasted as a cake, and I think maybe it's not such a good idea after all.

Growing Pains

What can I say about this one except that I still feel the same way as I did the day I wrote it.

I am a grown-up. I know this because this morning for breakfast I ate half a bag of Reese's miniature peanut butter cups. If I were a child, someone would have stopped me.

But I don't always feel like a grown-up. In fact, most of the time I sit around waiting for someone to tell me what to do next, as if the bell ending recess rang but I can't remember where my classroom is. I keep hoping a hall monitor will happen along and point me in the right direction. The peanut butter cups, clearly, were an act of rebellion.

Some people take to the whole grown-up thing with ease. They get jobs and plan for their futures. They have cocktails with friends, take vacations, and follow the financial news. These people frighten me. Sometimes I sit on the subway and look at them with their briefcases, neat haircuts, and stylish clothes, wondering how they got that way. Clearly we all started out on the same road. But at some point they took the exit leading to adulthood. I, apparently, was busy trying to find a really good station on the radio and missed my turn.

It's not that I don't do the requisite adult things. I pay my bills every month. I have a credit card. I have a car. But sometimes I still find myself in front of the television thinking, "You really should turn that off and go outside to play." And on more than one occasion I have had to remind myself that no one is *forcing* me to get up at 6 every morning, and that I really could grab another couple of hours if I wanted to. But I do it anyway, urged on by some kind of groundless fear that if I continue to sleep someone is sure to give me hell for it.

When my parents were the age I am now, they had a house and three children. I have a rented apartment and a dog, but it's hardly the same. For one, the dog's toys cost less, and he'll never demand to be taken to a Spice Girls concert because all his friends are going and if he doesn't they'll say he's not cool.

Sometimes, as I look at myself while shaving, I wonder if my father used to stand in front of the mirror in the morning in the same way and wait for the moment when everyone would figure out that underneath the suit and tie he wore to work he was really still 13 years old. Because that's what I do. Not that I own a suit or tie or have a real job. I sit at home in my boxer shorts and write. But I still worry that one day there will be a knock on the door and some official-looking person will announce in a loud voice that the jig is up and I have to go back to junior high with the other kids.

When I was in my early teens, I used to look at my sisters' college friends and think they were very grown-up. Then, when I was in college, I looked at people who had graduated and started their lives and thought that *they* were very grown up. A few years later, graduated myself and toiling in a real job, I started getting suspicious. The grown-ups were getting older and older, and I was always five or six years behind them. The height of the adulthood bar kept rising, and more and more it looked as if I would never clear it.

Growing Pains

Finally, I gave up. I admitted to myself that I am never going to be one of those truly grown-up people who knows what he's doing. And that's OK. That's why the world has people like Dan Rather and Oprah. They figure it all out and break it to the rest of us in terms we can understand. Thanks to them, I don't need to be able to talk about health plans and politics with any sense of assuredness. I can just sit around playing with blocks until Oprah and Dan fill me in.

Sometimes I'm fine, and for a while I go around feeling like I can cope. I'll be wheeling my cart through the grocery store, throwing things into it, and I'll realize I can do this any time I feel like it. Or I'll have the sudden thought that I can just get in my car and drive somewhere without permission. *Why*, I think excitedly, *I could buy a plane ticket to Tibet, or paint my bedroom some exotic color, and no one could say anything about it.* At those moments, being grown up seems almost worth it.

But most of the time it just freaks me out. Worse, I fear that others are suffering from the same condition and not letting on. As a kid, I looked at the adults around me and assumed they knew what they were doing: doctors knew what was best for my health; the people flying the airplane could handle it; and people in charge of the government were capable and worthy individuals. After all, they were grown-ups. Grown-ups could do anything, and someday I would be just like them.

Now someday has come, and if the other adults are anything like me, we're in big trouble. This frightens me. When I go to the doctor, I don't look at his framed degrees from Harvard and feel reassured. I study his face as he talks and conclude that he has no idea what he's doing and is making up all those big words to save face. When I sit in an airplane during takeoff, I imagine the pilot up front staring at the switches on his instrument panel, trying to remember what does what and hoping his copilot was more awake during class than he was. As for the government, let's just say I do not watch our elected leaders on television and feel any sense of pride or confidence. After all, people like me elected them, and what the hell do we know?

A couple of months back I spoke to a group of third graders at a local elementary school about what it's like being a writer. During the question-and-answer period, I looked around at the shiny faces staring at me, at the hands waving frantically in the air as they waited to be called on. Choosing one, I asked an eager little girl what she wanted to know.

"How old are you?" she asked. The other hands went down, as if every one of the kids wanted to know the same thing.

"I'm 30," I answered, having just endured that birthday.

All around me, eyes went wide. The children gawked as if I were a newly discovered relic pulled from the desert sands of Arizona or something.

"That's so old," said one boy.

"You're older than my mom," added another, disbelieving.

Things went on in this way for some time. The children wanted to know how someone as clearly aged as I was could write books, let alone walk to their school without the aid of a cane.

I, of course, was looking at them and wondering what I could possibly say that would ever be of any use to them. Tucked into one of their tiny chairs, I didn't feel much older than they were. Yet there they were, asking me for advice and answers. I knew that if I told them to stand on their heads, they'd probably all do it, simply because I was taller than they were. I wanted to say, "Don't you understand? I don't *know* anything."

When I left that day, the teacher accompanied me to the doors of the school. "You should never tell them how old you are," she said consolingly. "It's like throwing raw meat to coyotes. I just tell them I knew God when he was a boy. That shuts them up. Except for the ones who want to know if he was a good kickball player."

But I know how those kids feel. They look at me and wonder what their lives will be like a billion years later when they too are 30. I'm sure they have all kinds of plans about being models and football stars, and of having nice clothes, nice cars, and big houses. Next time, I'll tell them the truth.

"You still won't know what you want to be when you grow up," I'll say. "You'll wonder why everyone else has great jobs and wonderful relationships and dogs who sleep on the floor, because in all likelihood you won't have won that Oscar, your significant other really won't be that good in bed, and your dog will throw up on your shoes every chance it gets. You might luck out and make a lot of money, but chances are you'll be eating spaghetti and shopping at Wal-Mart while you try to pay off student loans and the credit card bills you rang up when you were 23 and thought it would all take care of itself."

Probably they will just stare at me for a few moments, wondering if I've succumbed to some hideous form of mental illness brought on by advanced age. And then I'll feel bad for ruining their lives.

"OK," I'll tell them gently. "It's not that bad. You can eat peanut butter cups for breakfast." That should give anyone hope.

Unnatural Causes

*This piece signaled a change in my writing. I've always very consciously attempted to use humor as a way of getting people to think about things in different ways. But while a lot of my earlier work had been a combination of humor with more serious observations underneath, this essay stripped away the veneer of laughter completely. It is, perhaps, more akin to the books I've published for young adults about subjects such as the AIDS crisis (*The Voices of AIDS*), what it means to be gay (*OutSpoken *and* The World Out There*), and spirituality (*Paths of Faith*). Although I've frequently used my religious upbringing as a source of comic material, I've remained deeply interested in spirituality of all kinds. The two events that conspired to bring about the creation of this essay touch on many issues that concern me: the role of religion in both society and in our individual lives, the hypocrisy of religious institutions that perpetuate shame and fear while hiding their own guilt, and the power of friendship, love, and genuine belief to cut through all of these things. While a number of readers didn't care for the change in direction this essay took, many more wrote to say how much they appreciated it. I received dozens of letters from clergy—both gay and straight—thanking me for the essay. I* *also received several letters from other former students of Dr. June Steffensen Hagen, the professor mentioned in the piece, sharing their own stories of how June had touched their lives. Sometimes the things we write take on lives of their own and lead us down unexpected roads. And although this essay first appeared several years ago, the importance of its message grows stronger. Even as I write this, the Catholic Church in America is coming under intense scrutiny for its inexcusably inept handling of years of sexual abuse incidents involving priests and children. Perhaps next they'll be forced to acknowledge the many other victims of their legacy of secrecy, lies, and shame.*

This morning I received two things in the mail. One was a clipping from *The Kansas City Star*, sent to me by a reader who thought I would find it interesting. It was an article about the frighteningly high death rate from AIDS among Roman Catholic priests and how for years church leaders have been covering up this fact. The second thing I received was a letter from my friend Dr. June Steffensen Hagen.

It's interesting how seemingly unrelated things take on new meaning when they're brought together. Ordinarily I might have read the *Star* article and filed it away to think about later. But then there was June.

June was one of my English professors in college. I was her assistant for two years. My job was to photocopy the endless stream of articles she clipped from *The New York Times*, manage her convoluted filing system, and wash the teacups that piled up on her desk at an alarming rate.

At a school that ran rampant with muddleheaded fundamentalist Christian teaching, June was a breath of fresh air, a fiercely intelligent, liberal Episcopalian determined to get her students to think for themselves instead of believing everything they were told. More than once she upset the powers that be, and more than a few people would have liked to see her ousted.

Knowing June changed my life. Not only did she introduce me to writers and ideas I'd never encountered, she was the first person to let me know that being gay was OK. She was also the first person I'd ever met who I think genuinely loved God. Having grown up with a lot of people who feared God or used him as a weapon, it was something of a shock to find someone who thought of God as her friend. Determined as I was because of my past experiences to believe the whole God thing was a lot of nonsense, June made me rethink that position. In fact, when it was time for me to leave school, I even applied to the Episcopal seminary. Ultimately I didn't go, which I know now was the right choice. But at the time it was an appealing option.

June's husband, Jim, is a retired Episcopal priest who for many years served a largely Spanish-speaking community in Queens. Her letter to me was filled with news about their lives: their recent trips to Ecuador and Mexico, the literature class June was teaching, her and Jim's involvement in the New York Choral Society and their parish, and the activities of their two children. These are the pieces of a full and happy life. They're what I think of when I think of June.

And then I think of those priests dying from AIDS. According to the *Star* article, many of them were sent to hospices outside of their parishes to die, alone and far from their friends and families so that no one would know what was killing them. In almost all cases, the cause of death was listed as "natural causes" and the occupation written on the death certificate was listed as anything but priest. In the end, these servants of the church were reduced to lies, their years of service to God wiped out with the stroke of a pen to protect the image of the institution to which they had devoted their lives.

Tucked into June's letter is a photograph of her and Jim, taken on one of their trips. June's hair is grayer than it was when I was her student assistant, and Jim's is more absent, but the smiles on their faces still reflect the love of life and each other that I remember. The most wonderful thing about it, though, is how much they look like a couple. Jim has his arm around June, and she's leaning into him in a way that radiates familiarity and friendship—a picture of a lifetime spent together exploring the world and all of its joys and challenges.

I can't help but compare this to the image in my head of priests dying, alone and frightened, among strangers because their superiors sent them away to hide their shame. I want to believe that someone was there to hold their hands, to tell them they were loved. I want to believe they died knowing that their lives meant something. But I don't think they did. I think that in the end they were betrayed in the cruelest way.

The Episcopal church and the church of Rome have been at odds since the beginning, and theologians and academics can argue points of doctrine until they're blue in the face. When it comes down to it, though, the only thing that matters is how a church serves its people, and the Catholic church gets failing marks in that department. I'm sure the church sees its dead priests as embarrassments best forgotten, the same way for years it ignored the rampant sexual and emotional abuse of young people by its clergy. What the Catholic Church should really be embarrassed about, though, is its refusal to acknowledge the needs of the men who come to it offering up their lives. In order to maintain control, they strip them of their humanity, forcing them to give up love and companionship and, yes, plain old sex in a misguided attempt at manufacturing piety. Sublimating desire in incense and robes and a rehearsed liturgy mumbled two or three times a day is a recipe for unhappiness. And for death by the most unnatural cause of all—shame.

One of the things June taught me was that God—in whatever form you embrace him—loves joy. It saddens me that the Catholic priests who came to worship God with joy were instead met with betrayal and fear in the hour when they most needed love. I am also angered—angered enough to want to comfort myself with disbelief in a God who would let this happen, just as I wanted to back in college.

But once again June won't let me do that. I've put the picture of her and Jim on the wall above my desk, right beside the picture of my Wiccan friend Archer dressed in a hat covered with enormous yellow roses and the one of the stone circle and phallic rock monument my Radical Faerie brother, Ron, painstakingly built on his Maine sheep farm. When I look at these pictures, I am reminded that even the fear of an institution as large and imposing as the Catholic church is nothing compared to the power of one or two people who truly understand what it is to live with joy. And I am reminded too that God comes in many forms, that the God those priests were searching for really does exist somewhere, waiting for them. I hope they've found him.

How Alec Baldwin Ruined My Life

I owe my early success in large measure to Alec Baldwin's chest. Actually, to what people thought *was Alec Baldwin's chest. When* Alec Baldwin Doesn't Love Me *first hit bookstores, more than a few browsers picked it up not because of my name on the cover but because of the photograph of a hairy-chested man that graced it. Some readers even thought the chest was mine, and one of the most confidence-shriveling experiences of those early days was arriving at a radio interview only to be greeted by the host with a disappointed "Oh, that's not you on the cover." No, it isn't me. Nor is it Alec. It is, in fact, porn actor Tom Katt. Anyway, people always want to know what the deal is with Alec Baldwin. This is the essay that explains it all. I'm sad to say, however, that even though Alec has divorced Kim Basinger since this was written, he still hasn't come calling. I did get a nice note from him, though.*

I'm saving myself for marriage. My mother would be so proud. Unfortunately, there's one small problem: The man of my dreams is taken, and I'm not getting any younger waiting around for him. Yes, the world is a sorry place indeed. Crime is rampant. Children can't read. People are homeless. It's enough to make any sympathetic person weep for days. But while these things are indeed terrible, they are not the worst things about the world, not by a long shot. No, the worst thing is that Alec Baldwin is married, and not to me.

Don't laugh. This is a serious issue. You see, Alec was my first and only real love. Ever since I was 17 and saw him on television in the homo-oriented *Dress Gray*, I've known I would marry him. From the moment he slipped off his attractive officer's uniform and I saw the dark line of hair peeking out over the edge of his crisp white T-shirt, I was hooked. Then there were the eyes, so blue and inviting. The secretive smile. And the voice. So sensual. So masculine. I could just imagine how it would sound whispering my name as he slipped into bed and put his arm around me. After the scene in which he lowers himself into a hot bath, I was a believer in love at first sight.

Once I'd found my man, I set about getting ready for him. Having grown up with two older sisters whose primary objectives in life were getting married as quickly as humanly possible, I knew how it was done. I prepared a hope chest, filled with everything my man could desire. I embroidered little linen guest towels with my new initials. I collected flatware in an appealing design, and chose a china pattern that was both homey and elegant. I loaded up on sheets I knew Alec would look the most handsome reclining on in his white boxer shorts on our honeymoon night.

Then I waited. I knew that if I was patient, Alec would come. No matter that we moved in two different worlds. I had fate and little linen guest towels on my side. In the meantime, I saw all of his movies—*The Alamo: Thirteen Days to Glory, Beetlejuice, Married to the Mob, She's Having a Baby, Working Girl, Talk Radio,* and even *Forever, Lulu.* No matter how brief Alec's appearances in a film, in my eyes he was the star. *Great Balls of Fire. The Hunt for Red October. Miami Blues.* With each movie, my love for Alec deepened. I sat in the audience, eating popcorn and wishing I could reach out to pat his thigh and tell him how magnificent he was on screen, even in the smallest roles.

Then came *The Marrying Man.* Oh, sure, I admit that I'd heard all the stories about his off-the-set romance with costar Kim Basinger. I'd secretly read the tabloids while waiting in line at the supermarket and seen the picture of them kissing. But I knew that it was just hype, a carefully orchestrated publicity stunt to boost the buzz around what was, with the obvious exception of Alec, a terrible film. I didn't sense any real danger. After all, surely Alec would never sully himself by touching lips that had touched Mickey Rourke.

What a blow, then, when I turned on the television one awful evening to hear Mary Hart chirpily announcing that not only was Alec really dating that horrible bitch, but he was going to marry her. My man—my Alec—was actually going to give himself to the woman who not only couldn't act to save her life, but who had gone out and bought *a whole town.* Even on my worst shopping days I had never returned home with more than a pair of shoes. And I sincerely doubted that Kim even knew what a little linen guest towel was.

I didn't understand it. How could Alec—my Alec—the man who spoke so eloquently about politics, acting, and human rights, the man who won accolades for his serious stage work, be marrying the human equivalent of cotton candy? It was yet another senseless act in a world gone awry. I went into a tailspin.

Lest you think that my love for Alec is based solely on his

on-screen image, I should tell you that I have met Alec in person twice in my life. OK, I've *seen* Alec in person twice in my life. The first time was when he played Stanley in the revival of Tennessee Williams's *A Streetcar Named Desire* on Broadway. I was first in line the day the box office opened. When the woman behind the ticket window asked me what kind of seats I wanted, I answered breathlessly, "As close to Alec as I can get," and flung my Gold Card at her.

Now, normally I wouldn't bother to plunk down $75 to watch some guy in a play. But the real genius of Tennessee Williams is that he was, when it came down to it, a frustrated queen, and consequently most of his leading men spend a great deal of time running about in undershirts and boxers. Because the parts are so gripping, the male stars seldom realize that the entire point of a Williams play is to see hunky men seminude. This makes it all a great deal of fun for the rest of us, who are in on the joke and wish that more actors would venture into live theater.

I do not actually remember much about the play. I'm sure Jessica Lange, who was also in it, was brilliant. After all, she won raves for it, even though I suspect the critics applauded her simply because she was able to touch Alec's chest while still retaining the ability to speak complete sentences. And I'm told that the writing is very good for that sort of thing. All I can vividly recall is that Alec took his shirt off six times during the two and a half hours he was on stage. In fact, the entire production seemed to have been conveniently choreographed around opportunities for Alec to undress. Whoever staged the thing should have won a Tony for it.

Alec himself *was* nominated for a Tony, and I have no doubt that this had less to do with the forcefulness with which he screamed out, "Hey, Stella!" than it did with his nightly striptease. I am not exaggerating in the least when I tell you that every time Alec reached for the buttons on his shirt, the entire house fell completely silent. When he casually shucked the shirt off and peeled his sweat-soaked T-shirt over his head to reveal his beautiful hairy chest, there was an audible gasp from every sensible person in the audience, the vast majority of whom were male. It was a moment I will never forget. Had my American Express card allowed it, I would have bought box seats for the entire run.

This brings us back to the night I discovered Alec was getting married. Tragically, the second time I saw Alec was on the day before his wedding to She Who Is Unworthy To Run Her Tongue Over His Chest. After hearing the news of the impending nuptials, I had called in sick for a week, unable to get out of bed except to change the Alec tape in my VCR. Finally, after wearing out my copy of *The Hunt for Red October*, I'd pulled myself together and returned to work. It was my first day back, I had somehow muddled through despite my pain, and I was coming home from my office in Midtown. I'd managed to get a cab at Second Avenue and 52nd Street. It was raining, as well as a Friday afternoon, and this was no small accomplishment. For a brief moment, I thought maybe things were looking up.

As the cab rushed past the corner of 48th Street, I noticed a man waving for a taxi. In the true manner of a New Yorker possessed of a cab while others wait in the rain, I laughed wickedly to myself. Until we got closer, and I realized that it was Alec—my Alec—standing there, rain running down his manly face and onto his coat as he vainly tried to flag a ride. Suddenly, everything seemed to move in slow motion. It was just like a scene from a 1940s love story. I pressed my face against the glass and wailed his name as we raced by. Try as I might, the Pakistani driver would not stop the cab, even when I grabbed him by the hair and screamed, "You don't understand—I must get my hands on that chest!" We sped down Second Avenue as I cursed the fact that real life seldom turns out like a Billy Wilder film.

Little did I know that Alec was, in fact, at that very moment on his way to his wedding in Long Island. When I saw it on the news later that evening, with a triumphant Kim smiling as she dragged an obviously confused Alec down the aisle, I wept bitterly. Fate had thrown me another chance, and I'd blown it. When I'd left him on that corner, I'd ruined forever any chance we might have had. I knew it was all over for me and Alec. I did the only thing a jilted lover can do. I bought 16 bags of Reese's Peanut Butter Cups, put my worn out copy of *Beetlejuice* in the VCR, and ate myself into a stupor.

In the days after, I tried to cope as best I could. At first, I hoped that the marriage would fall apart in the tradition of so many other ill-suited Hollywood couplings. Surely Alec would quickly see what a mistake he'd made and divest himself of the walking Barbie he'd given himself to. Then I would rush in to comfort the man who obviously had been destined for me all along, laughing cruelly at Kim as I put Alec's bags in my trunk and drove away to a secluded cabin in Vermont. Smiling sweetly, I would roll down my window and reduce her to tears with the two cruelest words I could think of: "*Boxing Helena*."

But he didn't leave her. In fact, over the next year or so, Alec and Kim seemed to become one of those rarities in Hollywood—a bizarre couple who manages to remain together despite the fact that they have absolutely nothing in common. Just like Bruce and Demi, they inexplicably weathered everything from financial ruin to critical pot shots of their films without a scratch. Not only did they thrive in the face of adversity, but they did it shamelessly.

Kim Basinger, of course, became my enemy. I rented her movies, searching them for some sign of the elusive quality possessed by the shameless hussy who had stolen my husband right out from under me. Like Arantxa Sanchez Vicario watching tapes of Steffi Graf in order to prepare a game plan, I studied her every move. She had to have something I didn't have, something that drove Alec crazy, and I was determined to find it and duplicate it. I watched *9½ Weeks*, *Batman*, and *Cool World* until I was sure my eyes would begin to bleed. I analyzed the way Kim flipped her hair, dissected her amazing ability to speak without ever moving her lips, and strived to copy her capacity to render a full range of emotions meaningless with the same vacant stare.

My friends begged me to stop my madness. "Please," my friend Katherine said. "Switch to Billy. At least he isn't married." This, of course, was pre–Chynna Phillips. But I wouldn't hear of it. "His face is too bony," I said, kissing my picture of Alec with a full day's growth of beard. "Try Danny," said another well-meaning soul, and I was briefly tempted, until I heard him talk. "Too stupid," I said decidedly, replaying my tape of Alec fervently discussing environmental issues on *Crossfire* with John Sununu and imagining myself walking a picket line with him, his manly hand gripped in mine. I suspected Kim's idea of saving the environment was using biodegradable bleach.

In the end, of course, my battle proved fruitless. Despite numerous voodoo dolls, rituals, prayers, and candle burnings, as of this writing Alec remains with Kim. They've even managed to produce a child, dashing my long-held hope that perhaps the relationship was never consummated and that Alec was holding out for me, wondering why I was so late in coming. When he decked the photographer trying to snap a photo of him on the way home from the hospital, I knew in my heart that it was out of frustration at not having found me.

Unable to have him for my own, I have devoted my life to celibacy. If I can't have Alec, I want no one. No other mouth will kiss mine. No other hands will caress my flesh. I have resigned myself to an existence devoid of love. Oh, sure, I've tried dating, but inevitably it ends up the same way every time. No matter how witty, charming, and handsome the man, at the end of the evening when he asks for another date I sigh, look into his eyes, and say sadly, "I'm sorry, but you're just no Alec." Like an unlucky princess in one of the sadder Grimm's tales, I am cursed to wander the world alone while another enjoys my beloved's bed.

Still, there may be signs of hope for me yet. A few weeks ago I read in a gossip column that Alec had started going to a salon to have his back hair removed, after Kim said it repulsed her and refused to do it for him anymore. All I have to say is, Kim, you better watch out, you bitch. Because I, for one, will be waiting outside the door with hot wax in hand.

My Life as a Dwarf, Part 2: Bashful

When his youngest daughter got married, Patrick thought it would be fun if we treated our new son-in-law to a traditional bachelor party the night before the wedding. By traditional he meant a night out drinking at a strip club in Vegas. "That's what you're supposed to do," he explained when I gently questioned whether this was really the excellent idea he thought it was. And since he has been married and I haven't, I assumed he knew best.

The event itself was largely forgettable. The drinking was minimal, the mood more exhausted than exuberant, and we were back at the hotel and in bed by midnight. I was left with the distinct impression that the heterosexual bachelor parties of lore are likely more about what everyone wished had happened than about what really did happen.

In our case, the strip club was one of Vegas's finest, lauded far and wide as surely the most wonderful place in the world if you're looking for lovely ladies anxious to show you their goodies. Patrick had selected it based on the praise of Howard Stern, whom he listens to regularly and considers an authority on All Things Tasteful.

I suppose it really was an excellent strip club. At any rate, there were women there and they were removing their clothing at an astonishing rate for the adoring male audience. But what struck me most about the experience wasn't the beauty of the women or how keen they seemed to be to show us what lay beneath their underpants—it was how completely unerotic the whole thing was. It was, to be perfectly truthful, about as exciting as a piano recital performed by profoundly untalented 9-year-olds.

Now, I know what you're thinking. Mike, you're a H-O-M-O-S-E-X-U-A-L. You're not supposed to find women taking off their underthings arousing. It's right there in the handbook, on page 173, just below the paragraph on mandatory back waxing.

Yes, I *know.* But even though I might not find female naughty bits exciting in an I-need-to-touch-myself-immediately kind of way, I can certainly appreciate sensuality for what it is. And this wasn't sensual. It was more, well, garish and tiresome, like a living room done over in a faux country style complete with wagon wheel furniture and badly done stenciling around the ceiling. As the men around us hooted and hollered while the women writhed in faux-Sapphic ecstasy with each another or pinched their nipples while making baby-doll pouts, I couldn't help think they should all be just a little bit ashamed of themselves.

I'm not a big proponent of shame, mind you. I grew up Baptist, so I know all about shame and what a job it can do on people. I've seen people overcome with shame do terrible things to themselves, worrying the shame like a dog with a bone until they've resorted to inflicting pain on their bodies or gone completely mad. I've seen lives that should have been beautiful and vibrant things become dried-up scraps blown away and forgotten because of shame's withering influence.

I do think, though, that a great number of us could do with just the littlest bit of shame, a tiny, vitamin-size dose downed along with our orange juice or milk in the morning. And not shame of the "look how awful you are" variety, but more of the "do you really need to do that?" kind.

For instance, what I really wanted to say to the men in the strip club that night wasn't, "Do you know what idiots you look like?" What I wanted to say was, "Do you realize that girl you just paid $50 for grinding around on your lap for five minutes could be your daughter or your niece?" Maybe if they thought about it that way, they wouldn't be so worked up over the whole thing.

As for the women, well, I have enough sex-worker friends that I've heard all the bullshit about how empowering it is and how it reverses traditional power roles and restores sexual energy and blah, blah, blah. I also know how lucrative it is, but I really doubt that if those women I saw in Vegas could make the same amount of money, say, dog walking or serving up coffee at Starbucks that they'd really prefer to bend over in high heels and have a hundred pairs of eyes glued to their assholes. As for all of those empowered sex workers, why is it that so many of them end up depressed, addicted, and dead? I guess empowerment demands a high price.

And of course it isn't just the women. I could easily make a list of female stars from the sex industry who have been devoured by the adoration of their fans and the demands of the business. But there are just as many male sex stars who have been empowered into oblivion. Remember Joey Stefano? He was billed as the most famous bottom in gay porn. Even in death he continues to have legions of fans, probably more than he did in life. His videos are collectors' items, and the biography of his brief and turbulent life topped best-seller lists for months. Or how about Ryan Idol, the self-proclaimed straight star of so many gay male fantasies? Ryan ended up (depending on whose story you believe) falling or being pushed from a hotel room window. And the list goes on.

What I find particularly interesting about many of the people we idolize for their blatant sexuality is that in almost every case they're described as children who were painfully shy. Most were completely unassuming, even invisible. Socially awkward. Wallflowers. Bashful, if you will. Childhood pictures show them hiding behind the legs of their parents, eyes lowered so as not to confront the camera. High school photos more often than not depict faces ravaged by the cruelties of adolescence: acne, braces, regrettable hair styles, and misguided fashion choices.

It may be surprising, then, that these ugly ducklings end up parading before us in the most revealing of ways. But is it? Many psychiatrists now believe shyness is an unnatural state, that the retiring child is in fact probably depressed, perhaps even mentally ill. Not merely a sign of a "delicate" personality or a "sensitive" nature, bashfulness has become a potential symptom of something much more sinister—a child who isn't quite normal. Perhaps, desperate to break out of this repressive state, the wallflowers see freedom in becoming the future porn stars of America.

From the ages of 11 to 17, I said perhaps 78 words. I hadn't said a whole lot before then either, but those years were particularly silent ones. I spoke little to my parents, even less to people my own age. I didn't have anything to say. I also almost never left my room. It was safer there. Safer from what, I wasn't really sure. I wasn't afraid of anything in particular. I just felt that being alone, with no one looking at me, was preferable to being out in the world.

My Life as a Dwarf, Part 2: Bashful

I still don't welcome being paid attention to. I'm not overly fond of doing interviews or public readings. I don't go to parties. I particularly dislike being focused on by salespeople or servers in restaurants. None of this is because I'm afraid, or because I feel overly uncomfortable in such settings. It's simply that I prefer to go unnoticed.

I used to feel badly about this. I thought I was disappointing people—first my parents, then my friends, and later my agents and publishers and partner—by not being more excited about being the center of attention. I tried very hard to get into the spirit of things, to enjoy it all. But the truth is that I don't, and there's nothing wrong with that. I suppose I could have rebelled against my bashfulness and just gone into gay porn, but I don't think I would have been very good at it. Writing seemed more feasible. And it requires fewer trips to the gym.

I don't want you to go away thinking I'm not excited about sex. Sex is fine. Seeing people naked is fine. If someone were to publish nude photos of, say, Russell Crowe or George Clooney, I would happily look at them. Maybe even two or three times. But the strip club thing and the porn thing simply holds no magic.

I like those old-time burlesque shows. You know, where women danced around behind giant ostrich-feather fans and maybe showed the audience a little bit of leg here, a glimpse of bare torso there, and a lot of suggestive eye contact in between. To me that's much more interesting than someone taking it all off and waving it in my face. "Oh, you have a penis. How nice. And look, it's coated in baby oil. Mmm. And my, but you did a good job shaving that scrotum. It's smooth as the day you were born. Kudos."

I don't think so. Shyness is much more appealing than brazenness any day. Again, not to bring too much of a religious aspect to this whole conversation, but one of my favorite stories from the Bible is about Esther. Way back before *Married by America, The Bachelor,* and *Are You Hot?* Esther was invited (well, commanded) to appear before King Ahasuerus (there will not be a quiz later, so you can forget this immediately if you like) along with every other available woman in the land so that His Majesty could choose a wife. Apparently he was quite a catch, because the girls were all very excited about this. So excited that they coated their faces with eye shadow and rouge, dressed themselves in colorful silks, and generally tarted themselves up. Then they all paraded around in front of the king in an attempt to get his attention.

All of them except Esther. Esther wore a plain white dress. No makeup. Very little jewelry. She was just Esther. And who do you think became the king's queen? That's right.

Since then poor Esther has been held up by legions of Sunday School teachers as proof that virgins always win out over whores. I think this misses the point entirely. Esther was, by all accounts, a beautiful woman. But she knew that revealing a little said far more than revealing everything. She understood the power of holding back. For her efforts, she gained a kingdom.

We could do with a little more of that these days. No one holds back anymore. We don't have to wait for Britney Spears's career to need a boost to see her bare it all in a *Playboy* spread, because we've already seen it in her videos. We don't have to guess what our favorite stars look like in the altogether because they show us on a regular basis. It's getting so you can't turn on the television without seeing some famous tit or Academy Award–winning ass.

The mystery has, unfortunately, gone out of sex. It's become way too easy, and as a result we've all become jaded about it. We no longer have to wait to see what a potential lover has beneath her or his clothes because chances are one of our friends already has a Polaroid of it hidden in a sock drawer or we've already been the recipient of an X-rated JPEG or GIF courtesy of an online chat room and the click of a mouse.

So back to the strippers, if I may. What's the thrill? Sure, you can sit there thinking about what having sex with them would be like. But here's the thing—you already *know*. What they do offstage isn't going to be any different from what you've already paid your money to see along with a bunch of other horny guys. Plus, they're probably a lot more slippery when you actually get your hands on them.

I have friends who have lusted after porn stars for years, only to finally sleep with them (sometimes by accident, more often after handing over a credit card) and come home disappointed by the experience. They're always surprised by this, and I'm always surprised by *that*. "What did you expect?" I ask them. "You already saw everything they've got to offer."

I'm sorry, but sex is always hotter, always better, always more satisfying when there's been some kind of buildup. Getting to know someone and *then* getting naked with them will win out over instant gratification every time. Sure, sometimes you need fast food, but when you think about your most memorable dinner it's not likely to be that Big Mac you gobbled down on your way home from work. If it is, that's sort of sad.

I love Jane Austen and Anthony Trollope novels. I love them because the heroes and heroines are so sexually worked up that they're ready to wet their knickers and soil their petticoats just from looking at one another. But do they rip each other's clothes off at the first opportunity? No.

They needlepoint and make witty remarks. They bring one another flowers and work out their horniness by banging on clavichords and engaging in fox hunts. Never in a million years would a Jane Austen character rip off her blouse and pinch her nipples, and I can't recall a single instance when one of Trollope's suitors sent another a lewd drawing of his erect penis enclosed in an invitation to afternoon tea.

Ah, for a return to decorum and civility. Is it too much to ask that instead of running around shaking our moneymakers at anyone who wants to see them that we sit quietly in the corner with hands in our laps, smiling shyly, and waiting patiently for the right moment?

Singing a Different Tune

Every time I do a public appearance, someone asks me about my nephew Jack. "Did he turn out to be gay?" "Has he read your book?" The answer, at least to the second question, is that yes, Jack has read my books. (We'll get to the first question later.) He loves them. He's even shared them with some of his friends at school, and as a result has become something of a local celebrity. In fact, out of all the members of my family I suspect Jack is the most pleased about having his life mined for fun and profit. Now almost 18 and getting ready to head off to college, he barely resembles the 10-year-old boy from this essay. Reading it makes me feel very old, and indeed the music references betray their early 1990s origins. Still, it remains one of my favorite pieces.

When my nephew, Jack, was about to turn 10, I called my sister well in advance of the actual date and asked her what he would like for his birthday. The 10th year is a big one for any child, marking a transition between the dreamlike world of kick-the-can and paper dolls and the horrors of adolescent life like spontaneous erections and big bullies named Kurt, and it should be commemorated accordingly. I still recall vividly the gold eagle pendant my cousin Jay, my childhood hero, presented me with on my tenth birthday. I wore it religiously, until one sad day the clasp snapped and it was lost forever, improving dramatically my choice of accessories but leaving me cheerless. I wanted Jack to have such a moment to remember.

Karen knew instantly what Jack would cherish above all else on this earth. "CDs," she said promptly. "He's really into music now."

This was good news. Children as a rule have no taste whatsoever, so when buying music for them, it's just a matter of going to the record store and picking up whatever is hovering at number one for that given week. Even if they have no idea what it is, kids will play it loudly and thrash about in some semblance of dancing, feeling very grown up and pleased with themselves. The week of my 10th, it was the soundtrack to *Grease* burning up the charts, and I received it with delight and some surprise, considering that my mother had forbidden me to actually see the movie after learning that the word "shit" was uttered freely. I played it endlessly, naturally taking Olivia Newton-John's solos, and to this day I wonder how my life would have turned out if, instead, AC/DC or Bruce Springsteen had ruled the airwaves in the fall of 1978.

"So what should I get him?" I asked. "Hootie and the Blowfish? Coolio? Maybe Garth Brooks?"

Karen laughed. "Oh, no," she said cheerfully. "Nothing like that. He likes soundtracks."

"Great," I said, visions of *Grease* filling my mind. "So maybe the music from *The Lion King* would be good." I had this vague notion that every 10-year-old thrilled to all things Disney.

"Actually," Karen said, "He wants the albums from *Cats* and *Les Mis*."

I was speechless. I wondered if my sister had any notion

of what implications were of what she had just said. Maybe, I thought, I'd just heard her incorrectly. "You mean the Broadway shows?" I asked doubtfully.

"Yep," she confirmed. "He loves those. We went and saw a touring show of *Cats*, and he's been humming the songs ever since."

I didn't know what to say. This was my sister talking, the one whose only response to my coming out was, "Well, you know I'm OK with it, but God says it's wrong so you're probably going to hell." Now she was telling me, in effect, that her very own son was exhibiting early signs of becoming a raging queen, and not only did she not seem to mind, she was enthusiastically supporting his bid for queerdom.

OK, I know the stereotype of the gay man singing show tunes is one many people find offensive. I know I don't happen to like them very much. And we all go out of our way to reassure kids that just because some boys like ballet and some girls like softball they aren't necessarily going to end up with rainbow flag stickers on their Volvos and mineral water in the fridge. But really, when's the last time you saw a little boy who could belt out "I'm Just A Girl Who Can't Say 'No'" grow into a fascination with Pamela Anderson Lee's breasts? Can you blame me for being suspicious?

Still, I knew I had to be careful. I certainly didn't want to out the kid to his mother, especially so near to his birthday. If he really was tripping gaily on the heels of Dorothy's ruby slippers, I didn't want her to freak out, which I knew she would. She was already worried about the effect it might have on him being raised by a single mother, and she'd probably go out and buy him a rifle to compensate. She still harbors a suspicion that I'm gay because our father never built a tree fort with me.

"Um, Karen," I said, trying to determine exactly how

serious the situation was. "Does Jack just kind of hum the music, or does he know all the words?"

"It's amazing," she said ingenuously. "He knows *every* word to every song. He hears them once and has them down. He can even do the motions Grizabella makes when she sings 'Memory.' You should see it; it almost makes me cry. Why?"

"No reason," I said casually. "I'll see what I can do."

I hung up and ran to the record store. Now, I'm not saying it's right to actively hope that a young child is gay, and far be it from me to suggest that we push those showing the slightest indication of a queer aesthetic along in any way. All I will say is that I skipped with a glad heart to the show-tunes section and snatched up Jack's requested discs. For good measure, I added *Phantom of the Opera*, and briefly paused at *Gypsy* before deciding that would be too much even for me. He had to be broken in slowly.

Once home, I wrapped the CDs up and shipped the whole mess off to my sister with a prayer to the Patron Saint of All Young Queens—Charles Nelson Reilly. On Jack's birthday, I called to see how things were going.

"Hello?" Karen shouted when she picked up the phone. In the background I could hear the swelling tones of "Music of the Night" filling the apartment.

"Hi," I said briskly. "How's the birthday boy?"

"Just great," Karen said. "He's absolutely thrilled with the CDs. You didn't have to send so many, you know."

"That's OK," I said. "You only turn 10 once. What's that shrieking?" In the background I could hear what sounded like a recent castrato bemoaning its fate.

"He's singing," Karen said proudly. "All morning it was 'On My Own' from *Les Mis*. Now he's learning *Phantom*."

I tried not to crow in triumph. "That's really great," I said.

"He'll be a singer in no time." I imagined what my sister would think when Jack started renting Joan Crawford movies. She'd probably blame it on me, but I didn't care. Score one for our side.

"Oh, he already is," Karen said. "You should hear him try to do 'Evergreen.'"

This was more than I could stand. "He sings Streisand?" I said incredulously.

"Oh, yeah," Karen answered. "He's been getting into my Barbra records since he was six. In fact, my present to him was his own copy of *The Broadway Album.* We sing it together."

I had to hang up.

So maybe 10 is a little young to know for sure. Still, I think the fact that I asked for an Easy-Bake oven when I was seven was probably some kind of early indicator, sexist or not, of what would come. My friend Anne agrees. She gave her Barbie a crew cut and rechristened her Alix when she was four. Now Anne drives a UPS truck and plays rugby for her wimmin's collective team. You can't ignore the facts. Jack's birthday is coming up again, and this year he wants to visit the Smithsonian to see the exhibit of first ladies' gowns. Karen says she's glad he's showing such a healthy interest in American history.

Guy Problems

After the popularity of my first essay about my nephew Jack and his questionable sexuality, it seemed a follow-up was a foregone conclusion, if only to stanch the flood of letters asking, "Well, is he?" In fact, Jack is not *gay. But don't weep tears of sadness, gentle readers, for this revelation actually caused me to realize something: We are all much more alike than we are different. It's a platitude of* Sesame Street*-esque proportions, I admit, but it's true nonetheless. This piece was as popular as its predecessor, particularly with Jack and his friends. It made the rounds at his school (where, coincidentally, I was also once a student), and although a small group of parents were less than enthusiastic, the kids themselves, many of them the children of my former classmates, were delighted to see the life of one of their own in print. Perhaps things do change after all.*

A couple of Wednesdays ago, my sister called for our semiweekly chat. We spoke for a while, and after we'd caught up on the latest news and she had filled me in on the details of her breakup with the most recent unsuitable boyfriend, she asked me to hang on for a second. I heard voices in the background, and when Karen returned, she said, "Jack has something he wants to talk to you about."

Jack is her son, and due to the laws of relativity, my

nephew. Some readers may remember him from previous columns as the young man who has shown an inordinate amount of interest in show tunes. Well, he's now 12, and entering middle school. While I find this difficult to believe, wanting probably to maintain the illusion that he is still 5 and I am not hurtling rapidly toward 30, the fact is that Jack is starting to encounter all of those pleasant adolescent hurdles like acne, voice changes, and, as I was soon to find out, more difficult challenges.

"You have to leave," Jack said to my sister after picking up the phone. "This is guy stuff."

Karen dutifully exited the room, and as soon as she was gone, Jack breathed heavily into the receiver. "I have a problem," he said. "A big problem."

"I told you last time, everybody does it," I said reassuringly. "Just make sure you lock the bathroom door this time. I don't think your mother has quite gotten over it yet."

"It isn't *that*," Jack said impatiently. "It's even more important."

I couldn't imagine anything more important than *that*, at least not when I was 12. In fact, I don't know many guys under 60 who think there's anything more important than *that*. But maybe that's just me. At any rate, I was curious to hear what was going on in Jack's life that was so significant that it eclipsed even the forbidden joys of masturbation. So I sat patiently as his tale unraveled. It took him a good 10 minutes to get it all out, but he managed. The result was worse than I'd imagined.

It seems he's involved in his first love triangle. Actually, it's more of a love square, involving as it does three other 12-year-olds. As I was soon to discover, Jack has a crush on a young woman named Amber Platt, who he assures me is the most bewitching girl in his class. But he also thinks Megan

Huckabone is rather swell, even if she is missing a front tooth from a confrontation with a softball. And standing in the middle of it all is Jack's best friend, Henry Bick, who also seems to think Megan is a cutie-pie.

"So, what do you think?" he asked me after he'd outlined in agonizing detail who liked whom and how much.

I stared at the diagram I'd made of the situation while he was talking. I am a visual person, and like to have things in lists before I begin to think about them. Now I had all the participants lined up before me, but I was at a loss for words. To tell the truth, I'd been dreading this moment for a number of years. Jack's father is out of the picture, and I'm the one he comes to with dad-type problems. Most of them, like how to put on a jock for Little League or what to get his mom for Christmas, had been easy enough to handle.

Even the masturbation discussion had been relatively easy. For some reason, I never think of jacking off as sex. It's more like playing a vigorous round of rock-paper-scissors or something. There's a certain amount of societal baggage attached to it, but ultimately it's just you and your hand and maybe some tissues. When Jack had brought up the subject of his own self-exploration, I'd been able to explain it to him calmly and reasonably, and hadn't even blushed when I informed him that of course his mother did it too and that it wasn't anything to be ashamed about. Why, I told him, even the president does it. It was nothing to worry about.

This, however, was different. This went beyond sex for one and straight into uncharted territory. This was all about the first stirrings of pubescent desire and, well, I wasn't sure how to talk to him about, you know...girls. More specifically, I didn't know how to talk to him about what boys did with girls. Girls and girls I could do. Boys and boys as well. But this was the stuff that had made me queasy even as a kid, and now he was expecting me to help him figure it out. I couldn't tell him that I haven't even figured it out yet.

When Jack's father had first left, Jack was very young, and I'd hoped that some other man would come along to take his place before he was old enough to wonder about things like this and ask me about them. I had also, given Jack's show-tune fetish, thought that perhaps he might one day come to me with other questions I could answer with more authority. But despite numerous attempts, my sister had managed to remain single, and regardless of the show-tune thing, Jack seemed to be developing at least some kind of curiosity about girls. So there I was, faced with his first big romantic question and no idea how to handle it.

"Well?" said Jack, bringing me back into the present. "Who should I go out with?"

"Um, I don't know," I said vaguely.

"But I have to pick one of them," Jack said plaintively. "I'm almost 13. I have to have a girlfriend soon. Everyone else already does."

"Wait until you're almost 30 and still don't have one," I said bitterly.

"How would you choose?" Jack asked.

"I'd pick the butchest one," I said automatically, thinking about my own personal proclivities in men.

"What?" said Jack.

"Never mind," I said.

It was rapidly dawning on me that Jack hadn't even reached the sex part of the equation yet, and was still trying to sort out the basic lineup. I was relieved that we wouldn't be delving into moister topics, at least not immediately, but I was still unsure of how to proceed. My own feeble adolescent attempt at heterosexuality had consisted solely of slipping Bobbi Jo Wagner a note in English asking her if she "wanted to go with me." Her response, "I like to go shopping with you, but that's it," was the first hard evidence that perhaps my romantic leanings lay elsewhere. If Jack is in fact a budding homo, I wanted to spare him the same experience. But in my heart I knew he had to go it alone.

"Look," I said finally. "Which one do you like the best?"

"Well, Amber is a great dancer," said Jack. "But Megan is really good at basketball, and you know that's my favorite sport."

Wondering if maybe Megan and Jack had more in common than either of them knew, I said, "Then go out with her." If nothing else, they could shoot free-throws together.

"But what about Henry?" said Jack.

"You want to go out with Henry?" I asked happily, hoping that the conversation would take a more positive direction after all.

Jack sighed. "*I'm* not gay," he said. "What I mean is that Henry likes Megan too."

We were back to square one. Wanting to be helpful, I tried to think about what I would do in the same situation. The problem was, the dating rules for gay men are slightly different than they are for grade-school children. Or, I thought, maybe they aren't so different after all. Maybe all I had to do was reverse the situation and half of the genders.

"Hold on a minute," I said to Jack. "I have to think this one through."

I then invented in my mind a theoretical situation involving my friend Ed and two guys at our gym, Jesse and Roberto. In my scenario, I liked Jesse, who had nice pecs and lingered near me in the showers once. Roberto was less well-defined, but was always very friendly, and told bad jokes that cracked me up so that I almost dropped the weights. Usually, and for completely shallow reasons, I would be more tempted by Jesse. But I knew that Ed also liked him. In fact, Ed thought Jesse was his dream man, and talked about him at every opportunity. Decisions, decisions.

"Can't you just date them both?" I asked Jack in frustration. "Or maybe share? You know, switch on and off."

"No," he said firmly.

I went back to work, weighing my friendship with Ed against how my tongue would feel running along Jesse's beautiful chest. It would be wonderful. But then I pictured us running into Ed in Provincetown and having all of his friends point at me. The word "slut" would be uttered. The weekend would be ruined for everyone. My mind raced as I went from envisioning nights in Jesse's arms to seeing Ed's dejected face as he spent yet another lonely evening watching *What Ever Happened to Baby Jane?* and downing pint after pint of Ben & Jerry's Heath Bar Crunch, gaining 50 pounds while Jesse and I made love to the serenading of Ella Fitzgerald.

It was an agonizing three minutes. But finally I gave in and went for Roberto, leaving Jesse to the man who really loved him. It was the hardest thing I ever had to do. But to my surprise, I felt great about my decision. And ultimately (at least in my version) it worked out fine after all. Ed was happy, and we were still friends. Best of all, I discovered that Roberto was not only funny, but hung like a horse.

"Let Henry go with Jesse—I mean Megan," I told Jack quickly.

"Thanks," he said. "But how did you decide that?"

"Years of experience," I answered.

I hung up, very pleased that despite my lack of enthusiasm for heterosexuality I had been able to use my own experiences to help out my nephew. Why, guy problems were guy problems. Straight or gay, we were the same when it came to matters of the heart.

A few minutes later, the phone rang again, interrupting a particularly enjoyable fantasy involving Roberto, some sweaty boxer shorts, and a locker room. Thinking it might be Jack needing more advice, I picked up. But it was my friend James.

"Hi," he said. "I need to talk to you about something. See, there are these two guys who like me, and I'm not sure which one…"

"Go with Amber Platt," I said quickly, and hung up.

Relationship Tips for the Neurotically Inclined

Relationships—in particular how bad I and most other gay people seem to be at them—has always been a central topic in my writing. This particular piece was written shortly after I began dating my partner, Patrick. It was, I suppose, my attempt at working out the various neuroses that were conspiring to get me to stop going out with Pat before, as I repeatedly told myself, "you have no one to blame but yourself." Luckily for me, I didn't listen. And in my defense I should point out that I never *looked through his wallet. It's too late now anyway—he started hiding it after reading this essay.*

Once upon a time, being neurotic was fun. Those of us with, shall we say, more finely tuned personalities were treated with utmost care, not to mention great psychiatric interest. To aid us in our endeavors we were presented with such intriguing items as fainting couches, smelling salts, and fans. The more ambitious of us could look forward to spending copious amounts of time in bed, being sent to spas for weeks on end, and perhaps being bled by leeches. It was a glorious time, marked chiefly by pallor, fidgetiness, and lots of sighing.

Things are not so good now. We as a culture have become far less tolerant of peevishness and fretting, and over the years neurosis as a defining personality trait has seen a sharp decline in popularity, to the point where it now it hovers somewhere between obsessive hand-washing and bed-wetting. This raises problems for those among us who stubbornly cling to our neuroses, refusing to let go like thumb-suckers hanging onto our favorite blankets for dear life.

But fear not. There is hope of a resurrection. A number of years ago someone published the enormously popular book *How to Live with a Neurotic Cat.* This was followed, inevitably, by the similarly themed *How to Live with a Neurotic Dog.* These were funny books, giving cat and dog owners much to chuckle about. But their chief value seems to have been overlooked, which is that they were wonderful training manuals for those who knew how to use them. They were, in short, filled with tips on how to be neurotic.

Now, constant furniture shredding and tail chewing are all well and good if you have four feet and answer to a single name. (No, Cher does not count, as she has only two feet.) But for those of us with brains larger than your average lemon, it takes slightly more than that. With that in mind, I offer here an easy-to-follow plan designed to take full advantage of the neurotic's natural abilities. This particular set of instructions is focused on relationships, as that seems to be the area where the neurotic excels and also where the most challenges are faced.

TIP 1: ASSUME THE WORST

Relationships, for the neurotic, are the perfect breeding ground for worry. When approached correctly, they can provide endless opportunities for exercising the natural inclination to believe that in any given situation the most unpleasant outcome is inevitable. This can begin on the very first date, where you can immediately begin thinking of reasons for there not being a second date. Should the relationship miraculously continue, each day that it goes forward is another occasion for gut-wrenching anxiety. Particularly excellent moments for perfecting this approach include promised phone calls that don't come, nights when your beloved is "out with friends," and the first time your partner answers "Me too" in response to your "I love you."

EXERCISE: Make a list of every possible reason why your relationship could fail. Do not forget to take into account differences in sleeping habits, food preferences, height, allergies, religious practices, age, blood type, income, toothpaste squeezing technique, television viewing habits, sexual turn-ons, musical tastes, and the absolutely-sure-to-be-devastating Yankees versus Mets schism.

TIP 2: KEEP IT ALL INSIDE

This can be a particularly difficult thing to master, but if you can do it, it will serve you well. In general, it is more satisfying for the neurotic to voice any and all concerns or worries that come up, as it puts one's partner in the position of having to be reassuring. There are, however, occasions upon which it may be far more pleasurable to keep your thoughts to yourself. Why? Because you're probably wrong in whatever it is you're worried about, and letting your partner know what you're thinking will deprive you of the delicious joy that comes from having something painful to gnaw on. This technique is most successful at times when simply asking a question would clear everything up, for example after finding an empty condom wrapper under your boyfriend's bed (he probably hasn't cleaned under there since long before he met you) and running into someone on the street whom your partner greets cordially but fails to introduce you to (surely a former trick). **EXERCISE:** Think about an offhand remark your boyfriend made that for some reason made you suspicious, such as the time you were out together and, indicating a man in the bar where you were getting drink, he said, "That guy has done *everyone* in town." Wonder—but don't ask—if this includes your boyfriend. Imagine what they might have done together. Become irrationally angry at him for saying something he should have known would make you unhappy. Again, do not say anything. It's so much more satisfying to seethe.

TIP 3: CONSTANTLY COMPARE YOURSELF TO HIS EXES

Exes are prime fodder for making yourself neurotic. After all, they've gone before you, so of course your boyfriend *must* be comparing you to them, right? It's only fair, then, that you do the same thing. This is particularly easy for gay men because we always seem to remain in contact with our exes (proof, I think, that we're all neurotic to start with). If your boyfriend keeps pictures of his exes, all the better. Visuals add depth and clarity to the worry. But even if there are no physical reminders, you always have mental ones. Be sure to note every time your boyfriend mentions an ex, and in what context. Examine his face closely (but covertly) to see if he smiles when thinking about the men in his past. Provide opportunities for him to comment on his exes, then go over and over his responses in your mind—preferably late at night, while lying next to your boyfriend and resenting him for being able to sleep while you fret. The more bold neurotic may even go so far as to be agonizingly direct, employing questions such as, "Did [insert name of ex] do that for you in bed?" "Did you love him as much as you love me?" and "Is my dick bigger than his?"

EXERCISE: If possible, make a list of all of your boyfriend's exes. Include one-night stands. Go through the list one by one, thoroughly outlining the reasons each of them annoys you. Wonder what your boyfriend did in bed with them. Wonder if he took them to the same places he takes you. Wonder if he called them the same silly names, or laughed the same way when *they* tickled him. Deeply resent every moment he spent with them. Most important, be sure to completely ignore the fact that *you* have just as many (if not more) men in your past and that those experiences have absolutely no effect on how much you love your current guy. This would be far too emotionally healthy and could threaten to undo all the hard work you've done.

TIP 4: LOOK FOR CLUES

Think of this as a scavenger hunt. Or perhaps a police investigation. You're looking for clues—any piece of physical evidence that will enable you to worry about what your boyfriend is up to and what he's hiding from you. Particularly good finds include scraps of paper with phone numbers, photographs showing your boyfriend with his arm around men unfamiliar to you, E-mails from people with suggestive screen names, pornographic magazines or videos, ticket stubs left in coat pockets, cards that accompanied flower deliveries and are signed only with initials, and phone numbers programmed into his phone. Be sure to check medicine cabinets, car glove compartments, shoe boxes in closets, and his wallet (make sure he's in the shower or asleep). More advanced techniques include secretly marking the lube bottle to see if any is used in between your visits, scrolling through the call log on his cell phone, and counting the number of condoms left in the box.

EXERCISE: Keep an evidence log. In it write down everything you find that seems suspicious. NOTE: It is important never to take the actual items. After all, you don't want your boyfriend to *know*, do you? That would take all the fun out of it (See Tip 2). Instead, repeatedly go over the "proof" you've collected, creating elaborate scenarios around each tiny morsel. That ticket stub from a ball game, for example. Who did he go with? What did they do afterward? That phone number. Is it a friend? Why does it just say "Carl" on it? And is that bar smell on the paper? Should you call it and hang up? Ah, the thrill of it all.

TIP 5: CREATE A SUPPORT GROUP

Being neurotic alone is satisfying; doing it with others is nirvana. Not only does having someone else to bounce your suspicions, worries, and general fears off of give you the opportunity to bring your neuroses to life, if you choose wisely you can have an unending source of inspiration. This is particularly true if the other person (or persons) in your support group are just as neurotic as you are. A good support person will know when to reassure you and when to egg you on. For instance, you know you've found yourself a perfect accomplice if, when you suggest that you think your boyfriend might be losing interest, your friend responds not with, "Don't be ridiculous," but with, "Well, he *has* been spending a lot of time without you." Good choices for support staff include your own exes (who knows you better?), fag hags (no matter what they say, they want you for themselves), and your mother (ditto on both previous examples). When employing this technique, be sure to schedule regular meeting times—nightly phone calls or Wednesday dinners out are good—so as to have something to look forward to.

EXERCISE: Begin interviewing possible candidates for your support group position(s). Make a list of the most neurotic people you know. Invite each one to lunch or out for drinks. During conversation, throw out a starter question. For example, "Do you find that you have less sex the longer you're with someone?" Gauge the response and mark the performance on a scale of 1 to 10 depending on how much more neurotic you feel about your own relationship based on their answers. Narrow your list of contestants to five finalists. Have brunch with all of them at once. Halfway through, turn the conversation to relationships again. Take notes (clandestinely) and rank the five in order of their ability to raise doubts and worries in your mind. This is your team. Number one is the captain; the other four are your backup squad.

High Times

The worst part about rereading this essay is realizing that when I wrote it I had no idea that "Republican candidate George W. Bush" would shortly turn out to be President George W. Bush. I still think it must all be a bad dream. Or, given the theme of this essay, a bad trip. Despite that one tiny blight, I'm really fond of this piece. I still laugh when I remember sitting in the car with my mother, pleased as hell that I was secretly a stoner. And for those of you who might be interested in knowing, I've still never tried drugs of any kind. There was a plot to introduce me to the forbidden joys of marijuana when I visited a friend of mine last year, but in the end we decided to stuff ourselves with doughnuts and play Mystery Date *instead. I really have to start hanging out with better people.*

You know you've lived a sheltered life when a presidential candidate has done more drugs than you have.

I was watching CNN the other night and they were interviewing Democratic presidential hopeful Bill Bradley. The issue about Republican candidate George W. Bush's alleged past drug use came up, and in the course of the discussion Bradley was asked if he'd ever smoked pot.

"On several occasions," Bradley answered without hesitation.

High Times

"And did you inhale?" joked the questioner, referring to Bill Clinton's infamous claim about having smoked pot without actually smoking pot.

"I did indeed," said Bradley.

Well, he's one up on me. I've never smoked pot. Well, once I tried, but I did it all wrong and ended up wheezing a lot. Besides, I hated the smell, and I never tried again. In fact, I've never done any drugs of any kind. No Ecstasy. No coke. Not even poppers, which technically aren't a drug but which gay men seem to go wild for.

Now please don't think I'm taking the moral high road here. I haven't steered clear of altering my consciousness through chemicals for any particularly pious reasons. It's just that I'm bad enough without them. I don't even take cold medicine unless I'm absolutely dying and convinced that my nasal passages are closing up for good. And even then I only take half the recommended dose, because it's sure to knock me out for hours and leave me nauseous afterward. When I had to have my wisdom teeth out, the doctor gave me a prescription for Tylenol with codeine. I took one and woke up three days later, convinced I was in a Turkish prison.

The problem is that my body doesn't handle stimulation very well. Things that give other people mild buzzes, like caffeine or sugar, send me into overdrive. A couple of years ago I decided I needed to start drinking coffee because that's what writers do. Besides, I liked the idea of having a coffee maker and a little machine to grind the beans. So I bought them and launched myself headlong into the exciting world of java. I trotted over to a coffee store, thrilled that such a thing could even exist, and got myself a pound of some exotically named beans. Then I ground them up, set the machine to perking, and waited.

The first cup was sort of OK. It woke me up, and I felt a warm glow as I sat in front of my computer drinking it. When it was done, I poured myself another. By 10 o'clock in the morning I had consumed six cups because I didn't want to waste what I'd made, Kenyan blue mountain coffee beans costing what they do. My whole body was trembling, and I found myself reading the same paragraph over and over and over, unable to make any sense of it and desperately trying to remember if "chrysanthemum" was really even a word. Finally I laid down on the floor and stared at the ceiling, wondering if my heart was going to leap out of my chest. That was my last experience with the coffee machine. The next day I packed it up and gave it to a friend whose years of coffee drinking had left her immune to anything weaker than 100% black Columbian roast injected directly into her veins. I went back to Ovaltine, and gladly.

While the physical issue is one thing, I admit that my inexperience with drugs is also at least partly because I fear losing control. This I blame on Angeline Kennedy. Angeline was my school's resident pothead. She and I were friends, and she made it her mission to get me high. While outwardly I protested, secretly I wanted her to make good on her threat because it seemed like such a bad-boy thing to do. But I was also convinced that if I touched a joint someone would surely get me for it, probably God.

One day Angeline arrived at lunch with a smile on her face and a small bag in her hand. It was, she said, marijuana. The real thing. I looked at it with a rapidly growing sense of alarm and wonder, and asked what she was going to do with it. She opened the bag, took a pinch of the green leaves, and proceeded to sprinkle them over the little carton of strawberry ice cream that was a part of our lunch that day.

"Dig in," she said, grinning.

I took a spoonful of the pot-covered ice cream and tasted it. Pot is not the culinary equivalent of chocolate sprinkles, but I figured that since I'd stuck my toe in the water I might as well go in all the way. I quickly ate the rest of it and put the dish down.

"I don't feel anything," I said to Angeline.

"Don't worry," she said. "It takes a while."

As it happened, that afternoon my mother and I were driving to my sister's house, which was about five hours away. She picked me up at school right after lunch. As I got into the car, I wondered if she could tell that I was high. Because I was sure that I must be high. After all, I'd eaten pot. I settled nervously into my seat and tried to remember all the signs of drug use we'd learned about in health class. I wanted to be able to hide them from my mother. I kept trying to look at my eyes in the rearview mirror to see if they were bloodshot, and I tried not to fidget. If my mother noticed, she noticed she didn't say anything.

For the entire five-hour trip I debated whether or not I was high. I didn't really feel any different, but I knew that I must be under some kind of influence. After all, I'd ingested real live marijuana. I even tried being more high than I seemed to be, squinting my eyes and giggling a little. But I just felt stupid, and eventually I settled into a morose silence, trying to console myself with the thought that I was in a car with my mother and I was stoned. Very movie of the week. Very after-school special. I imagined myself getting high on a regular basis, hiding the pot from my mother inside a hollowed-out Bible or something. My grades would slip, and I would start to have friends of dubious reputation. It would all be very wicked, and when it was over I would be a different person, edgier and streetwise like the girls in the novels I sometimes got from our church library who ran away from home, became hookers, and had to be rescued from foul-mouthed pimps by their dedicated and surprisingly attractive youth group leaders.

All weekend I remained in my newfound druggie persona. I sat on the couch, watching my sister and my mother and thinking, *They have no idea that I use.* If they asked me questions, I lied just for the practice. I knew it would come in handy later on. By the time we returned home on Sunday night, I was ready for the big time. On Monday when I saw Angeline, I asked her when she could score for me again.

"That wasn't pot," she said, laughing. "It was oregano. I was just fooling with you."

I've been getting high on oregano ever since.

The sad truth is I wouldn't know a real drug experience from the one I convinced myself I was having, so why bother? Plus, I worry that the very second my consciousness is altered the house will catch fire from some freak accident and I won't be coherent enough to get the dog out. I realize this fear is the vestigial remains of good old Baptist guilt, but it's there nonetheless. I just know that if I were to snort cocaine, it would inevitably come from a bag that had been cut with rat poison and my brain would explode on the spot. Or if I were to take acid (oddly the only drug that actually appeals to me, probably because I imagine that being on it would be a lot like watching Disney's *Fantasia*) I would end up believing I could fly and find myself climbing utility poles to prove it.

Honestly, I don't think I've missed anything by not playing with drugs. I have many friends who have done more than enough for both of us, and they assure me that, while sometimes amusing, overall drugs are nothing to write home about. But when a presidential candidate, of all people, has done more than you have, it makes you wonder if maybe you haven't been just a little too uptight. Besides, I don't want anyone to think I actually listened to Nancy Reagan in the '80s and agreed with her.

The problem is that it's too late to start now. Experimenting with drugs at 22 is sort of hip and expected, like announcing that you're a Communist for a week or two, but at 30-something it's like buying a red convertible and trading in your perfectly wonderful boyfriend for a moody French underwear model. It just means you're trying too hard. Instead, I have accepted that I am not the thrill-seeking kind when it comes to that kind of thing. I'll leave the coke and the Ecstasy and even the coffee to other people. I have the memories of my oregano weekend to get me by when I need to go back to my wild days. And if I want to relive them, all I have to do is eat one too many chocolate bars, wash them down with some Mountain Dew, and within minutes I'm flying high.

The Non-Writing Life

It's an interesting phenomenon that most people who want *to be writers spend a great deal of time thinking about writing, while most people who* are *writers spend a great deal of time thinking about not writing. I'm not sure who's actually* doing *the writing, but somehow it manages to work itself out.*

Writers who claim that they've wanted to write since the age of 6 and would die if they couldn't write are pathological liars.

I hate writing. In fact, I will do almost anything to avoid doing it, and actually getting me to produce something is no less a miracle than it must have been to construct the hanging gardens at Babylon. If it wasn't for the simple fact that I am totally unemployable in any other capacity, I probably wouldn't even write at all. And if someone were to offer me a vast sum of cash to stop, I would. Why Joe Eszterhas, the screenwriter of such classics as *Showgirls* and *Basic Instinct* and the highest-paid writer in Hollywood, refuses to make the same concession, I cannot understand. He's probably written since he was 6.

Discovering this about me amazes people who know that I have made a living as a writer for several years now. This is because people have interesting ideas about writers. Most think that we spring from our beds each morning and leap to the keyboard to get down all the fresh ideas that have been birthed in the subconscious while we sleep. They envision us spending joyous days at the computer creating marvelous new worlds and turning out witty phrases left and right until, breathless from the act of creation and weak from forgetting to eat, we repair to the kitchen for a light snack of leftover sushi before settling down to watch something stimulating on PBS.

I do know writers like that, but they are not to be trusted, and I do not speak to them. My own life, and that of most full-time writers I know, is far less glamorous. How books are written remains a mystery I do not fully understand, even though I have produced close to two dozen of them. I know only that, in my case, they generally are pieced together in fits of activity that come between extended periods of not doing anything at all.

Take, for instance, this past Tuesday, which is fairly representative of most of my days. At 5:30 I got up and, after stumbling about in the dark trying to find my clothes, took Roger, my black Lab, to the park for a swim and a run with his friends. Now lest you think my getting up at this early hour is an admirable display of affection for my loyal pet, I should explain that we do this because predawn is the only time that the park is not overrun by joggers and fishermen, two groups of people who neither Roger nor I need adding to our morning experience. It also means that I don't have to make elaborate excuses for going to bed at 8:30 in the evening and refusing to have dinner with people I don't like.

Returning several hours later, Roger enjoyed a leisurely breakfast on the porch while I ate potato chips and Lotsa Lemon yogurt and wondered why all the geraniums were yellowing. I then spent from 8:30 until 9 examining the plants and trying to cheer them up, unsuccessfully, by spritzing them with a mixture of fish meal and bottled water. What I was really doing was not working on the book I'd promised my editor would be on her desk by Friday, but which in truth I had not even begun to write yet.

At 9 o'clock I turned on *Oprah*, which I watch because my agent says that authors who appear on her show make millions of dollars, and I figure tuning in each day will give me some tips on how to write books that Oprah likes. On this particular morning, the guest happened to be Toni Morrison. I had sort of been hoping for Zack, a 70-pound 2-year-old who had been making the talk show rounds of late, but I settled for what I could get. Besides, it was literary, and was therefore not a waste of time. Everything went well until Oprah asked what Toni liked best about being a writer. "Oh, I don't think I can call myself a writer," Morrison said. "I don't think anyone can make a living by writing these days. It's just too hard."

I turned the TV off. Toni Morrison has several best-selling novels and a Nobel Prize to her credit, and she still won't call herself a writer. I don't even have a savings account. And I've written more books than she has. Surely it was a sign that I should just stop. I started to scan the "Help Wanted" for ads, but decided it was too much effort because they weren't listed alphabetically.

From 10 o'clock to 11 o'clock I checked my E-mail, none of which was important but all of which was deeply fascinating in comparison with trying to write something. I then answered it all, writing thoughtful and incisive responses in the event that a century from now someone will want to know what I had to say about things. Having sent it, I opened WordPerfect and began to look through all of my files, deciding that it was a wonderful opportunity to clear things out and, thus newly organized, begin my writing work with a fresh outlook.

The Non-Writing Life

At 1:30, while I was deeply engrossed in reading a self-help book on visualizing success (deleting the files had become boring when I realized there was nothing new since the last time I'd rearranged them), the phone rang. Visualizing someone calling with an offer of cash, I picked it up. Still, ever wary that it might be a disgruntled editor, I disguised my voice.

"Hello?" I said gruffly, adopting a slightly irritated tone, as though interrupted in the middle of composing something utterly brilliant.

"Relax, it's me," said my friend Katherine. Katherine is a writer too, and is almost as good at avoiding actually writing as I am.

"What are you doing?" I asked, pleased to have something to rescue me from almost working. Since Katherine had called me, I had the passive-aggressive advantage of having her to blame later on for my unproductive day.

"Nothing," she said flatly. "I got up at noon and watched a *Murphy Brown* rerun. I was thinking about going to the library, but I'm too tired."

Being tired is a central quality of all full-time writers. I cannot recall the last day on which I did not have a nap.

"Maybe you should write something," I suggested lightly. I was hoping Katherine might actually believe for a moment that *I* was really working.

"Right," said Katherine instantly. "When's the last time you wrote something?"

I thought about that. "I handed a manuscript in at the beginning of February," I said. "A novel. Rent was due."

Katherine was impressed. "I haven't handed anything in for months," she said. "In fact, I forget what it is I'm supposed to be working on."

"The article about lesbians in China," I reminded her.

While we seldom do any of our own work, writers can always remember the details of what our friends are not working on. That way we always know who would be ahead if anything was actually written.

"Oh, yeah," she said sleepily. "That's been due for weeks."

I sighed. "You know, I wish I had something interesting to work on," I said. "That would make it so much easier to be motivated."

"You have three books under contract," Katherine said.

"But none of them are *interesting*," I complained. "I didn't think they'd actually buy them when I sent in the proposals. I just needed to feel like I was doing something."

"Just write them," Katherine said. "What about your column?"

I needed to change the subject. Being reminded of everything I wasn't writing was making me tense. "Do you think Joyce Carol Oates and Stephen King have conversations like this?" I asked.

"Probably," said Katherine. "I bet she eats Oreos all morning and then calls him to see what he's doing."

"And he's sitting there playing solitaire on his Mac," I added. It made me feel better to imagine writers more famous than myself sitting around not writing too.

Katherine and I talked for a long time about not writing, and about what Joyce and Stephen were doing. By the time we were done, we had them engaged in trying to create a stained glass effect on their office windows while avoiding finishing first drafts of their new books, something Katherine and I had actually done a few years back. Then I looked at the clock. It was 3 o'clock, time for Roger's walk. I said goodbye to Katherine and hung up.

After Roger's walk, I gathered the mail and scanned it hopefully for 1) letters from publishers with checks; 2) letters from readers with kind words and/or checks, and 3. magazines which would give me something to do for the rest of the afternoon. Sadly, there were no checks or kind letters, but there was a new issue of *Entertainment Weekly*. Grabbing the cookies from the kitchen, I sat on the porch and started to read while Roger dozed in the sun. It would, I thought, help me relax for all the writing I would not do later in the afternoon.

About halfway through the magazine, I came across an article about a young writer, who was not Joe Eszterhas, who had just been paid $2 million for a script that apparently featured neither plot nor characters. I snatched up the phone and speed-dialed Katherine's number. She picked up immediately, using the same mock-annoyed tone I had adopted earlier.

"It's me," I said. "Listen to this." I read her the article. When I was done, I sighed. "It's not fair," I said plaintively. "I could have written that."

My Life as a Dwarf, Part 3: Sneezy

When I think of sneezing I think of cow shit.

I don't remember who taught me this or when I learned it, but somewhere along the line the secret was revealed: if you say "cow shit" very forcefully and deliberately when you feel a sneeze coming on, you will stop the impending nasal explosion.

I don't know why you would ever want to do this, but it works. I suppose it could be useful if, for instance, you were seated in the audience at a chamber music recital and wanted to avoid interrupting the players, or perhaps if you were part of an assemblage for whom the Pope was saying Mass. Then it might come in handy. In fact I quite like the idea of several hundred devout Catholics silently mouthing "cow shit" so as not to interrupt Papa's benediction.

At any rate, this tiny piece of knowledge is one I will likely never have occasion to use. I love to sneeze. I look forward to each one as if it were Christmas or, better, the Oscars. The first telltale sniffle that heralds a sneeze's birth fills me with anticipation. I've even developed a Sneeze Face, a look of expectant joy mixed with an anxious twitch. It isn't pretty, but it reflects the conflicting emotions battling within me as

I await the actual sneeze itself. Will it hurt? How many will there be? Will it result in spray?

I will say too that I am not one for sneezing tidily into a tissue or my cupped hand. That thwarts the whole experience. Sneezes, as far as I am concerned, are to be celebrated wholeheartedly or not at all. Let them come, I say, and loudly, and woe be to anyone who happens to get in their way.

By the way, I have a theory that the way people sneeze reflects what they're like in bed. Why? Because a sneeze is physiologically very much like an orgasm. Both involve involuntary muscular contractions. Both temporarily interrupt the body's natural processes. And both, when properly experienced, feel great.

Think back to that first one. Orgasm, I mean, not sneeze. You probably don't remember your first sneeze because it happened before you even knew what a sneeze was. Maybe you didn't know what your first orgasm was either, but I bet you remember it anyway. Maybe it arrived in your sleep, sneaking up on you unawares and leaving you with a sticky stain in your pajamas or wet sheets you tried to hide from your mother. Or perhaps it was self-induced, the result of accidental or intentional experimentation.

However that first one came, so to speak, it likely changed your life. From that moment on, your body was something dangerous and exciting, your times alone with it fraught with unbelievable joy and ever-present peril. Whether you had been told as much or not, there was something undeniably secretive about it. Only the bravest of us would dare speak of it to our friends, and none of us could even imagine mentioning it to our parents. Certainly we could never imagine they might do it themselves.

I was probably 10 or 11 when one afternoon on the school bus an older boy, asked by his buddy how he was going to spend his afternoon, replied that he'd "probably sit around and jerk off." He accompanied his statement with a hand motion, a quick back-and-forth at crotch level. I'm sure I'd heard and seen such things hundreds of times on the bus, but for some reason that particular time I took notice. What was he talking about? What was jerking off?

When I got home I was still thinking about it. The hand motion had been unmistakable. But why, I wondered, would someone bother doing that? The only way to find out, of course, was to try it and see.

Well, that was that. Suddenly I understood. I was amazed and delighted to discover that my body that had betrayed me in so many other ways—by sprouting hair and pimples, by developing new smells and growing at a seemingly out-of-control rate—had at last rewarded me with *something* to make up for it. All was immediately forgiven.

Think about this the next time you shake hands with someone: That hand has probably been responsible for hundreds, if not thousands, of orgasms. Those fingers you're grasping so casually for a few seconds have almost certainly been intimately acquainted with their owner's privates, wrapped around a hard shaft or plunged into a warm pool nestled between the thighs. Their skin has been soaked with the results of these unions, smothered with the scent of ecstasy. When we shake hands we are engaging in a most intimate encounter, joining the parts of us that have been responsible for innumerable moments of pleasure. Just food for thought.

Anyway, back to those first orgasms. Weren't they amazing? Remember how your entire body trembled, how it began with little fingers of electricity running over your skin and how it ended with a shudder you were sure was shaking the floorboards or the mattress so hard that everyone in the house would hear? Remember wiping away the evidence with a mixture of sadness and guilt, and then maybe promising yourself (or God) that you wouldn't do it again? At least until tomorrow.

I had a friend when I was 15 or so who decided he was going to save all of his come in a jar. I don't remember why, or why he told me this, but he did. I also remember his profound disappointment when the thick, creamy liquid that shot out of his dick turned overnight into a thin, milky fluid resembling the water-and-paste mixture we used for making papier-mâché in art class. Still, he continued to save it, secreting the jar in a shoebox beneath his bed.

Maybe he was trying to capture some of the pure happiness that accompanies those first moments of self-discovery, the way you might catch a caterpillar or tadpoles and put them on your dresser. It's a nice idea, if a little creepy. I also wonder what his mother thought if and when she decided to do a little cleaning or snooping.

As the years go on, of course, things improve. Your technique gets better. You realize you aren't going to die from it, or go to hell, or use it all up. You stop fearing that someone will catch you, and you relax a little. In fact, you may even slip into a sort of casualness about the whole thing. Perhaps it becomes part of your morning or evening routine, what you do before or after you brush your teeth and feed the dog.

This is not a good thing. With routine comes complacency. Rather than being the thing you look forward to, the reward you give yourself, masturbation becomes as exciting as flossing. Oh, it relieves the tension and all of that, but some of the fireworks are gone. A few minutes of whacking or thrusting or grinding and it's all over, sometimes accompanied by a feeling of relief. "*That's* done," you think as you wipe up. "Now I can vacuum the house."

Even worse is when jacking off begins to feel like a chore, something you have to do because maybe you haven't done it in a while and you feel guilty about ignoring yourself. Then out comes the porn and the lube, or you close your eyes and try to fantasize about something—anything—that will get you off. The mail carrier, perhaps. The mail carrier in boxer shorts. The mail carrier in boxer shorts sitting on your couch with your head between his legs. It's a good start.

Only then you start thinking about the mail itself. Why have you been getting so many credit card applications lately? And speaking of credit cards, where did you put your last Visa bill, and did you call to ask about that weird charge from Pottery Barn, the one for the table you never bought? And oh, shit, your mother's birthday is next week and you need to send a card. Or maybe you could just call her. That would be OK, wouldn't it? How old is she going to be, and how old does that make you, anyway?

Eventually you give up. Or worse, you determine to keep going until you come. An hour later, genitals rubbed raw and your carpal tunnel begging you to stop, you're still at it. Only now you can't quit because that would mean admitting defeat. There's an orgasm in you, and you know it. You just have to try *harder*. You have to *concentrate*. It's like meditation. You can't let any other thoughts in. Finally, of course, it's just all too exhausting and you give up. But the slight limp and stiff hand you have for the rest of the day is a reminder of your failure, and you hate yourself for it.

I've read that most men—gay or straight—continue to masturbate even after they've gotten into relationships. Women do too, I suspect, but not for the same reasons. I think women do it because heaven knows their partners usually can't get them there. Men, however, do it because we just can't keep our hands off ourselves.

My Life as a Dwarf, Part 3: Sneezy

It's true. Men are in love with their dicks. We love what they can do, the same way we love our cars or our baseball card collections or our Fiestaware. Touching them brings the same kind of joy that playing kickball did when we were kids, or that we felt at our first rock concert. It's a primal thing, and it's also incredibly silly. But still we do it, and every time we manage to squeeze another load out we think "Thank God. It still works."

A number of years ago when I was living in Boston there was a minor scandal involving a group of police officers from a nearby town. Apparently some of the guys had been using the back room of the station for jerk off games, the purpose of which seemed to be to see who could come the quickest and the farthest. There was a lot of speculation about *why* grown men responsible for the public safety would engage in such behavior. I'll tell you why—because they *could*.

For the most part we can't come in public and get away with it. But we *can* sneeze, usually without reproach. So the next time you feel one building up, don't condemn it to "cow shit" limbo. Welcome it with open arms. And when it comes, let it fly and think back to that first time your hand dipped south of your waist. It's OK—your mom won't walk in on you.

Too Much of a Good Thing

The piece that started it all. Although this was not the first essay I ever published, it was the first of the "My Queer Life" columns. The column debuted in Norfolk, Va.'s Our Own Community Press *under the editorial eye of the lovely Kathleen Vickery, to whom I owe a great debt for giving me that unexpected opportunity. Although I haven't written the "My Queer Life" column in a number of years, many of the old pieces remain archived online courtesy of the papers that eventually picked up the column and ran it every month. They say you never forget your first time, and in this case it's definitely true. I still get letters about this one, although I'm still awaiting my apology from Martha.*

My name is Michael F., and I am a Marthaholic.

That's right, I am addicted to Martha Stewart, Goddess of the Art of Living Beautifully. It started innocently enough. I would catch a glimpse of Martha's television show as I was flipping channels. She would be briskly dipping French toast into batter speckled with cinnamon, or deftly winding sage leaves into a cunning wreath. *I could do that*, I thought, and I did. It was easy. It made my life a little brighter.

Things went on in this way for a couple of months. I was satisfied by the occasional fix of Martha's helpful hints and her winning smile. Like a freshly baked muffin brimming with ripe blueberries, my encounters with her left me feeling content and happy. But then I found that these small Martha doses just didn't do it for me anymore. I looked at my perfectly poached salmon reclining on its bed of blanched endive, at the cheerful stencils dancing merrily along the edges of my walls, and I wanted more.

So I subscribed to *Martha Stewart Living*, the magazine devoted to my guru and her ways. Each month I had delivered to my mailbox a new installment of the Gospel According to Martha. What a joy it was to rip off the protective plastic bag and stroke the glossy pages with trembling hands before delving into the mysteries awaiting me inside that only She could reveal.

With Martha's guidance, I whipped up lemon tarts so light and fluffy they floated out the window. I learned how to refinish and install the claw-foot bathtub I'd always wanted. I tossed together a kitchen herb garden in no time and discovered everything there was to know about Fiestaware, which I began to collect with abandon.

Soon editors began to phone, frenzied when promised manuscripts failed to arrive. "It's almost done," I'd lie, cutting out gingerbread men with my free hand. Worried friends left pleading messages that went unanswered as I experimented with making my own lavender-scented soaps or made plans for constructing a charming Italianate grotto in the back yard. Finally, I unplugged the phone.

Free to immerse myself entirely in Martha's spell, I devoted my every waking moment to her. I copied her personal calendar (helpfully provided in each issue of the magazine), making sure that on the day Martha was ridding her gutters of fall leaves, so was I. On Martha's birthday, I built a chicken coop in celebration. I pictured

Martha pruning her apple trees, the stray hairs of her carefree bob clinging to her slightly damp brow, and wished for an orchard of my own.

Things finally came to a head the night of my annual Christmas party, which I went forward with only because it was an opportunity to celebrate all things Martha. The handmade invitations, addressed in my finest calligraphy, had gone out two weeks earlier. The fudge was finished, all 18 kinds individually wrapped in glistening cellophane boxes and decorated with found objects. Presents, all of them handmade according to Martha's own specifications, sat under the tree. And, oh, the tree. How it sparkled with the ornaments I'd spun from glass and carved from wood into fantastic shapes. The tiny hand-dipped candles twinkled as I sat sipping my mulled wine and waited for the guests to arrive.

By midnight, when no one had come, it hit me. After months of scorning my friends for the company of Martha, they had abandoned me. I looked at the dilled shrimp and plum pudding languishing untouched on the gaily laid table and wept. I was alone on Christmas Eve, and even the spirit of Martha couldn't save me from my despair. I needed professional help.

The next day, after a fitful night spent tossing and turning on the crisp linen sheets that graced my antique sleigh bed, I plugged the phone back in and called the mental health clinic. "Help me," I sobbed when someone picked up. "I can't take it anymore."

Much to my surprise, the young woman on the other end quickly referred me to a local chapter of M.A.—Martha Anonymous. It was held at a nearby address, and there was to be a meeting that afternoon. Knowing that I needed help to break my Martha addiction, I went.

The room was full. Men and women of all ages sat in

folding chairs in front of a podium. Some chatted quietly among themselves. Others sat, hands neatly folded, looking at the floor as though they were picturing in their minds exactly how it would look sanded and refinished in knotty Carolina pine.

A cheerful woman approached me. "Hi," she said. "My name is Anne, and I'm a Marthaholic. Is this your first meeting?"

I nodded. She seemed normal enough. I wondered what her addiction had cost her.

"Thanks for coming," she said. "Have a cookie."

My eyes widened in terror. A cookie! Wasn't that exactly what a Marthaholic would want? I pictured slim fingers of chocolate, delicately beaded with candied violets, or perhaps the thinnest of butter wafers dusted with a scrim of vanilla sugar.

Anne sensed my alarm. "Don't worry," she said reassuringly. "They're Oreos."

I sat down, sipping reluctantly from a styrofoam cup of bland instant coffee, and Anne began to tell me her story. "It started with the Good Things," she said. "I made little labels for my kids' clothes, covered old shoes with shells and painted them gold, wove ribbon into the edges of my pillowcases. Then it got worse. Soon I was making peach pie kits for people I barely knew. I emptied the kids' college accounts to pay for terra-cotta planters. I wore gloves so no one could see the marks on my fingers from pushing cloves into orange pomanders. It was sad."

"But you're OK now?" I asked hopefully.

"Oh, no," Anne said gently. "Once a Marthaholic, always a Marthaholic. I still can't walk past a yard sale without breaking into a sweat. But don't worry, we can help."

That afternoon I heard story after story of people whose lives had been devastated by Martha. People who, like me, had been brought to ruin by her promise of enchanted living—losing lovers, jobs, and friends in the process. From them I gained the courage to face my problem, and Anne became my sponsor. We started with the First Step. "I am powerless against Martha," I would repeat to myself every morning as I ate a plastic bowl of plain cornflakes, resisting the craving to improve it with fresh berries and honey from the hive I'd installed out back.

It was hard, but I was determined. Out went all the back issues of *Martha Stewart Living*. I emptied my closets of potpourri, the kitchen drawers of arcane Japanese cooking utensils. I ate store-bought baked goods, gagging on their mass-produced taste. Arugula became a forbidden word in my home.

Slowly, my system rid itself of Martha's insidious poison. I no longer felt the need to marble every bare inch of wall space. I found that I could indeed eat vegetables that were not grilled over mesquite and doused in raspberry vinegar. After several months of daily phone calls with Anne, I was even able to part with the collection of animal-inspired egg cups I'd collected in my heyday.

I am still not completely cured. Marthaholics never are. I still sometimes pine for a perfectly trained grape arbor, and some mornings I think I won't be able to get out of bed without a day of transplanting pearl onions or creating whimsical picture frames from antique ribbon to look forward to. Holidays are the hardest. But I persevere.

Besides, the other night I was watching PBS and discovered Norm Abrams and *The New Yankee Workshop*. Watching Norm turn ordinary pieces of lumber into beautiful pieces of furniture, I couldn't help but think that the grotto would look so nice with a Shaker table in it.

My Contract on America: A Fantasy

I originally wrote this essay for a newspaper that had commissioned a piece from me. The editor, who was straight, loved it. The gay members of her staff, however, were horrified. They thought it portrayed queers as hysterical terrorists and, in short, made us look bad. After a lot of discussion, it was killed in committee. So I sent it to another paper where I was published regularly. They too turned it down for the same reasons. So did approximately a dozen other papers and magazines, some of which bought it but then later decided to pull it before publication. Undaunted, I decided it would finally see print in the Alec Baldwin Doesn't Love Me *collection. However, my editor at the time was concerned that its tone might be too harsh. We argued about it for weeks, and in fact briefly stopped speaking because of the rift. In the end, he won and it was dropped from the book. Finally it was published in my second collection,* That's Mr. Faggot to You *(I had a new editor, who thought pissing people off was fun), but only after I added "A Fantasy" to the title, just in case someone thought I was serious. And after all that, I've never received a single letter about it. Oh, and in an interesting side note, years after I wrote this I actually got to interview one of the people mentioned in it, John Cardinal O'Connor, for a book I did called* Paths of Faith. *To my surprise, we had a lovely conversation. I think he was a horribly misguided leader, but he was also a funny, thoughtful man, and I want to state for the record that even though he died shortly after our interview, I had nothing to do with it.*

I'm thinking of going on a killing spree.

Don't worry. I'm not going to do it right this minute or anything. I still have a little bit of planning left to do. And if you want to know the truth, the entire plan is actually pretty shaky, primarily because it hinges upon my contracting a fatal disease. And not just me but my friend Katherine too. See, Katherine and I have decided that if we ever discover that we have some decidedly deadly disease (we use inoperable brain cancer in our scenario, but you may substitute anything you like) we are going to go out in a blaze of glory by taking some key people along with us.

By key people we mean people who, in our opinion, deserve to die because they just don't get it. This group consists primarily of congresspeople, lawmakers, religious leaders, and others with antigay, antiwoman, anti–health care, and generally stupid views. Stupid, just for the record, means those we disagree with. We are hardly impartial, and we freely admit that. On days when we're really crabby, or when we accidentally happen to catch a glimpse of a newspaper, we also include on the list certain world leaders who will go unnamed and Catholic figureheads who may or may not be Cardinal John O'Connor.

The way we figure it, the plan is foolproof. Once a weapon is secured—which can be readily accomplished by giving any third grader in New York $25—the actual act of assassination is relatively easy. The people who really deserve to die generally do not adopt adequate protection for such emergencies, as they can't imagine anyone not being impressed by their ability to always be right. Eliminating them is just a matter of being in the right place at the right time. With a little luck, we would probably be able to pick off several morons in the space of a couple of days or, if we concentrate on the Capitol Hill area of Washington, even a few hours. Even in the worst case scenario, the chances are that we could take out at least one jerk—say, just for the sake of argument, a senator from North Carolina or a sponsor of an antigay initiative—before anyone got suspicious. The way we see it, bagging even one member of the idiot brigade would make it worth it, and we could then die knowing that our lives had been fraught with purpose.

Now ordinarily, an undertaking such as the one we propose would be foolhardy at best. After all, in America you can't just kill someone and get away with it, unless, of course, you happen to be a highly popular sports figure or you chose as your victim someone from a minority group, meaning anyone who is not a heterosexual white male. In those instances, you can probably rest easy, knowing that the people in charge of investigating such things—notably heterosexual white males—will not feel endangered in the least, and will probably leave you alone. But neither Katherine nor I are particularly well-known in the sports world. And while some of our targets might come from other groups, the majority would be predominantly white, male, and heterosexual, at least allegedly. This makes it slightly more risky than it might otherwise be, especially for Katherine, since white heterosexual males do not take at all kindly to being shot at by persons with vaginas, as they somehow believe it shows flagrant disrespect for the supremacy of the penis.

That's where the fatal illness comes into play. While the

eradication of stupidity is always a good idea, there's no point in engaging in it at the expense of your own happiness. We are hardly selfless martyrs to the cause. But being practical people, both Katherine and I agree that if we're going to die anyway, we might as well have fun on the way out. After all, where is the joy in sitting around waiting to go when you could be outside getting some fresh air and meeting new people?

Besides, consider if you will the possible endings to our plan. If we ourselves are killed while carrying out our idea, then it's all over with one quick shot to the heart by a skilled SWAT team member. In that case, the police look foolish for offing terminally ill people, and we depart this life relatively easily. Surely a fast death after ridding the world of a little bit of evil is preferable, if not being downright patriotic, to lingering around uselessly and racking up huge hospital bills that would go unpaid after our deaths. Even someone like Pat Buchanan would have to admire our thoughtfulness, unless—and I'm not saying for certain that his name is or is not on our list—he happens to be one of the people we get to first, in which event he would likely have a less cheerful outlook on the whole thing. We would also, I'm sure, gain instant sainthood amongst oppressed peoples everywhere. Perhaps we would even get an alternative rock band named after us, which would be worth any small amount of suffering we might endure.

But before we go getting all excited, let's look at the other option. If, instead of becoming heroic victims of the despotic white patriarchy, we are merely captured and punished, in all likelihood we'd spend our remaining days in a facility where we were fed, clothed, and exercised regularly—at no expense to us. After years of living as freelancers with no health care and more than a passing acquaintance with ramen and Woolworth's white sales, even the barren cells of Sing Sing would seem to us to be the Ritz Carlton. Not only that, but we'd be sure to be extremely popular with the other inmates, who tend not to be inordinately fond of the sort of people who make up our intended targets.

Of the two most likely options, I think I prefer death, if only because I dislike the idea of having to spend so much time with other people and because I do not give good sound bites when interviewed. However, I am open to all the possibilities, and if a movie is made, I would just like it noted that I think George Clooney would make a wonderful me. Katherine casts her vote for Dianne Wiest.

Mind you, these two possible outcomes are assuming that capture, whether dead or alive, is a foregone conclusion. But really, there's no reason at all why things shouldn't go off without a hitch. In that case, we would be left to continue our merry death dance until we were too tired or bored to go on. A sort of demented Thelma and Louise, we would roll across America ridding the world of people who make life annoying, although in our version no one knows who we really are because we look like tourists from Connecticut and drive a very old Toyota. Blending in easily, we would remain undercover as long as possible, although we both agree that the whole thing wouldn't be half as much fun if it had to be carried out anonymously. After all, while we do think there is a generous amount of concern for the public good in our plan, primarily we just want to make ourselves feel better about lives that seem to have twirled out of control at the hands of Republicans and the Religious Right, and scaring the crap out of the miserable little bastards is a good start.

More than a few people are appalled by our annihilation fantasy, feigning politically correct liberal shock at the mere suggestion of murdering another human being, no matter how vile she or he may be. These gentle souls believe in the power of the political system and in the strength of voting. They insist that a voice raised in protest says more than a dozen stones thrown in anger. “Remember Gandhi,” they cry, renewing their memberships in the Human Rights Campaign and trundling off to recycle their bottles.

To those people we say: Get out of our way.

Really, if we’re honest about it, how many of us would be at all mournful to hear that someone like, say, Senator Helms had been murdered by vigilantes, or even by people who merely found the activity amusing. When it comes down to it, there’s a thin line between finding something acceptable when other people do it for us and doing it ourselves because we’re tired of waiting. All it takes is a willingness to cross that line, a state easily reached simply by watching the latest congressional hearings regarding gay marriage on CNN, where yet more heterosexual white men debate whether or not they should *give* us equal rights under the law. Whether or not you favor gay marriage (and I don’t favor marriage of any kind), listening to these guys talk about our lives as if they have any clue about them is infuriating. And who has time to wait for them to die? When you think about it, isn’t our plan a lot more effective than pledging another $50 to PBS or plastering a Greenpeace sticker on the Subaru?

Actually, I’m surprised that no one else has thought of this earlier. Katherine and I were sure that some clever person in ACT UP would have done it years ago, and we briefly thought about copyrighting our idea before it could be co-opted by other activists far more pissed off or motivated than ourselves. After all, if they can make a condom fit over Jesse Helms’s house, surely they can figure out how to work a handgun. Then there are the women fed up with inadequate breast cancer research, people who suffer from easily treated illnesses because of unaffordable health care, victims of the tobacco industry and its lobby, and really anyone with any sense at all who finds themselves in the position of having limited time left, lots of pent-up energy, and no desire whatsoever to get in touch with their anger through interpretive dance.

Ideally, I suppose, the most impressive thing to do would be to marshal all of these folks into one big army. The problem with that, of course, is that a militia of the dying and angry is hard to organize effectively. Debilitating illnesses develop at different rates, and it would be no small feat to get everyone ready to go on the same day, which we see as being crucial to a successful national operation. That's why we think it's better to work in small teams of two or three. Large groups are easily caught or divided, which can ruin things for everyone, and lone gunmen are too risky, tending to be too flashy at the last minute and thus proving unreliable. Besides, in the later stages of illness, it's sometimes difficult to aim steadily, and a partner can provide helpful suggestions, as well as being able to drive a getaway car.

In the end, it's all theoretical anyway. As I said, most likely neither Katherine nor I will ever find ourselves in a position where we actually have a chance to set our operation in motion. And if we did, I'm sure we'd have better things to worry about than a handful of idiot heterosexual white men trying to keep their gasping vision of a perfect world alive for another day. But I admit that it's nice to think about. Sometimes when I see another hatemonger spewing forth about protecting family values or whining about how straight people have it so rough in this country,

I close my eyes and imagine how he (or she) would look standing in his (or her) driveway, staring with bemused surprise at the gun in my hand. In my mind, I gleefully pull the trigger and hop into the convertible as he (or she) ceases to irritate me. Katherine steps on the gas, and we roar off accompanied by the sounds of Melissa Etheridge blasting from the stereo.

Selling Out

As I prepare this book to go to the editor, Rosie O'Donnell is coming out of the closet. Good for her. If she can't win over Middle America, I don't know who can. I hope she starts a chain reaction in Hollywood. Even if she doesn't, I'd still like to see my game show on the air. Fox, are you listening?

OK, I've been watching *Who Wants to Be a Millionaire?* But not to see if I can guess all the answers. The questions are those random kind that you just either know or don't know. No, the best part, for me, is seeing people get totally confused about the simplest things on national television. By the time the contestants get to the highest levels, they're so unnerved that they'll convince themselves of anything. Except the gay players. They all seem to do pretty well. When a poor straight guy got confused the other night on a question about which of the following is not a type of mushroom, and thought a morel was a kind of eel, I snickered, knowing that any self-respecting queen would have answered correctly in two seconds flat and ended up with $64,000. The same with the fellow who didn't know how many children Captain Von Trapp had in *The Sound of Music.* He passed on the question rather than risk losing a little money, and you could just hear queens all across

America shouting, "Do, re, mi, fa, so la, ti, you hetero idiot!" as they counted the seven children off on their fingers.

Anyway, it seems that everyone is obsessed with this show, and that's no big surprise. Americans are fascinated by money and by other people trying to win money. And who doesn't want to be a millionaire? Although really the show should be called *Who Wants to Be a Half-Millionaire?* since the taxes on those prizes are 49%. But you get the idea. Those of us who don't have a half million want to see other people get it, or at least try to get it while we sit at home going, "I would have gotten that one."

While ratings for *Who Wants to Be a Millionaire?* have been stellar, the show's popularity seems to be dipping a bit now that there are several other more interesting shows like *The Weakest Link* and *Survivor*. I think, though, that with a little bit of tweaking they could get the show back on top. The trick is to simply play to other great American obsessions.

Imagine, for example, *Who Wants to Weigh 500 Pounds?* Next to money, weight is the great American obsession. Many of us are trying to lose a few pounds, and thin is most definitely in. But what would happen if we offered people money to *gain* weight? In this variation of the game show, thin, beautiful people would be given the chance to make big money by getting fat. For every pound gained they would be given a cash prize, with the amount increasing at various levels.

The first few pounds probably wouldn't be a big deal. Most people would be willing to pack on 10 or 20 pounds if they were given, say, $5,000 or $10,000. But what would happen when the bar was raised to 50 or 100 pounds? How many of us would gain that much weight for cash? Especially if we were really weight conscious to begin with. It would be a fascinating struggle between beauty and wealth. If you had, for example, a bunch of supermodels or aerobics instructors, watching them decide between thinness and early retirement would provide weeks of fun. Every episode would involve weighing the contestants and asking them if they wanted to progress to the next level of obesity. The host could wave platters of Hostess products before their anxious faces, tempting them to ever-greater levels of hugeness just for the sake of taking home that elusive half a million. It would be human drama at its most theatrical.

Or what about *Who Wants to Be a Homosexual?* This would be even better. Heterosexual contestants—preferably men—would be presented with a series of choices, each one leading them closer and closer to a queer life. The first step might be agreeing to spend a night out dancing in a gay bar, say for $2,500. From there they would be challenged to march in a pride parade wearing only leather shorts, walk down a main street of some medium-sized Midwestern city holding hands with someone of the same gender, coming out to a family member, and attend a Liza Minnelli concert. As the weeks went on, they would have to decide if a same sex kiss was worth the cash payout, whether being the passive partner in oral sex for $16,000 was preferable to being the active partner for $25,000, and, in the final week, if the indignity of being anally penetrated on national television could be paid for with that much desired half a million.

Just like on *Who Wants to Be a Millionaire?*, contestants would be allowed to stop at any point and walk away with the cash they'd accumulated. If they agreed to go on, and did not perform the assigned task successfully, their money would be taken away and they would be left with nothing. And should a contestant reach the final level and pass the anal sex test, he would be rewarded with not only the money but a Hugo Boss wardrobe, an entire collection of Erasure albums, the keys to a condo in South Beach, and a lifetime subscription to both *Out* and *Genre*.

This would be even better than the fat thing. Imagine watching people decide how much being perceived as gay was worth. Would they stop at $32,000, or would they only be willing to be gay for $120,000? How much would it take to buy off male fears about sucking dick and taking it up the butt? I'd love to find out.

Of course, we already have some idea of the answer. Porn actors regularly get paid different sums for assuming different positions in their films. Much of the gay world watched, literally, as former porn icon Ryan Idol went from being a straight guy who would only allow other actors to blow him to a skilled cocksucker himself. With each film, Idol did a little more, as long as he was paid more. And he isn't alone. Hollywood is filled with actors who will play gay as long as the paycheck is right. Remember Will Smith? When he had to kiss Anthony Michael Hall in *Six Degrees of Separation* a few years back, he made sure every interview he did talked about how awful the smooch was.

We won't even get into all the Tinseltown figures who have donned drag or feigned queerness in the past couple of years just because the money was right. Or those who have kept their real queerness secret for exactly the same reason. How many people are there who are willing to trade who they are for the security of a paycheck and continued status? How many of us choose to do it in both small and large ways on a daily basis? Like the contestants in these proposed game shows, do we continually weigh what our identities are worth, selling ourselves for another week of living large? Yes, money can make people do a lot of things they would never do for free. But you have to wonder: at what cost?

Trial by Fire

A year or so after this piece first appeared in a Los Angeles gay magazine, the first episode of Will & Grace *aired on NBC. Almost immediately I started getting letters telling me how cool it was that someone had based a television program on my essay about my best straight girlfriend, Grace. I wish, people. Sadly, I have nothing to do with the program. Nor does my life even remotely resemble that of the male title character. It is, as I have said before, much more like* Roseanne *around here. And by the way, the real Grace is now happily married to an accountant.*

As a queer man, I've made a concerted effort to stay away from that harpy of gay life—the Fag Hag. I'm referring of course to that peculiar breed of heterosexual woman who finds it some kind of a thrill to hang around men she'll never get into bed with and who remarks frequently that spending time with her beautiful but untouchable boyfriends is just like having a pajama party with all her girlfriends, minus the thrilling conversations about tampons and armpit shaving that we men missed out on in our teens, and which it can be argued that some segments of our population have been making up for ever since by clumping around in glitter wedgies and dresses that would scare Gloria Swanson back up her staircase.

While some men find the company of these women amusing, I am not one of them. I grew up in a house with two older sisters, and consequently the feminine mystique was demystified for me very early on. The esoteric rituals of depilatory creams, sanitary napkins, and the appeal of a smart vinegar and water spray hold absolutely no fascination for me, and the world of straight women is one I haven't wanted to spend time in since I first discovered the joys of man-to-man sex in a men's room at the local Sears.

As a result, over the years I've carefully honed my Hag Radar to the point where I can spot clingy heterosexual women immediately and avoid them like an ex walking on the street with a new, more handsome lover. I refuse to spend a minute with any woman who begins a sentence with, "If only you weren't gay," forces me to go shopping to help her pick out something for her nephew's bar mitzvah that is both tasteful and will make Stacey Schermer green with jealousy, or asks me to share oral sex techniques that will make her boyfriend babble uncontrollably and promise her emerald earrings. If I wanted to hang around a lot of straight women, I'd have a Tupperware party.

Because of this aversion, the fact that Grace and I are such good friends surprises most people. Thoroughly heterosexual (except for one drunken confession about a fantasy involving Cindy Crawford and a bottle of lemon-scented oil that I promised never to tell another living soul), Grace is one of the few straight women I know who doesn't expect me to be able to offer decorating advice. She never asks me to go to weddings with her as her "special friend," never teases me for not knowing anything about opera, and not once has she asked me if her favorite actors are gay. We met in line waiting to buy tickets to a k.d. lang concert. Each of us thought the other one was a dyke.

What enables Grace and I to remain friends is that we respect each other's views. She knows not to try and make me appreciate modern painting, and I in turn have stopped trying to explain to her why hockey is the only perfect art form. Her idea of indulging in Italian food involves sun-dried tomatoes and basil-infused olive oil; mine is eating Spaghetti-O's straight from the can. I cannot understand her fascination with nerdy academic men who take her to lectures on the underlying Christ figure metaphors in Renaissance sonnets. She finds my obsession with big jocks who like to go to Steven Seagal movies appalling.

Despite these differences we have managed to stay close, and for five years this partnership has run smoothly. But a few months ago something happened that tested the strength of our friendship, and it was the last thing either of us expected.

It started when I dragged Grace to Sam Goody to look for the latest John Michael Montgomery album. She had just forced me to sit through an agonizing French movie that involving subtitles that had no pronouns and featured lots of pale men and women throwing leaves at one another while weeping, all set to a score comprised mostly of bassoons and what sounded like small children being crushed to death by stones. I had fallen asleep halfway through, and was still aching from a persistent cramp in my left leg that refused to go away and made me limp around like a wounded bear. As my revenge, I had brought Grace record shopping because I knew she would hate it. As expected, she was being a pain in the ass.

"You just didn't understand it," she said as I pulled her though the doors. "It was all about how men and women relate to one another."

"Nothing blew up," I said. "There were no cute men and far too many breasts for my liking. And what was that business with the nun and the bowl of tomatoes?"

Grace snorted. "Just because Harrison Ford didn't run through wearing a fedora and fending off a bunch of natives with only his manhood and a short piece of stick doesn't mean it was stupid. Not everything is about sweating and saving the world. You know nothing about art."

I ignored her, rounding a large Garth Brooks cutout whose considerable cardboard bulge poked invitingly over a display of his latest album. "I don't know why you have to listen to this stuff anyway," Grace was droning as I pulled her down the aisle of the country section. "It's so...twangy."

"Shut up," I told her venomously as I tugged on her upper arm. "It's better than that Eurofag–Pet Shop Boys–mindless computer dance crap you listen to. And I think you need to do some more water aerobics; you're getting a little thick up here, and you'll look doughy in that off-the-shoulder thing you bought to pick up boys at the opera."

She responded by kicking me viciously right where my cramp was, so that I stumbled and lost my hold on her arm. Sensing an opportunity for escape, she made a worthy attempt at dashing back toward the jazz section while I tried to regain my balance. Fortunately, I was able to cling to a surprisingly sturdy Mary Chapin Carpenter stand-up, and regained my balance quickly enough to give Grace a head start of only a few feet. Before long I was right behind her.

I had just managed to get a good grip on her hair, and she was in the process of trying to step on my foot, when the fireman came into view. He rounded the corner near the vocals section and made his way toward us, striding by the Olivia Newton-John section briskly. Without a word, we paused mid battle, an unspoken truce brought on by the appearance of the only thing on earth that could get us to stop—a Fire God.

I should explain that Grace and I both have a thing for firemen. More precisely, we have an obsession with anything remotely to do with firemen. We walk the long way to the subway so we can go past the firehouse and linger while we watch the guys wash the trucks or straighten the hoses or even put the recycling bags at the curb. We always stop to pet the Dalmatians at our respective houses—High-rise at mine, Domino at hers—and chat up their owners, Fireman Steve and Fireman Robert. When the fire department had a big subway ad campaign last year, we had a contest to see who could steal the most posters. STAY BACK 200 FEET means nothing to us when the sound of sirens calls.

This man fully lived up to my vision of what a fireman should be. His very broad shoulders were packed into the telltale blue fire department T-shirt; the rest of him into jeans and boots. His short dark hair begged to have someone's hands—preferably mine—run through it. He had the shadow of a beard. He was the most beautiful thing I'd ever seen. I glanced over and saw that Grace's eyes had practically rolled back in her head and she was beginning to drool like one of those pictures of a medieval saint in ecstasy over being pierced by God.

We stared in awe as our firefighter walked through the aisles, both of us carefully searching for signs that he might be available. Whenever he passed behind a pillar or display, we held our breath waiting for him to reappear. We bobbed and ducked and scurried after him, following silently. After a minute of watching him, I surmised that there was no one near him who might be a potential significant other, and a quick scan showed that the ring finger of each hand was bare.

"It's not real," Grace murmured.

"I can practically smell the smoke," I said.

We looked at each other suspiciously. There was only one fireman and two of us. The answer to the problem was simple, and we both knew it. One of us would have to die.

"I'll invite you to the wedding," I said, and started after my soon-to-be-husband.

I got about five feet before a violent force knocked me flat against a display of Amy Grant Christmas CDs. In my daze, I could only vaguely wonder where Grace had learned to body check like that. I felt like the casualty of a Ranger-Canuck run-in as I peeled myself away from Amy's oversize smiling face.

"Get out of my way," Grace hissed as she streaked by. "This one's mine."

Pausing momentarily to check her lipstick in a metallic theft-prevention sticker on the back of *Juice Newton's Greatest Hits*, Grace made her way across the store, softly humming "On Top of Old Smoky." She was wearing her short skirt, and I knew I was in trouble if I didn't think of something fast. My mind raced as I ran through a list of possible diversions, watching in horror as Grace moved closer and closer to my intended. Finally, when she was halfway down the aisle, I stopped her dead in her tracks by shouting, "Forget it. He's heading for the show-tunes section."

The fireman, who was in fact intently perusing that area of the store, turned around, the original cast album from *Carousel* in his manly hand. I quickly ducked behind a stack of Judds boxed sets, leaving Grace to fend for herself and congratulating myself on my cunning.

Forced to think quickly, Grace relied on her years of experience in dealing with men. "You know," she said cleverly, "I just loved *Backdraft*." She followed this with a little laugh and a swing of her hair. The fireman smiled. *That bitch*, I thought bitterly.

Peering out from behind the Judds, I could clearly see every move Grace made. She was standing as closely as possible to the fireman, laughing at everything he said and swinging her hair 13 times a minute. Her hand rested lightly on his masculine forearm, her nails purposefully stroking the soft dark hair as she babbled on and on, holding him captive. At that moment, I hated her more than I'd ever hated anyone in my life. She wasn't my friend; she was a husband stealer.

I had to think of something to get her away from the man I was sure I would spend the rest of my life with. Grace was working herself up into her "if you take me home I'll do things to you that you only thought were possible in European soft-focus films" mode. I'd seen it before, and was all to familiar with her success rate. Unfortunately, I was too busy thinking about the fireman's hairy forearms to concentrate fully on my next move.

"Can I help you find something?" a voice asked from behind me, startling me back to the real world.

I turned around to find a store clerk watching me. I stared at his wide, innocent face and blinking eyes. He reminded me of a big, stupid dog waiting for a bone. What I did next was the act of a desperate man.

"Actually, Walter," I said, glancing at his nametag and whispering conspiratorially to gain his trust. "I'm just watching that girl over there."

Walter looked over the stack of grinning Naomis and Wynonnas with their big red hair and squinted at Grace, then looked back at me. "She sure is pretty," he said.

I put my hand on his shoulder. "No, Walter," I said seriously, "you don't understand. I think I saw her stick some blank tapes in her backpack."

Walter blinked again while his brain processed this new information. "Are you sure?" he asked, his demeanor growing bolder as the enormity of the situation sunk in.

I nodded, hoping I looked innocent and believable. Walter, eyes gleaming, pulled his pants further up his belly and squared his shoulders. Then he walked over to where Grace was playing out her seduction scene. "Excuse me," he said politely, interrupting a gale of girlish laughter as he tapped her sharply on the shoulder, "But would you please come with me?"

Grace looked as if he had slapped her. "Why?" she said defensively, her eyes narrowing. Walter, his adrenaline churning out of control from this unexpected power opportunity, turned stone-faced. "Just come with me, please, ma'am. We'll talk about it downstairs. In the security office."

I knew Grace wanted to put up a fight, especially over being called ma'am, but she also didn't want to make a fool of herself in front of her prey. The fireman was looking from Walter to Grace, and she knew she was in trouble if she said anything unladylike. She went quietly, remarking over her shoulder to the fireman as she left, "There must be some mistake. I'm sure it will be cleared up in a minute. Don't go away."

As Grace marched past me, I avoided looking at her, pretending to rifle through some Patsy Cline CDs. She tried to stop and say something, but Walter pushed her ahead of him. "It's always the innocent-looking ones," I said, shaking my head sadly as they went by.

Once Walter and Grace were out of sight, I made my move. I knew she would be back once Walter opened her backpack and found nothing but breath mints and notes for her doctoral thesis in early English pastoral poetry. I only had a few minutes to get the job done and get Mr. Fireman of My Dreams out the door before Grace would be on the loose again. I strolled over to my beloved, my heart beating wildly as I planned my strategy.

"I wonder what that was all about," I said casually as I sidled up next to him, checking out the way his butt looked in his jeans and resisting an overwhelming urge to run my tongue down his neck.

He looked over at me quickly, then looked again. A good sign. "I don't know," he said. "She seemed like a nice enough girl. I can't imagine she did anything wrong."

"I'm not sure," I said, determined to crush once and for all any positive thoughts he might have about the evil vixen who almost took my man. I was pretty sure he was playing on my team, but these days it's hard to tell, and I always end up going for the straight ones anyway. If I was going to end up disappointed, I was going to make damn sure Grace was right there with me. "I think I smelled liquor on her breath."

He looked at me again and grinned, his perfect lips parting to reveal white teeth that appeared to have benefitted from years of orthodontia as a child. I thought I'd pass out when I saw the way his chin dimpled. Then, just as I was getting a good look at his beautiful brown eyes, he went back to his work. He appeared to be looking for a particular album, pawing through the stacks of CDs intently.

I know absolutely nothing about musical theater apart from the fact that at some point someone sings something, but I decided to improvise. If my man liked musicals, I could learn to like them too. Besides, I'd seen that movie where Mary Poppins dresses a bunch of kids up in curtains and takes them on a bicycle tour through the Alps while they're all pursued by nuns and eat strudel while playing the guitar, and that had to count for something. I hummed something I thought sounded vaguely show tune–like and snatched up the nearest CD without looking at it, pretending to read the back intently.

"Isn't this the show Liza was in?" I asked, throwing out the only name I could come up with that I knew might have anything even remotely to do with musicals. I saw her sing in a Diet Coke commercial once, and figured she must have been in something along the way to deserve that kind of exposure.

He glanced over. "I doubt it," he said, looking at me strangely. "That's the soundtrack from *Terminator 2.* You must be thinking of *Cabaret*."

"That must be it," I said lightly. "I'm always getting them confused." I put it down again and wondered what he'd do if I just tackled him and threw him to the floor. Things were not going well. Then, to make matters worse, before I could come up with another conversation starter, Grace reappeared at the top of the escalator. I could see by the way her lips were set as she stormed up the aisle that whatever was left of Walter would regret the day she walked into his store. I quickly moved to the other side of the fireman, so that he was between us. I knew she wouldn't risk damaging him just to get at me.

"It seems," she said pointedly as she came to a stop and rearranged her face into a mask of sweetness, "that someone made a mistake."

I tried my best to appear sympathetic. "That's terrible," I said, leaning in to smell my fireman's manly scent and noticing the hair that peeked over the collar of his T-shirt. "Some people will just do anything to get noticed."

"Some people," said Grace, shredding a CD wrapper with her nails, "Are going to be sorry forever when I get my hands on them."

The fireman had made his way to the Rs, and seemed to have found just about everything he wanted. Grace and I glared at each other balefully over his back as he bent to retrieve one last item. We both knew that time was running out, and both of us were desperate to get the man's clothes off. Now it wasn't even about him, it was about which one of us was a better flirt. Grace decided to go for broke. She brushed the hair out of her eyes and pretended to see the fireman's shirt for the first time.

"Oh, wow," she gushed, "a fire-department T-shirt. What company are you with?" We both know the location of the Manhattan fire departments by heart. I held my breath, hoping he was closer to my apartment than hers.

"Oh, it isn't mine," he said. "It belongs to my brother. I would never go near a burning building. I'm in the Shearson-Lehman accountant training program."

Grace and I looked at each other, our eyes welling up and our bottom lips trembling. Our mighty fireman was a fraud. It was all a cruel joke. This was worse than finding out there was no Easter Bunny, or even that Newt Gingrich was running for president. Far worse. This was as bad as finding out that the hole in the ozone layer was caused by excessive chocolate consumption.

After that, it didn't matter whether the guy had a boyfriend, a girlfriend, or a Golden Retriever named Jack. He had the shirt, he had the boots, and he had the look. But he wasn't the real thing. He would never come home from work sweaty from a practice run. He would never let us wear his T-shirts around the house. We would never be able to make love on top of the hook and ladder with him wearing nothing but his heavy black boots. We both knew that, despite his looks, there was nothing exciting about tax-exempt status or itemized deductions or plant amortization, and that sex on a pile of account ledgers would never be as exciting as the feeling of yellow rain gear on bare skin.

Once again, we united in our desperation.

"Look at the time," I said miserably. "*60 Minutes* is going to start soon."

"I'd better get going then," Grace played along. "I don't want to miss Steve Kroft's piece on the decline of family values."

The faux fireman waved farewell, oblivious to the fact that he had broken our hearts, and we headed off. Dejectedly, we walked out the door of Sam Goody and into the black night. Outside, we looked up at the empty sky and cursed our bad luck.

"Just think," I said after a minute in which we both contemplated our mutual loss. "We almost killed each other over an imposter."

Grace put her arm around me. "Why don't we go get a beer and laugh about it? I'll even let you drink out of the bottle instead of forcing you to put it in a glass."

Arm-in-arm, we headed down the street to our favorite bar. We might not have firemen, but we were content to have one another as friends. Before we'd gotten half a block we had already started to laugh about it and were finding fault with the man we had so recently thought a god. "His nose was a little crooked," I pointed out. "And that single eyebrow look isn't for everyone," Grace added thoughtfully.

Then we spotted the hunky policeman standing next to the subway entrance, handcuffs gleaming seductively against his thigh. I could feel Grace stiffen next to me as she thrust her chest out to maximum advantage, and her arm slipped from mine. This time I wasn't giving her any chances.

"Well," I said cheerfully, breaking away from her. "I think it's time to ask directions to somewhere."

As I dashed toward my God in Blue, I heard Grace's heels clicking on the pavement right behind me.

Thank-You Note

Like a surprising number of "funny" people, I've battled depression for most of my life. It's one of the ironies of being human that mental darkness so often results in the creation of the light of laughter. When I finally reached a point where I needed to confront the depression with more than just laughing at it, I feared the ability to laugh would be swept away along with the depression. I'm pleased to say it wasn't.

This morning I had some tea. It was some kind of mixed berry tea, herbal because caffeine does weird things to me that makes me think I probably need to go to an emergency room. But the flavor is not important.

What is important is that I drank the tea out of a mug that was sent to me two years ago at Christmas by the literary agency that represents me. It's a plain white mug with a drawing of the building that houses the people who, like the Greek Fates, weave the thread of my career and, I am convinced, sit there with their golden shears ready to snip that thread at any moment. It probably cost them all of 85 cents per mug, and I recall vividly the thought that went through my head when I opened the little box and saw what was inside: *Well, this is clearly your last chance.*

I am convinced that the quality of the Christmas gift I

receive from my agency is directly related to my worth to them. The first year I was with them, I received a lovely big box of apples and a cheery card welcoming me to the family. For weeks I chomped apples as I sat at my desk writing, sure that everything was going to be perfect now that I had someone who believed in me. The second year, when nothing I'd given my agent had sold, my Christmas gift was a strange little book that I believe my agent plucked from a pile of review copies she had sitting around. There was a short, awkward, note in it that I took as a veiled threat to produce something, or else.

When the mug came, I left it in its box and didn't look at it. It was too painful. It reminded me that I had yet to pay off for this big New York agency that had taken me on with such high expectations. Of course, this didn't stop me from putting the box on the kitchen counter, where I couldn't help but see it every time I had to open the cupboard or needed to clear space to chop something. Whenever I picked it up or moved it, I was reminded of my diminishing worth as a writer, of the painful fact that, as of that year, I was worth only an approximately 85-cent investment.

About two months ago, my roommate finally took the mug out of its box. He needed something to put paintbrushes in. He thought the mug would be perfect since, as he remarked casually, "You're not doing anything with it."

But I was doing something with it. I was letting it depress me. As a mug, it wasn't particularly pleasing to look at, but I got great satisfaction from knowing that it was there, like a sweet little cancer waiting to take over whatever space I would allow it to fill. Being forced to move it whenever I needed to tend to a basic physical need like eating allowed me the dark pleasure of handling a talisman of my failure, reminding me of everything that stood between me and receiving a really good Christmas gift, one of the gifts I imagined the agency's successful writers were all getting.

Now the mug was out of its box. There it sat, filled with murky water and an assortment of stained brushes. I passed it several times a day as I went in and out of the kitchen. Even though I tried not to, I glanced at it every time. And every time, that scab was ripped off again and I would have the pleasure of thinking, for maybe half an hour, about how awful it was that I hated the things I was writing to make a living and how unfair it was that writing the things I loved wouldn't pay the rent. Once or twice, I considered knocking the mug onto the floor. But I knew I would have to pick up the broken pieces, mop the paint-muddied water off the linoleum. Part of me was attracted to this picture. Something else to be depressed about. Another indignity forced upon me by my lack of motivation. But then the mug would be gone. I left it where it was.

Along with my depression about the mug came another kind of depression, a darker and more oppressive one. At first I assumed it was just the general moodiness that I am subject to from time to time, a kind of overall grayness that sweeps in and clouds things for a couple of days. But when a week went by, and then another, and I was still depressed, I started to wonder.

True, I was under more stress than usual with work. True, I had been thinking lately that maybe I'd made a terrible mistake in choosing writing as a career. These were not new things, however. In fact, they're regular visitors, and over the years I've learned to recognize them, let them have their whiny, raucous stay, and then kick them out when even I can't stand the sound of their voices in my head anymore.

I knew I was really depressed because I'd stopped eating for the most part. I would pick at things here and there, but more and more I was going all day without putting anything in my mouth until, around 10 o'clock, I knew I wouldn't be able to get to sleep unless I quieted the howling in my stomach with something, however small. Even then, I fed myself reluctantly, resenting my body's inability to control its needs. For several weeks I lived on bread and butter sprinkled with cinnamon and sugar.

One particularly bad day, when I woke up in the morning and knew that even hearing the phone ring would send me over the edge once and for all, I took myself to a matinee of *Girl, Interrupted.* I was feeling a little crazy myself, and sitting in a theater alone with my anxiety seemed like a good idea. Like being forced to acknowledge the mug on the kitchen table, I think what I really wanted was to stare at the crazy girls on the screen and dare them to ask me what my problem was. Or maybe I was hoping that they, with all their vast experience, would tell me.

As I sat there in the dark, watching the characters peel away the layers of their lives to reveal the causes of their various behaviors, I began to feel a little better. It always helps, when you're feeling not very good about yourself, to look at people who are worse off. At the same time, though, I had a vague suspicion that maybe I wasn't so far away from becoming those girls, especially if anyone was paying close attention. When I left the theater, I made sure no one was following me.

That night, because I couldn't sleep, I turned on the light and read. I picked up *Traveling Mercies*, Anne Lamott's book about faith. Anne and I are pretty much the same person, except that she doesn't have a penis and I'm not an alcoholic. I've always loved her books because I just know she's writing them specifically to me. Except for this latest one, which is all about her attraction to Christianity, a faith that left me cold long ago. Still, Anne is funny and clumsily wise even when I don't get into her particular brand of spirituality, so I kept reading. And almost at the end of the book, when I was so tired I could barely keep my eyes open, I read the following:

> The truth is that your spirits don't rise until you get *way* down. Maybe it's because this—the mud, the bottom—is where it all rises from. Maybe without it, whatever rises would fly off or evaporate before you could even be with it for a moment.

I read this section several times, with a growing resentment. I was angry at Anne for tricking me into realizing what I'd been doing to myself. I hated her for so swiftly and mercilessly ripping off the scab that I'd been picking at piece by piece for the past two months. I was so mad that I almost picked up the phone and called her to tell her what a shit she was.

Instead, I got out of bed and took the dog for a very long walk in the cold, thin light of a winter dawn. We walked for a long time, while the sun came up and I finally let go of the depression I'd gathered around me like extra clothes. I let go of the anxiety about work, and money, and the future. I let myself enjoy, for the first time in weeks, the fact that I can do something wonderful with my writing. And when I came home, I took the mug from the kitchen table, rinsed it out, and made myself some tea. Sitting at my desk, I drank from the mug that no longer symbolized failure to me. And I began to write.

The Condensed History of Gay Pride

For my third essay collection, It's Not Mean If It's True, *I wanted to write some shorter pieces to break up the flow of the book. The result was a series of "Condensed History" essays, each one taking a tongue-in-cheek look at a different aspect of gay culture. This is my favorite.*

It has recently been brought to my attention that a great many people are unaware of the history of our community. I made this amazing discovery while standing on the sidewalk watching our local pride parade. As the Dykes on Bikes roared past, breasts to the wind and mirrored sunglasses glinting in the morning light, a young man to my right sporting rainbow-colored running shorts and a pink tank top turned to his friend and said, "I wonder how all of this started anyway." His companion took a sip from the rainbow-colored spring water in his hand and said, "I'm not sure. I've been coming ever since I was a kid. I just assumed it had always been going on."

Ah, the innocence of youth. Can it be that there really is a generation of gay people who don't know why once every year we hold pride celebrations all across our fair land? Why, pride is the single biggest party of the queer calendar. It is our Christmas, our Fourth of July, and our Halloween all rolled up in one. It's the one day a year we get to take center stage and have ourselves a big old whoop-de-do. Not knowing about pride is like not knowing how to cruise. For any self-respecting gay person, it's unthinkable.

Clearly this ignorance of our heritage cannot remain unaddressed. If you don't know where you come from, you can hardly be expected to know where you are going. And as even the quickest of glances will reveal, the changing face of pride is a reflection of the changing face of queer life. In its pageant of banners and signs, its people and its music, we see our dreams and our joys, our accomplishments and our challenges.

So, in the spirit of education, I offer this handy time line of gay pride, from its origins through its present. My hope is that it will enlighten the uninformed and remind the already aware of what we have achieved and what we have yet to do. Remember, to know pride is to know ourselves.

1543 B.C.: The residents of Sodom and Gomorrah hold a spontaneous week-long orgy. When one enthusiastic participant runs through the streets waving a come rag over his head, it is mistaken for a parade and an annual event is born. Sadly, its history is short-lived due to an Act of God.

1542 B.C.–A.D. 1968: Referred to by historians as The Time of No Floats, this dark period in gay culture saw very little in the way of organized events for queer people. Occasional parties and festivals were attempted, but were generally not well attended because of little inconveniences like the Bubonic Plague, the Inquisition, and the inability of the Merrye Gaye Fellowes Chorus and Chamber Orchestra to agree on an arrangement of "My Lover is the Sweetest Fruite" for their subsequently canceled spring concert.

1969: The birth of a new era. Following the historic Stonewall Riots, everyone is filled with the power of liberation and a celebration is planned. When it is pointed out that late fall is hardly the time to be marching in the streets shirtless, the event is rescheduled for the summer of 1970, giving participants time to pump up and tan adequately.

1973: Thanks to the sponsorship of alcoholic beverage companies, gay pride events become a bit too reminiscent of the whole Sodom and Gomorrah thing. When shocking images of drag queens and leathermen appear on the evening news and frighten viewers, organizers decide to capitalize the name of the event—Gay Pride—to make it seem like a movement and thereby gain some legitimacy. Feeling left out, lesbians everywhere refuse to participate, but no one notices.

1974–1979: Considered by many to be the shining moment in the history of Gay Pride, the details of this happy period are nonetheless shrouded in mystery, primarily because everyone involved was too stoned to work their cameras properly. However, the by-products of this time, which include pierced nipples, the porn star as celebrity, and a renewed sense of humor, can still be felt today.

1980: Following the death of disco, Gay Pride organizers worry that attendance will drop. Fortunately, increased oppression provides a new theme, and the focus shifts from parades to rallies featuring long-winded speeches by hitherto unknown people about how being disliked really sucks. Lesbians everywhere enthusiastically applaud the decision, but no one notices.

1987: After several "downer" years marred by the AIDS crisis, Gay Pride festivities pick up steam again with the introduction of Freedom Rings, the "We're Here, We're Queer, Get Used to It" chant, and the mysterious ability of Alicia Bridges to appear simultaneously at every single parade singing "I Love the Nightlife."

1993: The era of political correctness. After voting to change the festival name to Gay, Lesbian, Bisexual, Transgendered, Transsexual, Queer, and their Friends, Families, and Supporters Pride, organizers panic when they realize the new name cannot be easily emblazoned on pins and T-shirts. Like Madonna and Cher, the name becomes, simply, Pride. Feeling left out, lesbians everywhere refuse to participate, but no one notices.

1997: Those born after Stonewall, annoyed at having missed out on all of the good drugs and easy sex, attempt to make up for it by creating zines and poetry slams expressing their angst. Their older brethren insist they have no sense of history and loudly cheer floats featuring members of Senior Action in a Gay Environment before attempting to pick up tricks from the queer youth contingents.

2000: Having become "just like everyone else," Pride celebrants are no longer distinguishable from straights. Many onlookers at the New York parade—dubbed Pride?—believe the event, featuring Grand Marshals Bruce Bawer and Andrew Sullivan riding in a wood-paneled station wagon, to be a convention of Promise Keepers. Gay men who remember when Pride actually meant something join the lesbians and refuse to participate, but no one notices.

My Life as a Dwarf, Part 4: Grumpy

When I was 7 I discovered the most magical books in the world, the Moomin books written by Finnish author Tove Jansson. There are eight books in the series, each concerning a family of peculiar little trolls (they look more like hippos, really, in Jansson's delightful accompanying illustrations) and their large circle of eccentric friends. They live in a big house in Moominvalley, and they were unlike anything I had ever encountered.

My favorite book in the series was *Moominvalley in November*. Surely one of the oddest things ever written for children, this dark and wonderful book is the sole entry in the group to not feature the Moomin family directly. Instead it focuses on an assortment of characters all of whom, moved by some unnamable loneliness, find themselves traveling to Moominvalley in search of something they don't quite understand. Arriving and finding the Moomins gone (it's never explained exactly where they've gone, which only adds to the atmosphere of loss), the group must form their own family of sorts as they inhabit the empty house and wait. In the process, each comes to terms with her or his personal ghosts in one way or another.

My Life as a Dwarf, Part 4: Grumpy

As I said, it's a strange book, filled with delicious Scandinavian pathos and a fondness for the darkness, and I loved it. I particularly adored a character called Grandpa Grumble. As Jansson describes him, "He was frightfully old and forgot things very easily. One dark autumn morning he woke up and had forgotten what his name was. It's a little sad when you forget other people's names, but it's lovely to completely forget your own."

Bored with his life, Grandpa Grumble sets out to find Moominvalley, which he thinks he may have once visited but perhaps has only heard about or dreamed about. It doesn't matter to him; the journey is the thing. In due course he arrives and, finding the family gone and the house occupied by others like himself, settles in to see what will happen.

I won't ruin the story for you; you'll have to read it for yourself. And you should read all of Jansson's books, including her marvelous work for adults, *The Summer Book.* They're truly remarkable, and even more so because their audience is children.

Even at 7 I identified with the 100-year-old Grandpa Grumble. I too was a grump who wanted to be left alone. I wanted to follow him into Moominvalley and climb the steps of the Moomins' house. Instead I re-created their world in paper, covering the walls of my room with construction-paper cutouts of the characters and places I longed to know. At night I turned out the lights, and my paper world came to life, bustling with adventure until the sour grin of dawn stilled the voices and returned my friends to one-dimensional stillness.

As I grew older, my paper world came down and was replaced with posters of Shawn Cassidy and Farrah Fawcett, pictures of KISS and Parker Stevenson torn from the pages of *16* magazine. But I never forgot the Moomins, and many years later when I was myself working in the world of children's books I wrote to Tove Jansson and told her what her books had meant to me.

To my surprise, she wrote back. Then in her 80s, she had trouble seeing, she said, and could no longer write books or do the painting for which she was (at least in Scandinavia) equally famous. But she wanted to say hello and let me know she had appreciated my letter. She also enclosed some of her picture books, unavailable in America at the time, that she thought I might enjoy.

We began a sporadic correspondence, made difficult not only by Tove's advanced age and failing health but by the fact that she spent a large part of each year on a remote island, away from the demands of city life. For my part I tried to bring her books back into print in the United States, but my bosses found them too dark, too strange. (Ultimately they were resurrected by the wonderful people at Farrar, Straus & Giroux, who continue to keep them in print.)

After several exchanges of letters, I finally asked Tove a question that had been on my mind for a number of years. Rereading the books as an adult, I'd begun to wonder if some of the feelings of isolation and loneliness experienced by so many of her characters might not be somehow related to my own feelings of isolation as a gay child. I'd read that the books were highly autobiographical, and I knew too that Tove lived with a female companion, a woman who appeared as a character in at least one of the books (*Moominland Midwinter*). I also at the time happened to be writing a book for young people about being gay (it was subsequently published under the title *The World Out There*). Nervously, I wrote to Tove and told her how much the books meant to me as a gay man, and I asked her if she would be willing to be interviewed for my book.

The answer, when it came, was both disappointing and rewarding. No, she couldn't participate in the book. Her partner didn't like the idea of making their relationship any more public than it already was. But yes, the stories were very much about her own feelings of isolation as a gay person. She was very happy, she said, that I had made the connection.

We wrote a few more times after that. Tove's health continued to decline and my own life grew increasingly busy. She sent me books, I sent her holiday cards and get-well letters. I made vague plans to visit her but never did.

Tove died last year. The obituaries mentioned her awards, her worldwide popularity, her status as one of the most beloved writers and artists in Finland. None mentioned her partner, who survived her, although *The Advocate* did eventually print a short story about her, for which I was thankful.

When I heard of her death I looked for the letters Tove and I had exchanged. I found many of them tucked into the pages of the books she'd sent me but, oddly, not the one regarding our shared secret. I can't imagine why I didn't put it somewhere safe, but if I did I've forgotten where, much like Grandpa Grumble was always misplacing his spectacles. It was as if Tove decided to take it with her to the grave.

In all my searching I found too a story I'd written for Tove, a gift to thank her for her kindness after receiving yet another shipment of books one Christmas. I don't think I ever got around to mailing it. So here it is now, out of place perhaps in this collection of essays, but better late than never.

Sara

for Tove

"Islands are foolish," I say to her. "They just sit in the sea all of their lives getting in the way of ships and being teased by the waves."

Sara laughs. She does this a lot, which is one of the reasons I like her.

"The veranda shouldn't be blue," she points out. "It should be yellow."

"I know," I tell her. "But it's all I could find."

Sara climbs onto the veranda railing and swings her legs through the flowers that grow along the side of the porch. "I just think an island would be nice sometimes, so we would have somewhere to take the boat. What's the fun of having a boat if all you can do is float around in it?"

"I'll think about it," I say.

The bedroom door opens. It's my mother.

"Thomas, come down to dinner *now*. I've called you four times already."

"I'll be right down," I mumble.

"Now," my mother says again.

I follow her downstairs.

"Hi, sport," my father says as I sit down at the table. "How was school?"

He says this every night.

"Same as usual," I answer. "Stupid." I don't know why he always asks. I guess he thinks that one night the answer will be different.

My father takes some peas. "It can't be that bad." He smiles.

"It's worse," I say.

My father won't give up. "Mrs. Wilkins says you wrote a wonderful report for her."

I forgot about conferences. They were this afternoon. I pretend one of the peas is Mrs. Wilkins and cover it with an avalanche of potatoes and gravy.

My mother joins in, trying to sound cheerful. "That's great, Thomas. I'm really proud of you. What was the report about?"

"Robin Hood," I lie. It was really about sheep, but that doesn't sound very interesting. Besides, I really did want to do Robin Hood. Mrs. Wilkins told me he wasn't real, though, and that sheep would be easier. When I told her I was going to tell Robin Hood that she said he wasn't real, and that she better watch out the next time she was in a dark forest, she told me I read too many of the wrong kinds of books.

"She also said," my father continued, "that you still aren't getting along with the other kids very well."

I take the Mrs. Wilkins pea and feed it to Max, who is sitting under the table. *Mrs. Wilkins screamed horribly as the wolf messily devoured her*, I think.

"She says you won't play kickball during recess or team up with anyone for science projects." My father is still going on from across the table. "And that all you do is sit under a tree and read."

I make a tree out of some broccoli and plant it in the potatoes. I decide that Mrs. Wilkins is buried under it, and I'm not sad.

"Why don't you try harder?" I hear my father finish.

I push some potatoes onto my fork and the broccoli falls over. *Timber*, I think.

"Do we have any green paper?" I ask.

"Thomas," my mother says, exasperated, "your father is trying to understand you. The least you can do is listen."

"I am listening," I say. "Don't we have some of that wrapping paper left over from last Christmas?"

"Thomas, this is important," my father says. "You don't seem to be getting along well at school. Your grades are fine—excellent, as a matter of fact—but you come home every day and lock yourself in your room. You never do anything with the other kids."

I put the entire fourth grade onto my fork and swallow them. "I'm fine," I say. "Really." I smile for extra effect.

My mother looks at me. "Well, why don't you ever have anyone come over, or go to anyone else's house?" she asks.

"I don't want to," I tell her. "I don't like any of them."

She sighs. "You must like some of them."

"Why?" I ask her, interested.

"Because it's normal to have friends," my father says tiredly. "People to call on the phone, go to movies with, that kind of thing. You can't always be alone."

"I like to be alone," I say, for about the millionth time. "And anyway, I'm never all alone. Usually Max is with me." Max pokes his nose onto the table to prove this. I feed him a piece of steak.

"Hey, that's good food," my mother shrieks. "Don't waste it on the dog."

"He's not just a dog," I say angrily. "And I like him better that most people around here." I think to myself, *He doesn't ask stupid questions.*

I put the broccoli tree in my mouth like a cigarette. I'm Bette Davis. "Besides," I drawl like Bette, "the children at school are awful. Simply awful." I love Bette Davis. I know fourth graders are supposed to like movies where about a billion people get blown up and the hero drives around in a big truck, but I don't. I rent Bette Davis movies from the video store all the time. They think I'm weird too. Of course, no one else will watch them with me. My mother says she's the wickedest woman she's ever seen, and my father says she gives him a pain and why don't I like Arnold Schwarzenegger like everyone else.

But Sara and I love her movies. Our favorite is the one where Bette looks around this room and then says, "What a dump." Sometimes we sit around saying "What a dump" and laugh so hard we can't breathe.

My Life as a Dwarf, Part 4: Grumpy

"Put the broccoli down," my mother orders.

I ask to be excused and carry my plate into the kitchen. Max comes with me, and I feed him everything but the broccoli. We hate broccoli. I name it Mr. Schrader and behead it with my steak knife; it's a guillotine. Mr. Schrader is our principal. At least once a week Mrs. Wilkins sends me down to see him, and he tells me I have socialization problems.

At the top of the stairs I sit and listen to my parents talk about me. This is nothing new; they usually do it after dinner. More often than not, they end up saying they just don't understand me. I could have told them that, but they never bother to ask me.

Once my mother said she thought I should go see a counselor. This was after I told her that there were ghosts in the second-floor clothes cupboard. Now I don't tell her anything. Her or my father. They don't really understand much of anything that's important, although my father can take apart the tractor and put it back together. Sara says that's worth something.

I don't tell them about Sara. I started to once, but my mother got the same look she got when I talked about the ghosts, so I asked for a peanut butter sandwich instead.

When I get back to my room, Sara is busy picking roses off the bush by the window.

"There you are," she says. "Did you get an island?"

"I forgot," I answer, and fall onto the bed. Max jumps up and lies down next to me. I rub his back hard, and hair flies all over.

"Look," I say to Sara, "a blizzard."

She laughs. She thinks this is hysterical. She laughs so hard she falls over the rose bush. I notice that one of her feet is torn. There's some black paper on my desk. I get a scissors and cut out a new foot. It's a little different from the old one, and Sara says thanks after I tape it on. She likes to be different.

The door opens again. It's my mother.

"Thomas, here's the green paper you wanted," she says and sits on the edge of the bed. She looks at Max and starts to say something, but then she stops.

She looks around my room. "This is really creative," she tells me. "You've made a whole world in here." She points to the house near the closet. "Why is the house blue?" she asks. "And why is there such a pointy roof on that tower?"

"They like it that way," I tell her. "Besides, we had lots of blue paper left over from art class. Miss Roberts said I could have it."

"That was nice of her," she says. She points toward the window. "What's that over there?"

"The sea," I tell her. "And maybe an island," I add, looking at Sara, who is lying on the bedside table.

My mother picks up Sara. "What a funny shoe." She laughs.

I take Sara and put her near the boathouse.

My mother sighs. "If only you would put this much effort into making friends," she says. "We only want you to be happy, Thomas."

I don't say anything, and she goes out. She shuts the door behind her.

"I think the dinghy has a leak," Sara is saying when I turn around. She is standing on the beach throwing stones into the water.

I pick up the green paper my mother has brought and cut furiously. Soon I have a rough round shape. I take my dark green marker and scribble a little, then I put the paper on the wall with tape.

"Look," Sara says excitedly, "an island. And it has trees on it. Let's go explore."

My Life as a Dwarf, Part 4: Grumpy

I get in the dinghy, and we push off. The sea is calm, and we row quickly. The island gets bigger and bigger. Finally, we slide onto the beach, and I pull the boat away from the waves.

Sara gets out and looks around. "Beautiful," she cries, and runs through the sand.

I chase her. She shrieks and hides behind a tree. I find her and we collapse, tired and happy, on the ground.

"I like it here," I say, and Sara smiles.

"So do I," she says.

We explore all over the island. We pick up shells and flowers and three kinds of bird eggs, one of them pale green. We find a dead crab, but Sara says it's too sad and we let the sea have it.

Then it begins to rain. It falls on the sea and sends spiderwebs across the water. It hits the rocks and makes them look like marble.

Sara points to a spot in the trees. "A cave," she says.

We run to the cave. Inside it is dry, and there are soft piles of leaves to sit on. We sit and watch the rain come down. The leaves crunch when we move. Pretty soon it starts to thunder.

Sara goes to the mouth of the cave and yells into the wind. "Isn't it wonderful," she screams. "So big and terrible and beautiful."

The rain comes down harder and lightning crackles across the sky. In our cave, Sara and I dance. We take flowers we have picked and throw them into the air. The wind scurries them around and around. We dance in a circle, holding hands and swinging each other around until we are dizzy. Sometimes we stop to watch the rain. Once when we look out we see the dinghy floating far out on the sea. We look at each other and laugh.

We dance until we are tired, then lie down on the piles of leaves and go to sleep.

Sometime during the night I wake up. My mother is shutting my window. She asks me if I am frightened by the storm. I look over at Sara and she is sleeping quietly.

"No," I say, and go back to sleep.

Where Have All the Flowers Gone?

My dating ineptitude has been a central theme of my work from the very beginning. Because of this, I was particularly shocked when, after the publication of my first book, I started receiving letters from men asking me out. Didn't they read the book? I asked myself. Don't they know this is a losing proposition? Apparently not, because the letters kept coming, more with every subsequent book. And no, I didn't go on any dates. I was too busy writing. Much later, when a friend set me up on a date with one of his buddies, I was relieved to be told, "Don't worry, he's never even heard *of you." As it turned out, Patrick* had *read one of my books, but he didn't realize it until later. By then it was too late. I'd already sent him flowers. And this time, he sent some back.*

It's official—romance is dead.

The tragic event occurred at 9:36 last Tuesday night. That was when a group of friends and I were sitting around in a bar after a reading that several of us had taken part in. Basking in the glow of post-performance relief, we were knocking back a few beers and talking about all of those important things that people talk about when they're slightly buzzed. We had already discussed which childhood comic-book heros we'd had crushes on, what our favorite songs of the 1970s were, and the relative appeal of corduroy pants. Now it was my turn to choose a topic for debate.

"Here you go," I said after thinking for a minute. "I want to talk about flowers."

"Flowers?" said my friend Anna. "What about them?"

Truth be told, I wanted their advice. I was thinking about sending flowers to a man I had recently met and was considering asking out, but I wasn't entirely sure it was the right thing to do. Not being the most adept dater, I find that it's always advisable to run my plans past people more experienced in romance than I am.

"Say you meet this guy," I theorized. "At a party or something. He seems really nice, and you have a great conversation. A couple of days later, you get flowers from him and a note saying he really enjoyed talking to you and would like to maybe have dinner or coffee or something."

"How did he get my address?" asked my friend Jackson suspiciously.

"What?" I said, momentarily caught off guard. "I don't know. What difference does it make? That's not the point."

"I just wouldn't want any of you giving out my address or phone number to some guy who wanted to stalk me," he said.

"Who said anything about stalking?" I said. "It's just flowers. Besides, he's a friend of a friend, not just someone off the street."

"I don't know," said Anna, taking a drag on her cigarette. "It sounds like too much commitment to me. I mean, I feel like I owe a guy sex if he buys me dinner. Starting with flowers would be like asking me to swallow on the first date. I'm not ready for that."

"He just wants to have dinner," I said. "No one even mentioned sex."

"It's always about sex," said Jackson bitterly. "No one sends flowers just because he's a nice guy. He wants sex. And if he wants sex, why can't he just call me and ask to come over? Why send flowers? What's that supposed to mean, anyway?"

"It doesn't have to *mean* anything," I explained in exasperation. "He likes you. He wants to tell you that, and he wants to ask you to dinner. What's the big deal about flowers? They're romantic."

"It's just sort of creepy," said Anna. "You know, desperate and clutchy and all that."

I couldn't believe what I was hearing. Granted, I am not exactly an expert in the area of interpersonal relationships. But even I would be thrilled if someone sent me flowers. You know, as long as I liked him. But even if I didn't, I wouldn't turn him in to the local sex-crimes unit. Apparently, my friends felt differently.

"I don't like all that flowers and cards crap," said Jackson. "Next thing you know, he'll be calling my dad asking for my hand in marriage. I prefer your standard gay date—go to dinner and then go home and have sex all night. Say goodbye in the morning. Maybe exchange numbers if you want to do it again. That's it."

"Amen," said Anna.

"But you're a straight girl," I protested. "You're supposed to love all that romantic stuff."

"No one I know does," she insisted. "That's all just a cover-up for getting you into bed. Any girl I know would be really suspicious if some guy sent her flowers. He's trying too hard. It's like not waiting a day to call someone back."

"Waiting a day?" I asked, confused.

Anna sighed. "I forget that you're dating challenged," she said. "It's the one-day rule. You never call someone back the same day he calls you. That makes it look like you don't have anything better to do. But if you wait a day, then that makes him think you didn't get home early enough to return his call, like maybe you were having a fabulous night out at the opera or hanging out in SoHo with Robert De Niro or something. Then he thinks you're really fabulous and interesting."

"But what if he knows about the one day rule?" I said, cleverly thinking ahead.

"It doesn't matter," said Anna patiently. "Even if he does, he still won't know for sure if you didn't call him back because of that or because you really were out all night. So you win either way."

"OK, but what if you're both playing the one day rule. Then no one ever calls anyone."

"You're reading too much into this," said Jackson. "It's really not that difficult."

"*I'm* reading too much into this?" I said. "You're the one who thinks anyone who sends you flowers should be under psychiatric care."

"He should," said Jackson. "Or at least heavily medicated. I prefer my men to be the no-nonsense kind."

"I just don't get this," I said. "I can't be that behind the times."

"You are," said Anna. "I'll prove it to you. Let's take a little quiz. Question one. You've managed to ask someone out, and you're deciding what to do on your date. Where do you go?"

"To a movie and dinner," I answered confidently. That was an easy one.

"Wrong," said Anna instantly. "Jackson, tell him the right answer."

"Coffee," said Jackson. "Always coffee first. It's too much

of a commitment to do anything more than that, and if things don't go well you can always leave after 20 minutes. With dinner you're talking at least an hour. Add a movie to it and there go three hours of your life."

"You do get two points for the movie idea, though," said Anna kindly. "At least if things are going badly you don't have to talk to the guy, and it might be something you wanted to see anyway. But don't even think about paying for his ticket unless you want him to run screaming for the nearest door."

"And no sharing popcorn, insisted Jackson. "You both buy your own."

"Gee, thanks," I said. "I'll try to remember not to scare anyone off by offering him a Milk Dud. OK. Next question."

"It's time for the first sexual get-together," Anna said. "Where do you go?"

I thought for a minute. I tried hard to remember everything I'd learned in my SAT preparation classes about picking the right answers by eliminating the obviously wrong ones. "Um, to my place?" I said finally, figuring I had a 50-50 chance of being right. I also thought going to my place would be a nice gesture, a first step on the road to intimacy.

"Wrong again," said Jackson. "You always go to his place for the first time. That way you can check out what it looks like and get clues about what kind of guy he is. I like to go through their drawers while they're in the shower. Once I found an entire scrapbook filled with cut-out pictures of Kate Jackson and poems about her hair. We never had a second date."

"I always take a look in the refrigerator," added Anna. "If it's got lots of leftovers, I know he's a loser who stays home every night. But if there's nothing in there but some moldy Brie and a bottle of flat seltzer, it's a go."

"So we go to his place so I can spy on him," I said, making a mental note to throw out all of the Tupperware containers in my fridge.

"Right," said Anna. "Besides, if you're at his place, you can always leave afterwards. But if he's at your place, it's harder to get him out."

"But what if I want him to stay?" I said.

Both Anna and Jackson shook their heads. "You never stay over the first time," said Jackson. "You shouldn't even think about staying over until at least the seventh time."

"And even then, don't even think about bringing a toothbrush with you," said Anna. "I know what you're thinking. But that's just asking for trouble."

"Oh, here's a good one," said Jackson excitedly. "Bonus question. You've been going out with this guy once or twice a week for three months. One Friday night you go out with some friends—say with us—and you see him having dinner with someone else. What do you do?"

"If we've been going out for three months, shouldn't we be spending Friday nights together?" I said, confused. "Why is he out with someone else?"

"That's exactly what I thought you would say," crowed Jackson. "See, you're hopeless. You think a couple of months of dating means you're married."

"Well, it should mean *something*," I said. "Why bother dating someone if it doesn't mean something after three months?"

"We can't put you into the dating pool," said Anna sadly. "You'll get eaten alive. Face it, you're doomed."

"Well, I don't believe you," I said. "There have to be some men left—and women too—who want romance. There have to be some people left who like being courted."

Anna and Jackson looked at each other and laughed cruelly.

Where Have All the Flowers Gone?

"This is why you never go out with anyone," said Jackson. "You haven't learned the rules yet. Just screw 'em and get out. That's how it's done. If you happen to find one you want to keep around, don't blow it by sending him flowers or singing beneath his window or whatever stupid thing you have in mind. It'll just backfire. You have to play hard to get."

"You are a bitter queen," I said. "And I'm going to prove you wrong. Both of you."

The next day, I called up the local florist and sent the man I was interested in a dozen roses with a card that read, "I've enjoyed getting to know you. How about dinner on Friday?"

Then I waited. I knew he'd call. After all, since we'd met we'd spoken several times on the phone and had great conversations. He was smart, and funny, and all of those things men generally aren't these days. Surely he would understand that flowers don't have to mean something sinister.

He did call, about an hour after the roses arrived. I was out walking the dog, and came home to find the message light blinking on my answering machine.

"Hi," said his voice when I hit the button. "Thanks so much for the flowers. They're really, um, nice. Look, about Friday. I guess I should have explained that I'm, um, not really ready to date anyone seriously."

It went on, but we needn't get into the grisly details. Suffice it to say, it was not a joyous moment and it involved the phrase "still be friends."

That Friday, instead of going out with my would-be beau, I went out with Anna and Jackson. "You win," I said as soon as we sat down. I told them what had happened.

"See," said Anna jadedly when I was finished. "It never works. You scared him."

"You should have just sent him E-mail saying you wanted

to savage him if it was convenient," suggested Jackson. "That's more to the point."

Before I could argue, the waitress appeared at our table, interrupting our discussion. "Here you go," she said, setting down a votive candle. "Especially for my favorite customers."

She smiled at us and left. As she walked away, I picked up the candle.

"And just what's this supposed to mean?" I said, blowing it out. "I bet she just wants a bigger tip."

"See," said Anna, patting me on the back. "Now you're catching on."

Dyke the Halls

No one believes the events in this piece really happened. They did, although I confess that they didn't all happen at the same party. Please forgive me.

I have always had a close group of lesbian friends, so having the girls over for a little Christmas get-together seemed like a fine notion. Perhaps encouraged by faulty memories of my own childhood holidays, one day I decided to invite some of them to come help me select and decorate a tree. We would, I thought, go out and cut one of the many pines that grew wild on the land around my house. Then, warmed by good will and vast quantities of hot chocolate, we would trim it while listening to carols and eating homemade cookies, perhaps even with green and red sprinkles on top. It would all be wildly fun, and a wonderful way to celebrate with our extended gay family before the annual horror of going home to our real ones. Really, it seemed like a good idea at the time.

The first sign of trouble came with the first telephone call, made to my friend Willow.

"Christmas is an Anglo-patriarchal holiday that bastardizes traditional goddess worship celebrations," she said after I asked her.

"I always thought it was about presents and singing and elves," I said.

"Furthermore," continued Willow grimly, "The whole Judeo-Christian concept of the season is a reprehensible fallacy that completely minimizes the spiritual belief systems of other cultures. All of those horrible Nativity scenes that pop up all over shopping malls across America—they're just representations of what the Church would like us to think Christmas is."

"But the presents...," I countered.

"I just can't condone participating in that kind of perpetuation,"said Willow. "I mean, this whole celebration—which really you should call Yule anyway—is supposed to be about the coming of the Horned God and the cold winter months, not about some fat white man in a suit abusing endangered animals by making them pull a sleigh, which is really probably far too heavy for them anyway..."

"OK, so it's a Yule celebration," I said.

"But the point I'm trying—"

"We're having cheesecake," I said.

Willow said she'd be there by 6.

Next on my list was Rachel. She had just finished meditating, and seemed to be in a good mood. I took this as a positive sign. "I'm having a Christ...er...Yule party," I said warmly. "I was hoping you'd come."

"I'm Jewish," she said. "We don't do Yule. Christmas either."

I sighed. "What do you do?"

"Nothing," Rachel said. "Well, there's Hanukkah, but I find the whole thing ridiculous. People rushing all over buying crap no one wants just because they feel bad that their kids don't get to visit Santa. It just makes me crazy."

She was warming up for a lecture, so I cut her off. "Look," I said. "This isn't about presents. We're just getting together and it happens to be Yule or Christmas or some damn thing. I haven't seen you in a month. Are you coming or not?"

"Well, if you're going to make me feel guilty about it, I guess I have to."

I took that as a yes and told her what time to be there. Anne was the last person to call. Prepared by my encounters with Willow and Rachel, I told Anne I was having a holiday party, which I would like her to participate in so that we could nondenominationally celebrate nothing and have a good time communing in one another's company.

"Fine," she said.

"Fine?"

"Yes, fine. What did you expect me to say?"

"Um, I don't know."

"I'll be there," she finished, adding before hanging up, "I'll bring my new girlfriend." So excited was I by her smooth acceptance that I failed to register the last part of her sentence. I would live to regret it.

The day of the festivities dawned cold and gray. By noon, a light snow was falling, the perfect backdrop for what I hoped would be a pleasant evening with my friends. As the hour neared, I made the last batches of cookies and set them out to cool. Everything was ready, and all I needed was the guests. I began to think happy thoughts. I put a Windham Hill Solstice sampler album on, pleased that it contained no religious connotations whatsoever but still sounded wintry.

They all arrived simultaneously, bustling into the house like a pack of cats caught in the rain and trying desperately to get out. "It's snowing," said Rachel glumly. "It's practically a blizzard."

Willow handed me a package wrapped in brown paper and tied with twine. "Here," she said. "It's a candle to burn for Yule. It brings happiness."

"I thought we weren't giving presents," Rachel said defensively. "I didn't bring anything because you said—"

"It's not a present," I said hurriedly. "It's a…a…a ceremonial object."

"I thought we weren't doing anything religious," Rachel started again, but was cut off by Anne, who entered accompanied by a tall, thin woman wearing an Army surplus jacket and John Lennon glasses.

"This is Hannah," she said. "We met at the co-op."

Thankful for the distraction, I picked up a plate of cookies. "Nice to meet you," I said. "Would you care for a gingerbread boy?"

"Person," said Hannah.

I looked at her blankly. "Gingerbread person," she repeated. "Not boy. Do they have sugar, butter, or eggs in them?"

"Yes, yes, and yes," I said. "Why?"

"I don't eat anything with animal products or processed sweeteners. No wheat either."

I glared at Anne over Hannah's shoulder. "Would you like some mulled wine then?"

"I don't drink alcohol," Hannah said. "But never mind. I brought my own soy milk and some rice cakes." She pulled a bag from her oversize Guatemalan peasant's pouch and proceeded to snack.

Thankfully, no one else had any qualms about sugar or fat, and dove into the piles of cookies. After a half hour or so of munching and chatting, I announced that it was time to go get the tree. "Tree?" Rachel said, her mouth overflowing with chocolate chip–macadamia nut crunchies. "You didn't say anything about a tree."

"I forgot," I said. "We're going to get a tree." I looked over at Willow, who seemed to be chanting under her breath. "It's a Yule tree."

"*Oy*," said Rachel, heaving herself out of her chair. "The things you goys do."

Eventually, I got everyone dressed and out into the yard. After a short trek through the now-snowy woods, we came to the tree I'd preselected earlier in the week and tied with a red bow so I could find it again. "Here it is," I said proudly. "The Yule tree."

"You're going to cut down a tree?" said Hannah. "A living tree?"

I smiled at her, gritting my teeth. "Yes," I said evenly. "Why?"

Hannah snorted. "Well, go right ahead. But what with all of the destruction of the rain forests in South America and all, I'd think maybe you'd want to leave this tree in peace."

I produced the hand saw from the bag I was carrying. "I'm sure this one tree won't cause the ozone layer to instantly evaporate," I said, waving the saw menacingly in Hannah's direction.

"She's right," said Willow. "I mean, you didn't tell me you were going to cut down a real tree or anything."

I looked at her through squinted eyes. "Just where did you think Yule trees came from?" I asked. "Do you think the Yule people or goddess worshippers or whatever they were made them out of old newspapers?"

"At least say a prayer to its spirit," Willow insisted. "Really, if you're going to kill it and all, the least you can do is tell it you're sorry. You owe it something."

We all joined hands around the tree. I stared at it, wishing it would just fall over on its own. Everyone was waiting for me to say something. I cleared my throat.

"Dear tree," I said, feeling like the biggest ass on earth. "Thank you for giving your life that we might have a joyous Yule season."

I looked over at Willow. "Happy?"

She nodded. I picked up the saw and knelt beneath the tree. I put the edge of the saw against the trunk, only to hear Willow and Hannah break out in violent weeping.

"OK," I said, standing up. "Everyone into the Volvo."

We piled into the car and drove to the tree stand set up at the end of town. My Christmas-Yule-holiday celebration was turning into one gigantic nightmare, but I was determined to have a good time. We all got out and started to walk through the aisles of trees, searching for the perfect specimen. Although Willow still sniffled a little as she ran her hands over the branches of the fallen trees, she behaved herself.

After looking at every single tree in the entire place, we were finally able to select one that looked decent. Although Hannah said that she was sure it was some kind of endangered fir and threatened to turn the owner of the place over to the Sierra Club, Greenpeace, and Robert Redford, I plunked down $45 and tied the hapless tree to the roof of the car. Everyone got back in, and we went home.

With a minor amount of fuss, we got the tree into its stand and settled into a corner of the living room, where it seemed a little overwhelmed. I hauled out a box of ornaments, and we set to work trimming it. I put Rachel in charge of stringing lights; Anne was responsible for hanging balls; and Willow and Hannah volunteered for tinsel detail because it involved the least amount of physical contact with what they insisted on calling "the wounded soul." Cookies were eaten and drinks were drunk, and soon things were humming right along. At least for five minutes.

The lights were the first problem. I should have been watching Rachel more carefully, or at least been suspicious when I heard her cackle every few minutes as she bustled around the tree. "There we are!" she said triumphantly, plugging them in so the room filled with merry color. The lights were on the tree, all right, and for once they all worked. But they were arranged in a strange pattern that defied explanation.

"What did you do?" I asked. "It looks funny."

"I arranged them in the shape of a vulva," she said proudly. "See how the labia wrap around the sides? Isn't it great?"

I sighed. "It's lovely," I said. "Let's just hang the decorations."

"I don't know about these," Anne said, looking doubtfully at my box of ornaments. She held up a frosted glass ball in one hand and a hand-blown icicle in the other. "How come these are all phallic-oriented? Don't you have any pink triangles or labryses or busts of Gertrude Stein?"

"Pretend the balls are breasts," I said. "And the angels are drag queens from the Stonewall Riots."

Anne was skeptical, but she went to work, hanging balls and icicles and angels with abandon until she'd gone through the entire box. "Are there more?" she asked.

"In the guest-room closet," I said, busy trying to arrange holly on the mantel. "Top shelf."

Anne disappeared. I stood looking at the tree, munching on a cookie. "This hasn't been so bad after all," I said to Rachel, who was trying to get a red light to line up with where a clitoris should be.

All of a sudden, Anne ran back into the room crying. She grabbed her coat and headed out the door. "What's wrong?" I asked her.

She turned around. "Willow is in the guest room teaching Hannah the basics of tantric yoga," she sobbed before getting into her Subaru and pulling out of the driveway.

A moment later, Hannah and Willow appeared in the

doorway, looking slightly flushed. "Hey, what's going on?" Willow asked.

"Anne saw you two playing O Come All Ye Faithful," I said menacingly. "Now she's gone."

"Oh, shit," said Hannah. "She still had my Womyn for a Free Tibet T-shirt in her trunk."

Willow snatched up her coat and left, followed closely by Hannah, who ran down the driveway yelling, "Wait, I need a ride," her Birkenstocks making patterns in the snow.

I shut the door and turned to Rachel. "Well, that was fun," she said. "Now, shall we hang this tinsel or not?"

I grabbed a handful and flung it at the tree, where it landed and hung like some cheap stripper's bedraggled fright wig, reflecting the changing colors of the lights as the vulva twinkled gaily. I sank into a chair and moaned. On the table, cheesecake sat untouched while the wine mulled on in silence.

"Look on the bright side," Rachel said, unwrapping Willow's Yule candle and lighting it. "There's always New Year's."

Ah-Choo! A Guide to the New Hankie Code

This piece was written purely for fun, on a day when I was wishing that men came with warning labels. I was gratified when it was later picked up for inclusion in Michael J. Rosen's More Mirth of a Nation: Best American Humor Writing.

For years, gay men searching for sexual fulfillment have been aided by the convenience of the hankie code, the wearing of different colored handkerchiefs in the back pocket to alert the careful observer to the wearer's particular fetishes. While this code has worked nicely for some, those of us who would like to identify potential partners by means other than what they do in the bedroom have been left to our own devices. This is not fair. So in an attempt to right this wrong, I have developed the following hankie code based not on sexual proclivities, but on general personality traits.

Green Hankie: Eats only organic produce. Will drag you around the co-op for hours searching for locally grown cilantro and pesticide-free lemons. Takes a multitude of vitamins, but is still tired most of the time, requiring numerous visits to acupuncturists, herbalists, and crystal healers, none of whom are covered by a health plan. When on a dinner date will complain loudly that the nonorganic lettuce in the salad will surely result in a sore throat, but will have no problem eating the entire piece of chocolate cheesecake you ordered for yourself. Advantages: Always has homeopathic remedies on hand for sudden colds, interesting collection of New Age books, makes great smoothies. Disadvantages: Will ban meat from the refrigerator, spends most weekends at self-actualization retreats, listens to music by whiny girl singers.

Yellow Hankie: Amateur activist. Has a membership in every gay group you can imagine, from the Human Rights Campaign to the gay swimming club. Has memorized every acronym imaginable, believes in the educative power of the bumper sticker, and leaves articles clipped from the newspaper on your kitchen counter with salient points underlined. Frequently unavailable for dates due to a heavy schedule of petitioning and volunteering for local gay political candidates. Advantages: Gets invited to parties with pseudo-celebrities, able to converse on numerous subjects (as long as they're gay), enthusiastic in bed because sex is seen as a political statement. Disadvantages: Makes movie-going difficult because of constant boycotts of allegedly homophobic films, tends to accuse friends of holding less evolved opinions, thinks Bette Midler is frivolous.

Red Hankie: Processing junkie. Enthusiastically codependent, and will not hesitate to reassure you that your personality defects are completely normal and most likely the fault of your parents. Has an entire library of self-help books and knows the schedule and meeting location for every conceivable 12-step program. Generally has a degree in social work. Dates will involve talking about how you feel about the previous date. Advantages: Always concerned with your welfare, generally doesn't abuse any substance except Prozac, very organized. Disadvantages: The phrase "How do you feel about that?" quickly becomes tiresome, has many depressed friends who need constant attention and call at odd hours, worries that having sex more than four times a week constitutes an addiction.

Blue Hankie: Enjoys foreign films, particularly when playing in inconveniently located theaters with no parking and surrounded by ethnic restaurants of ill repute. Will frequently tell you that anything made in Hollywood is crap and insist on attending only movies featuring arcane plots, actresses with three names, and children carrying balloons. A typical date will consist of sitting through three hours of subtitles and an additional three hours of exposition, during which you are told as many times as possible that you "just don't get it." Advantages: Selecting a date activity is easy, extreme length of most foreign films renders conversation impossible, seldom recognizes sarcasm. Disadvantages: Wears too much black, refuses to attend Oscar night parties, seldom recognizes sarcasm.

Lavender Hankie: Overly fond of Siamese cats. Probably has at least two, who will sport unsuitable matching names like Melissa and kd or Joan and Bette, even if male. Will frequently cancel dates because one or the other of them is sneezing, and will not understand when you ask that the cats not be allowed to sleep on your face at night. Dates will involve neurotically prepared dinners followed by looking at high school yearbooks and hearing endless stories about all of the people in them. Advantages: Tends to be very loyal, enjoys giving back rubs, clean. Disadvantages: Likes to call you "Pussums" in bed, high-strung, allows pets to use sex toys as playthings.

Pink Hankie: Bad poet. Has an entire shelf filled with notebooks of badly rhymed sonnets dating back to the sixth grade, and will spend hours reading each and every one of them to you. Easily breaks into tears while listening to Elton John or Jewel albums and says, "Can you believe how deep that is?" Dates center around poetry slams and exhibits of black and white photos of body parts with accompanying text from the work of Sylvia Plath. Advantages: Often has interesting friends, does just about anything sexually, will paint a mural on your dining room wall just for fun. Disadvantages: Works at Starbucks or The Gap because part-time work allows more time for "creating," has tentative grip on reality, will break up with you just to have something to write about.

Orange Hankie: Tanning booth afficionado and gym bunny. Insists that every season is swimsuit season, and always looks the part. Spends hours in the gym, and then even more time in front of the mirror. Comes with a startling array of hair and face care products, and considers the Abercrombie & Fitch catalog acceptable bedtime reading. Dates will involve shopping at J. Crew and repeatedly answering the question, "Does this make my ass look big?" Advantages: Takes a good picture, easy to shop for, likes just about anything. Disadvantages: Has many friends named Kyle, obsessive about fat intake, tends to go rapidly downhill after age 26.

Black Hankie: Depression queen. Medicine cabinet is filled with half-used prescriptions for every mood-altering medication known to science. Stays on each drug for a month before announcing, "It just isn't working" and trying another. Partial to career paths almost certain to result in failure, and frequently laments that it's too late to become a model, write a novel, or learn French, so why bother? Dates will consist of recounting everything said at the last therapy session and the therapist's reactions. Advantages: Loves Janeane Garofalo, makes your life seem comparatively wonderful, has low expectations. Disadvantages: Misery loves company, won't go outside if sunny, will blame you for the breakup.

White Hankie: Virgin martyr. Never does anything wrong, but makes sure that you know when you have. Is adept at sighing and looking disappointed, particularly on birthdays and anniversaries. Passive-aggressive, and will answer almost any question about making plans with, "Well, if that's what you want to do," without suggesting an alternative. Favorite phrase is, "I don't want to talk about it," particularly when uttered while sulking over situations of unclear nature and origin. Dates will revolve around discussions of exes and everything they did to ruin the relationship. Advantages: None. Disadvantages: Reminds you of your mother.

My World

While watching something on The Discovery Channel the other night, Patrick said, "Who do you think figured out that you could get iron out of rocks?" Clearly it wasn't one of my *ancestors. Had it been up to my bloodline, we'd all still be trying to* eat *the rocks.*

Imagine, if you will, a world without electricity. Or airplanes. Or Hollywood. Think about what kind of world that would be.

What it would be is the world that would exist if things had been left up to me. Not that I don't like electricity or airplanes or Hollywood (well, I'm not wild about Hollywood). It's just that, frankly, I would never have gotten around to inventing them. It would have taken far too much effort.

From time to time—generally while I'm supposed to be writing a book—I spend long hours simply looking around me at all of the things that exist despite the best efforts of people like myself. It's overwhelming, really, to know that had I been running things we probably wouldn't now be enjoying such wondrous creations as Hello Kitty, blue cheese, and public education. In fact, we would probably all be sitting around, naked, in fairly damp caves, gnawing on sticks.

My World

This is disconcerting. I like to think that I am at least marginally intelligent. I like to think that, if stranded in the wilderness, I could last perhaps 10 minutes or so before succumbing to heatstroke, lack of water, or hyenas. And perhaps I could. But I know with absolute certainty that had the development of the civilized world been in my hands, our entire planet would currently look like an Alabaman trailer park just after a tornado has passed through: lots of piles of formless refuse and crowds of bewildered people staring up at the sky.

Had I been running things, we wouldn't know there *was* China, let alone be enjoying takeout sweet and sour chicken. Not for us would be the joys of cello suites, gin rummy, and the flush toilet. In all likelihood we'd be standing at the edge of the ocean, waiting for something to happen.

Last year I went to India with my friend Katherine to look at temples (OK, to get away from my editors). One morning we were standing in the middle of a particularly beautiful temple, looking all around us at the intricately carved statues and decorations. Each stone of the temple walls fit perfectly against the next. The archways between the rooms were marvels of engineering. The temple rose hundreds of feet into the air, each level more exquisite that the last. It was, in short, breathtaking.

As we stood there, gazing at the statue whose shrine it was, Katherine turned to me. "You realize that they did all this using basically their hands and some little bits of metal, right?"

I knew exactly what she was getting at. Only an hour before she and I had been totally unable to remove the child-proof top from the bottle of malaria pills we were supposed to be taking. But hundreds of years earlier, some enterprising people had built *an entire temple* without the aid of machinery, computerized drafting programs, or chilled drinks. It was demoralizing.

Perhaps I'm not being fair. Maybe our ancestors built and discovered and set forth to conquer because there was nothing else to do. Nowadays we have responsibilities to keep us at home, not to mention air conditioning, frozen pizza, and Sony PlayStations. It isn't our fault that Lewis and Clark, Thomas Edison, and all the rest of them beat us to the punch, is it? After all, they weren't really doing anything else. I'm sure that they too would be hard-pressed to wander around in the wilderness or spend hours in a lab trying to make a light bulb if they knew that they could just as easily be trying to reach level 17 on *Crash Bandicoot.*

Or perhaps not. Perhaps the drive to invent and build has simply been bred out of us. Still, it's astonishing to think of how bleak things would be if people like myself had had our way. Take pretty much anything from modern culture and you can safely assume that it would never have gotten any help from me in its creation. Railroads? Never. We'd still be plodding along dirt tracks, taking six months to get from our huts in New York to those important pitch meetings in L.A. If New York and L.A. even existed, which I sincerely doubt.

Or what about this computer that I'm typing on? Forget it. I can barely understand what it does; the very idea that someone *invented* it is utterly unbelievable. Someone once tried to explain to me how hitting the L key on my keyboard is translated into a string of 1s and 0s that the computer does something with. I do not believe this. I do not understand how it is possible. This is a pile of plastic and metal with some electricity running through it. As far as I'm concerned, there are little people inside busily writing down everything I type, like that bird on Fred Flintstone's typewriter. I have proof of this: Sometimes I leave food out for them, and it's always gone in the morning.

It's not that I can't grasp the concept of *wanting* to invent things. I can, for example, fully appreciate that somewhere along the line someone looked at a tree and thought, "This would make nice lumber." That's where my interest in the subject stops, however. I cannot even begin to comprehend having the wherewithal to get from that fleeting thought to making a saw to turn the tree *into* lumber. This is way beyond me. As for turning the lumber into anything else, forget it.

Of course there are other things that I'm very proud *not* to have had a hand in. I hardly think, for example, that claiming responsibility for things like the Inquisition, textured ceilings, or electronic dance music is something to put on your résumé. But I can't help but feel slightly jealous of the people who came up with these things. At least they *made* something. I do not make things. I buy things. I like places like Banana Republic and IKEA and Ralphs because they do all the work for me. (Well, really, I suspect underpaid children in Taiwan do all the work for me, but I don't like to think about that.) I am happy to pay them for doing this, because I know that without them I'd be sitting in a tree somewhere, scratching myself and waiting for the fruit to ripen.

During all of the fuss about the millennium, when people were stockpiling food and building bunkers and whatnot, I did nothing. I knew there was no point. If the world as we know it was going to come to an end, I was going to go with it. Sure, I might have been able to buy up lots of cans of Spaghetti-O's and lay in a supply of bottled water. But what would happen when those ran out? I'd be dead meat. And really, I probably wouldn't have lasted even as long as the Spaghetti-O's. As soon as I wasn't able to check my E-mail 16 times a day, what would be the point of living?

Michael Thomas Ford

Some people aspire to be the first one living on Mars, or to invent the next microprocessor. I aspire to be Amish. There was a large Amish community near where I grew up, and it was always a treat for me to visit them when my mother went to buy eggs or quilts, which happened once or twice a year. “Don’t stare,” she’d warn as we drove up the long dusty road to their cluster of houses. “Remember, they’re different.”

Yes, they were different. And yes, I stared. But not because I thought they were weird. It was because, secretly, I wanted to live with them. I knew *they* would understand the comfort I found in a way of life that didn’t require me to know anything more complicated than how to light a candle or stick a seed in the ground (and I was even doubtful about my ability to do these things). Free of electricity and cars and telephones, they existed in a simpler place, one where no one expected anything of anyone. (I sincerely doubt that any Amish person has ever called up a writer demanding to know where his manuscript is.) What a relief it would be, I thought, to be among such people.

Now it’s too late. I’m far too used to my cable television and my Palm Pilot and the Internet. Although I will never understand how they came to be or how they work, I am happy to ride on trains and use my credit cards and stick contact lenses in my eyes every morning. And I am thankful for the people who did invent these things, because without them I would be nothing. I just hope they don’t expect anything in return.

Diary of a Would-Be Porn Star

Every year I look at the annual list of best-selling gay books, and every year I'm amazed to see that the top five to 10 titles are generally gay video guides, biographies of porn stars, and photo books of porn stars. What is it with our obsession with porn stars? Do we really think they lead these glamorous, fulfilling lives that we don't? Why do we even call them stars? *It's all a little surreal.*

For a short time a few years ago, I reviewed porn movies for a now-defunct magazine. Once a month a package would arrive, discretely wrapped in brown paper, containing five or six new flesh flicks for me to watch and give my opinions of. The pay was almost nonexistent, but I did it anyway, happy to be able to do my part in educating the smut-viewing public about the merits of these fine pieces of cinematic beauty. "Anything for art," I told my friends when they pretended to be appalled.

Watching these entertaining videos provided more than the occasional moment of pleasure, but after a while I had a disturbing thought: None of the things I saw in the movies ever happened to me. Oh, sure, the men in the films did things that I did. They went to the beach. They went grocery shopping. They took their dogs for walks. But that's where the similarities ended. When I took my dog for a walk, no handsome man asked me if I needed help burying my bone. When I returned books to the library, the shy man behind the desk didn't follow me into the periodicals section and show me his Dewey decimal system. It just didn't happen.

Because I firmly believe that life imitates art, I knew that the filmmakers couldn't possibly be lying. Surely all across America men were having hours of hot, oily fun with pool boys, pizza delivery men, and neighbors they happened to meet in the hall while wearing nothing but a jockstrap. Behind every bush there had to be two guys engaged in carnal knowledge of one another with barely a hint of polite introduction preceding it. Clearly, I was just going about things the wrong way.

I decided that with a little effort my life too could be as exciting as a porn movie. Even better, it could actually *be* a porn movie. All it would take was a little bit of planning and some daring-do. If I just put my mind to it, I would soon be romping from one exciting sexual encounter to another. I anticipated days of endless orgies with beautiful men who fulfilled my every fantasy.

I chose a Friday to begin my new life, since I had deduced from my film-watching that on Fridays everyone in North America became incredibly horny and ready for fun. I woke up that morning raring to go, and leapt from my bed in search of the first orgasm of my porn star life. Wearing nothing but my bathrobe, which was strategically left hanging open so that any men I happened to encounter would have easy access, I strolled to the front door and opened it.

Now, I'm sure the paper boy (who of course had just celebrated his 18th birthday) didn't mean to scream as loudly as he did. Still, at such an early hour it was a little unsettling. And certainly there was no need for running away in such an hysterical manner and leaving all of those papers on my lawn. As I shut the door, I made a mental note not to leave a tip at Christmas. In porn films, the paper boy was always most accommodating. To find that mine wasn't was a bitter disappointment indeed.

I decided I was going to have to take a much more active approach if I were going to be successful at porn stardom. I sat down and made a list of the most popular locations for finding sex, based on the porn films I'd seen. The list went like this (in order of frequency):

1. Apartment complexes in Laguna Hills
2. Beaches on deserted islands
3. Gyms
4. Locker rooms in high schools after football practice
5. Video stores (X-rated sections)

This, as you might well imagine, was not entirely helpful. California was on the other coast. Deserted islands are hard to come by. And high school administrators are not frequently as open minded as one might think. In the end, the gym and video store were the only real possibilities. I decided to try the gym first, since the video store didn't open until noon, and I was ready for action immediately. Throwing on some shorts, I packed up my bag and left.

The gym at 9 o'clock in the morning bore little resemblance to the stud-filled athletic facilities of my porn viewing experiences. Instead of rooms crammed with well-built men wearing tight shorts, no supportive gear whatsoever, and lots of oil, I found myself surrounded by 52 middle aged women in floral print leotards and headbands gyrating to Paula

Abdul while attempting to get in shape for their daughters' weddings. It was hardly the stuff of homo fantasy.

Undaunted, I checked out the sauna, which according to porn movies was frequently the site of some vigorous groping. Inside, it was just as misty and hot as the porn films had promised. And hidden within its steamy interior I could see a scantily clad man reclining on one of the wooden benches. Casually carrying my towel (no one wears them in porn movies), I went in and sat down next to him. To my satisfaction, he was quite a looker. Just my type.

I nodded, and he smiled. In porn movies, this always means, "I want to suck your cock." So I did what any good porn star would do—I spread my legs and waited for him to pounce.

"Hey," he said, putting a hand on my waiting thigh. "Have you ever read *The Book of Mormon*?"

I was out of there in a flash, leaving my towel behind as I high-tailed it out onto the street. This was *not* the way things were supposed to go. I checked my watch—only 15 minutes until the video store opened. I started walking.

Entering the store, I ducked behind the black curtain separating the adult videos from the rest of the store. To my surprise and joy, a cute college jock type was busily looking at the covers of the boxes. I looked at the one in his hand and, seeing that it featured two men and not a silicone-laden, red-lipped woman, congratulated myself on my good luck.

I played it cool, knowing full well that these things had to involve a little bit of play before the kill. I walked a few feet down the row and picked up a tape. Out of the corner of my eye, I could see that Mr. Frat Boy was taking quick glances my way. I moved closer, reaching for a tape near him.

"That one isn't so good," he said.

He'd taken the bait. "Really?" I said. "Is there one you like better?"

He turned and smiled. "Why? You interested?"

Finally. Sex was imminent. "Maybe," I said, already ripping his rugby shirt off and sucking on his nipples in my mind.

He looked around to make sure we were alone. "I really like to do it to *The Little Mermaid*," he said. "Disney makes me hard as a rock. Especially if you can talk like the crab."

Clearly, it wasn't my day. I suddenly remembered somewhere I had to be and excused myself before Jocko could launch into a chorus of "Under the Sea."

As I walked home, I pondered my plight. I couldn't understand why it was so hard to get laid. In porn movies, men with brontosaurus-size erections practically fell out of the sky. It was impossible to turn a corner without tripping over a luscious piece of beefcake, rump in the air and ready for fun. But all I seemed able to find were the rejects who never made it past Dropping and Sucking 101.

Back in my own home, I tried to think what Ryan Idol would do in my situation. After a minute, it came to me. I picked up the phone and dialed the cable company.

"Yes," I said when the weary operator's voice crackled through. "Something seems to be wrong with my box. It isn't working. Can you send a guy over?"

Much to my delight, it worked. The operator said a man would be by in about 20 minutes. I hung up, thanking the Porn Gods, who obviously had decided to smile upon me after all. I then raced into my bedroom and set the trap. I grabbed a tape from the pile by the VCR, shoved it in, and hit PLAY. My plan was simple: I would pretend the cable was out. When the technician tried to turn on the television, a porn film would be playing. Then I'd make my move. I'd seen it once in a movie, and it worked brilliantly.

I paced around the apartment until I heard a knock on the door. Still wearing my gym shorts, I opened it. Standing outside was a hunky young stud fair near bursting out of his uniform. I ushered him inside. His shirt had BILL stitched on it.

"Right this way," I said in what I hoped was a husky voice dripping with innuendo. "I'm not sure what's wrong." I led Bill into the bedroom, where he went straight for my cable box. I watched as he turned it on and off, checked the wiring, and did something with a little tool he pulled out of his back pocket. He never once turned the TV on.

"That should do it," he said, turning to go.

"Wait a minute," I yelped. "Shouldn't you check it? I mean, what if it's not fixed?"

"Oh, it's fixed," he said. "Trust me." He headed for the door.

"No!" I yelled, practically pushing him back into the bedroom. "Please, just check it."

Bill gave me an odd look as he turned on the television. I held my breath, waiting for a shot of Zack Spears doing what he did best to appear and get the ball rolling, as it were. Instead, what came on was a close-up of Mary Tyler Moore tap-dancing madly in an elevator in *Thoroughly Modern Millie*. Her big toothy grin spread across my TV where Zack's hard-as-iron cock should have been thrusting in and out of some lucky orifice.

"Happy?" Bill asked, glaring at me.

Dejected, I nodded. It just was not meant to be. I watched as Bill left the house, pulling the door shut behind him. "You bitch!" I screamed at Mary as I turned the tape off. "Why couldn't you at least have been a come shot?"

I was running out of possibilities. It was now mid afternoon, and I still hadn't gotten off. I sat down to think, wishing bitterly that I had an outdoor pool to lounge beside naked, a gardener with poor English skills and hours of staying power, or at least a handsome neighbor whose wife just didn't like to do certain things. But all I had was a faulty sprinkler, a pimply kid who raked up the leaves once every October, and old Mrs. Krumbach, who complained ceaselessly about her joints. The stuff of wet dreams, my life was not.

Then I had an idea. I'd once seen a movie in which a young man had engaged in a stimulating encounter with another man in the men's room at the local mall. Surely I could do that too. I hustled out the door to the local Galleria. Then it was but a quick turn past the Sunglasses Hut to the rest room. I threw open the door and commenced scouting out my lucky partner.

There were a couple of possible candidates lined up at the urinals along one wall. I picked the one who seemed the most pornlike (he had on work boots, which I was convinced was a sign) and squeezed in next to him. As I unzipped, I tried to remember what the actor in the movie had done. I casually looked over at my neighbor and smiled slightly.

"Hey," I said.

"Hey," he said, smiling back.

I had no idea what to do next. I couldn't for the life of me remember how it had been done in the movie. I reached inside my fly so I could at least pee and pretend to be doing something. But there was no fly. As I scratched around frantically inside my jeans, I realized that in my haste to leave the gym earlier in the day I'd put my boxers on backwards.

Mortified, I tried to find a way to free myself from my underwear. My waiting partner watched as I ran my hand around inside my pants, looking for a way out. I looked at him and tried to manage a lighthearted chuckle. Hoping to distract him, I winked seductively.

My contact tumbled out of my eye and fluttered gently into the urinal, where it swirled around in the water, bobbing over the fluorescent pink disinfectant tablet like an inner tube. I squinted, trying to locate it while simultaneously attempting to rearrange my boxers from the outside. With only one good eye, it was proving difficult.

Finally, I managed to pull the waistband of my boxers down. Even though my contact was way past rescuing, I decided that I could see well enough for my thrilling encounter to continue. I looked at the guy next to me.

Unfortunately, he was gone, and in his place was a burly mall guard. He took one look at my half-closed eye and the rapidly deflating erection in my hand and frowned.

Now, in the movies, security personnel are notoriously horny and ready for all kinds of fun. I was disheartened to discover that in real life, this is seldom the case. Noting the look in the man's eyes, and sensing that somehow trying to explain things to him would probably not help matters any, I beat a hasty retreat from the bathroom. Using my good eye, I managed to make it home, where I collapsed onto the couch.

My day had not gone at all well, and I blamed it all on porn movies. They had promised me a fun-filled existence of sexual freedom, but they had lied. Grabbing an empty box, I moved through the house, gathering up all of the tapes I could find. When the box was full, I taped it shut and hauled it out to the curb. Dusting off my hands, I went back inside and slammed the door shut on the world of randy men and their empty promises. It was time to come back to reality. Picking up a copy of *Pretty Woman*, I slipped it into the VCR and sat down.

Now, there, I thought happily, *is something I can believe in.*

My Life as a Dwarf, Part 5: Dopey

I do very little to excess. OK, every once in a while I'll do something like eat an entire bag of peanut butter cups in one sitting, but mostly I do things in moderation. It's simply not in my nature to overindulge. I don't eat until I'm stuffed. I don't smoke or do drugs. I've only been drunk a couple of times, and that was years ago when I was in college and it was more or less a requirement.

Because of this tendency it's a bit surprising to me to realize how many friends I have who go exactly the other way. It seems as if everyone I know has an AA anniversary to celebrate or stories to tell about the many times they did a little too much coke and woke up in a Dumpster behind a bar.

It was even more surprising to me that I ended up living for many years with a man who was an addict. As most such stories go, I didn't know he was an addict when I met him. I'm not sure even he knew. But he was, although it took almost two years for me to recognize the signs. Like most addicts, he was an excellent liar. It wasn't until the morning we ended up in an emergency room because he had a seizure in the middle of the street that I discovered the truth.

Then, of course, I decided to save him. To my logical self,

it seemed simple enough. If you could become addicted to drugs, I reasoned, you could become unaddicted. It just required a little effort. I made a plan. He pretended to follow it. I pretended it was working.

This went on for almost eight years. Finally, an arrest for prescription fraud brought everything to an end. The man moved out. The day he left I cried for hours. I thought I missed him, but I was really grieving the life I'd lost while we were both in the grip of his addiction. When the next morning I woke up without feeling like I was being strangled, I realized I hadn't breathed freely in years.

I know this man blames me, at least in part, for what happened to him. He's said as much. I'm sure he believes I didn't love him enough, or perhaps that I wanted him to remain addicted because it gave me some kind of control over him. And maybe in some small way that's true. Once you've lived with an addict long enough, you no longer know what to think about anything. Lies and truth weave together in an intoxicating dance, like the entwined tails of cats.

What I do know is that this man was brilliant, talented, and, when his mind wasn't clouded by the drugs, kind and funny and caring. I've seen him take an old woman's hand and listen patiently to her tell the sort of long, meaningless stories that the very old are masters of. But I've also seen him lie to get what he wants, and steal from people who trusted him. Now it's difficult to tell which was the real him, the two have become so fused in memory.

For years my friends told me to kick this man out of my house. "You're not responsible for him," they said when I objected that he had nowhere to go, no one to help him, no way to survive. "He'll survive," they said wearily. I didn't believe this, so convinced was I that all he needed to do was decide to get clean. Secretly, I accused my friends of not having as much compassion as I did. They were cruel, I told myself, and bitter.

Several times, though, when things got very bad, I did tell him to leave. Twice I hit him, convinced it was the only way to break down the wall he'd built up between addiction and the life he should have had. If it could just come down, I told myself, be torn down, he'd see everything that he was missing.

The problem, of course, was that he didn't want to see. It took me a very long time to understand that for him staying addicted was preferable to getting sober because if he removed the addiction from his life and was still unhappy, he would have nothing left to blame. All along I had believed the pills were making him unhappy, when actually they were making the unhappiness bearable.

This is something I cannot even begin to imagine living with. I don't like to feel numb. I don't even like painkillers when I have dental work done. It's a control issue, I know, but it's also a reaction to seeing how easily using a smoke screen to cover up pain can become a dependency on chemical or even mental sleight-of-hand. I don't want to lose myself in illusion, no matter how comforting it may be at the time or how magical it may appear.

For a long time after this man left my life I wouldn't even take aspirin. I had a manic aversion to drugs, to the tablets and pills and caplets that had filled our lives for so many years. I'd dumped too many bottles of pills down the toilet, searched too many drawers for stray specimens and then looked them up frantically in the *Physician's Desk Reference* to see what they were and what they did, as if attempting to identify various poisonous bugs so that I could find the antidote to their toxic bites.

I never did find the antidote, and for several years I considered this a failure on my part. Despite the relief I felt over having this destructive force gone from my life, I couldn't stop myself from thinking there was more that could have been done. I completely ignored the fact that scores of doctors, several treatment centers, and even the courts had done everything they could to help this man. Something, I thought, had been overlooked.

Thankfully, distance and my own survival instinct told me that it was no longer my problem. Actually, it had never *been* my problem. But I had let it become mine, or at least convinced myself that it was, and if I made any mistake during those eight years this was it. The truth was that it never had been, but accepting that took time. Frankly, the thought that I had wasted so much energy on this man and his problems was far more distressing to me than anything he'd done during our time together. I could forgive him; I found it much harder to forgive myself.

As it turned out, my friends had been right all along. After leaving, this man did survive. He found other people to use, other excuses to explain his behavior, other ways of feeding his addiction. He didn't need me, which was at first perversely disappointing, then dispiriting, and finally enraging. He'd learned nothing from all of his ordeals except how to manipulate more effectively, how to use his natural skills to prolong his relationship with chemicals and continue to be a fugitive from his own life.

It seems inadequate to say that addiction robs those afflicted with it of life. It's far subtler than that. Addiction makes promises. It gives just enough to make a person feel comforted, but when they aren't looking it takes back far more than it gave. Then, just at the point where a person is ready to turn his back on the addiction, it comes crawling back whispering words of contrition, saying it's sorry, that it will never hurt them again. Wanting to believe, they cradle their addiction in their arms, looking down at its smiling face and forgetting that its fingers are at that very moment reaching into their pockets to see what it can find.

In this way, bit by bit, addiction picks apart the soul. Like a greedy child tearing pieces from a cloud of cotton candy, it stuffs its mouth with morsel after morsel until its face is sticky and it's flying high on a sugar rush. Then it collapses in a stupor, sated for a time until the high wears off and it's time to feed again.

For those of us watching this process the answer seems simple enough: Take away the cotton candy. Who, after all, would keep eating until they were sick? It isn't rational. And therein lies the problem. Addiction isn't rational. Nor, in many cases, are our reactions to it. No one wants to let a child wander off alone down train tracks when we hear the whistle blowing and see lights in the distance. But that's what we ultimately have to do.

I have a friend who recently discovered that a relative is dealing with addiction. "I want to help her," she said to me the other night.

"All you can do is listen," I told her.

"That's not enough," she said. "I want to do something."

I closed my eyes and heard myself saying those very same words to another friend. When was it? Had I just discovered the first bottle of pills? Or was I sitting, years later, surrounded by literally hundreds of empty bottles discovered hidden in a closet? The timeline is difficult to piece together now. Was it after the 2 A.M. call from the hospital following a high-speed crash into a 100-year-old oak tree, or the one from the police asking me to come in for questioning because someone driving my car had attempted to use a forged prescription at a pharmacy three hours away?

"Don't let her problem become your problem," I told my friend.

I could feel her recoil, shocked at the harshness of my words. *How cruel,* I imagined her thinking. *How unfeeling.* She said goodbye, telling me she was going to research treatment programs.

A week later she called again. Things were better, she said. Her relative had not gone into treatment but had voluntarily cut back on her drug of choice. "I think she'll be able to wean herself off it," my friend said.

No, she won't. They never do. But my friend needs to believe she will. She needs to believe that she's being supportive, that her efforts aren't being wasted. She needs this as badly as her relative needs her drugs. I can feel them dancing around one another, each holding out a hand and waiting for the other to take it.

My friends who have also dealt with addiction—either their own or those of others—can joke about it now. We tell each other stories about the stupid things we did. We marvel that we're all still more or less sane. And sometimes we watch as other people in our lives take those first terrifying steps that we once took. Still the tendency is to hold out a hand, to shout warnings and offer advice. We don't want to see anyone fall.

But ultimately we know we have to sit, hands clasped tightly and lips pressed firmly together, and let them go off into the darkness alone. Only then will they discover they have the light inside themselves to find their way back.

It's Not Mean If It's True

I like to think of this piece as my literary version of tough love. I thought people would be more annoyed by it. Instead it was a favorite at readings. By the way, the image on the cover of the book It's Not Mean If It's True *was inspired by the video for Bob Dylan's "Subterranean Homesick Blues."*

My friend So Young (yes, she's heard all the jokes about it, so don't even go there) comes from a very traditional Korean family. When she was growing up, her family went to Korea every other year to visit her mother's relatives. This was a major event, but not an entirely welcome one. Because once there, her mother's sisters and their children—all daughters—would congregate in one place to catch up on one another's lives and engage in a ritual that So Young calls "Name That Flaw."

Name That Flaw involved all of the aunts and cousins crowding into the kitchen. The aunts sat around the table, and the girls hovered on the periphery, trying to remain as invisible as possible because they knew what was coming. After some preliminary chit-chat, the aunts would gaze around the room at the assembled girls and begin.

Whichever aunt had been selected to go first would choose a girl and sit, looking her over, until she was ready to speak. Then she would make her pronouncement: "Anna is thinner than last time," she might say. "That is good. But she has crooked teeth. Boys don't like that."

As her daughter had been the subject of the initial verdict, it would now be Anna's mother's turn to go. "Jin's eyes are a little too Japanese for my liking," she might say, or, "It is a good thing that Karen has such a lovely face, because she is not very bright."

Round and round the table the aunts went, each one dissecting the perceived faults of their sisters' children. No woman ever commented on her own child, as that was not allowed. Nor did they automatically choose to judge the daughter of someone who had criticized theirs. It was not a competition.

When So Young told me about this family tradition, I asked what had been said about her.

"Last year they said my butt was too big and that I didn't know how to cook rice very well," she said. "I got off pretty easily. They told my cousin Trish that she had a man's feet."

The most interesting thing about this ritual is that none of the aunts saw anything wrong with it. When So Young once questioned her mother about why they did it if it made the girls feel bad, her mother shrugged and said, "It's all true, isn't it? How can it be mean if it's true? We are just pointing out things that need to be corrected, if possible. And if not, it is still good to know about them."

It's not mean if it's true. There's logic in that. Harsh logic, but logic nonetheless. And perhaps a kind of logic we should employ more often. Ours is a culture that doesn't really like hearing the truth very much. We prefer to believe that everything is fine the way it is. In fact, we go out of our way to reassure one another that things are great.

When I was editing children's books a number of years

ago, one of the most successful series being published for young readers at that time was called "Coping With." Each book in the series addressed some issue that children might find themselves dealing with, so there were titles like *Coping With An Alcoholic Parent* and *Coping With Diabetes.* Each book assured the reader that things would be OK and that whatever the given situation was, it was manageable. It was all very Marianne Williamson and empowering.

The running joke in my office was that we should do our own series ("Coping With" was published by a rival company) called "Face It." The "Face It" series would be similar in scope to "Coping With," but it would tell the truth. And the truth is that being different really sucks sometimes.

So we wanted to do books like *Face It: You're Fat* and *Face It: No One Likes You.* Instead of doing a lot of hand-holding, these books would give kids practical advice for dealing with a situation that in all likelihood was going to cause them misery. Telling a fat kid that people have different kinds of bodies and that's OK is great, but it doesn't really help him deal with taunts of "Moby Dick!" on the playground. Reassuring a child that her parents' divorce has nothing to do with her doesn't prepare her for the horror of being dragged back and forth between their respective houses for holidays. Much more useful would be chapters like "Why Your Big Ass is Going to Make it Hard for You to Fit into Airplane Seats" and "Manipulating Mom and Dad Into Giving You Gifts."

We never did get the "Face It" series off the ground. It was always more of a fun fantasy than a practical possibility. But there could still be some use for it. Only now I think I'd turn it into a series for delusional adults who don't want to admit what's going on around them. It would be a wonderful way to encourage people to actually look at the issues that affect them instead of pretending they aren't there or that the problem is about something other than what it is.

Imagine, for instance, *Face It: Gays in the Military.* Instead of going on and on about how gay people can be just as loyal and brave as everyone else, we could talk about really crucial issues such as, "Yes, We're Going to Look at Your Dick in the Showers, So Deal With It," and "If You Want Me to Blow You After You've Gone Six Weeks with No Sex, You're Going to Have to Put Out Too." These are the things straight people *really* need to know, the issues they *really* worry about, so we should give them answers. Hiding the truth behind arguments over rights and sensitivity training just muddies it all up.

Another favorite of mine would be *Face It: Queers Have More Fun Than You Do.* This book would outline the ways in which gay people have better lives than straight people. I think chapters like "Only Other Women Know How To Eat Your Pussy Right," "No Kids Means More Vacations," and "You May Have Marriage, But We Have Bette, Liza, and Barbra" would be just the thing. It would force homophobic readers to realize gay people have really cool lives, and it might help them understand that the reason they treat us badly a lot of the time is they're jealous.

Not that straight people are the only ones who need a dose of reality. Queers could also use a couple of volumes of "Face It." One of my absolutely favorite magazines of all time was *Diseased Pariah News.* Born out of the AIDS crisis, this irreverent zine gave its readers the information they needed about living with HIV. For instance, the "Get Fat, Don't Die," column offered high-calorie recipes for people trying to counteract the weight loss often associated with AIDS. Essays about how contributors contracted the AIDS virus detailed the ways gay men were (and weren't) responding to the crisis. The writing was sarcastic and (to some people) offensive, but it was always on the mark.

That's what we need more of. If we had *Face It: If Relationships Were Easy We'd All Have Them*, for example, we could address the issues gay men looking for love encounter. "If You Meet Him at a Bar, Don't Be Surprised When It Doesn't Work Out" would be my choice for the opening chapter, followed by "There's More to Love Than Picking Out a Great China Pattern," "No One Likes a Whiner," and "When the Boyfriend Within Is an Asshole." Enough of this pie in the sky relationship nonsense. Give men the cold hard facts about how it actually works and they might have something they can use.

For our lesbian sisters, might I suggest *Face It: You Have Bad Hair*. This volume would get to the heart of dyke life. Beginning with "You Really *Can* Have Too Many Cats," the book would progress through "Lingerie Is Not Made of Flannel" and "Not Everything Is a Patriarchal Plot" before finishing up with "Just Because She's a Dyke and Plays Guitar Doesn't Mean She Can Sing Well."

And how about *Face It: You're Aging*? Many gay people do not, sadly, grow up with grace or dignity. We aren't encouraged to. But this book could change that. With chapters such as "No One Your Age Should Wear Shorts That Small," "When It's Your Turn to Stop Tanning," and "Transitioning from Circuit Party Queen to Opera Queen," we could launch a revolution—as long as people take the message to heart.

But I doubt that they would. Humans, as a rule, are a delusional species. Asking us to really look at ourselves is asking too much. I suspect, for example, that a book like *Face It: The Gay Community Is a Myth* would not be met with enthusiasm. We have too much invested in pretending that because we're all queer we all like each other and have the same agendas. Just ask the organizers of the March on Washington. It's far easier to force people to embrace a version of reality that, while wonderful, simply doesn't reflect the truth. It's easier to pretend things will be better for all of us if the ones who want gay marriage get it, or if the ones who think antidiscrimination legislation will end hate crimes get it, or if the ones who want to be Boy Scout leaders get to do it, than it is to face reality.

And maybe those things would all be great. Maybe I want some of them too. But I know they don't solve things for all of us, and I know some queer people who don't want them just as badly as others do want them. Instead, maybe we should look at some of the fundamental problems facing us as a community struggling to stay together. Maybe we should start by asking ourselves why gay men are so reluctant to support (or even acknowledge) lesbian issues, why almost two decades into the AIDS crisis young gay men are seeing a shocking rise in new cases of infection, or why older queer people are almost invisible in our world. Despite our many gains, some of the basic problems haven't gone away, but we don't often talk about that.

Maybe we need So Young's aunts to herd us into the kitchen and pick us apart. If they do, will we listen? Or will we stare at the floor and think about something else, hoping they'll move on to the next girl so we can try to forget about our fat thighs and bad skin?

Time

I've sometimes been accused of being bitter. I don't think I'm bitter. I think I just resent things more fully than others.

Time does not heal all wounds. This is one of the great lies of the modern age. Just ask the Jews, who are still smarting over the whole "wandering in the desert" thing. Or the African-Americans, who can hardly be expected to shake off that little slavery incident simply because it didn't happen yesterday. Or, perhaps most tellingly, women, who really haven't quite gotten around to seeing the humor in being blamed for the invention of sin.

Or, if you will, take me. True, I have not been cast out of my homeland, sold to the highest bidder, or christened the destroyer of Eden. But I can hold a grudge with the best of them. I refuse to accept the notion that just because something happened a long time ago—even if it was before I was born or had absolutely nothing to do with me—that I'm not entitled to be pissed off about it.

This is particularly true when it comes to relationships, where I have repeatedly demonstrated that I am fully capable of resenting my partner's past even when it occurred years before I came on the scene. Now, I am a reasonable person, and I truly do believe that what my boyfriend did before he met me has absolutely nothing to do with me. Really, I believe this. After all, I tell myself, he didn't even *know* me. I didn't know *him*. There's no reason at all why what transpired between him and anyone else should bother me in the slightest.

But it does. And this is where the whole time problem comes in. More than once, when discussing the past—or, more precisely, my annoyance over someone else's past—someone has very reasonably said to me, "But that was a long time ago." This is true. However, it was not a long time ago for me. It was moments ago. It is new information. The fact that it happened to you one, five, or 10 years ago is not the point; the point is that for me it is recent history. And I don't like it.

Take, for example, the unpleasant issue of one-night stands. Now, we've all had them. This is simply a fact—ugly as it may be—of gay life. No man can be expected to have gone his entire adult life without having occasionally ended up in bed with someone he chose not to ever see again. This does not, however, mean that I want to be made aware of it. Nor does it mean that just because it happened before I came along—perhaps even many years before—that I am going to receive the news of its having happened with anything approaching calm acceptance.

No, I am going to be irritable about it. Very irritable. Irrationally irritable. Because the fact is, it wasn't *me* my partner had the one-night stand with. It was someone else. And that is not a good thing. This is particularly true if the one-night stand happens to be unattractive, because the inevitable thought that naturally arises is not, "I'm so glad my boyfriend is with me now," but "What the hell was he thinking, and what does it say about me?"

It has been explained to me again and again by people

much more mentally well than myself that this is not a rational position to take. As if I don't know that already. Those who attempt to convince me of this simply don't understand, however, that this is a situation that defies logic. This isn't about being rational. I've never claimed to be rational. This is being deliriously irrational. It's about having something to poke at, like a loose tooth or a scab. It feels good, in a weird way, to work on it for a while. Eventually I'll get bored and move on to something else, but for the moment I'm having a good time.

I have a friend whose first lover was a notorious cheater. After several years of this, my friend finally dumped the jerk and moved on. Recently he let it slip that the two of them were talking again after almost seven years of not speaking.

"Why?" I asked instantly. "After what he did?"

"That was a long time ago," my friend said. "I'm over it."

Over it. This is not a concept I understand. "But you wanted to kill him when you walked in on him with that guy," I protested.

My friend laughed, as if this was funny. "I'll never forget the look on his face," he said. "It was priceless."

"I can't believe you," I said, stunned. "This man *cheated* on you, and you're talking about it like it's no big deal."

"It's not a big deal anymore," said my friend. "Like I said, that was a long time ago."

No. Absolutely not. It may have happened a long time ago, but it happened. The fact that this guy was in bed with someone else, having sex, does not change just because 2,534 days have passed. The fact that he was in bed with someone else, having sex, does not change just because my friend has lived in three cities, buried a dog, eaten 7,436 meals, and slept with probably 16 other guys since then. He still did it.

I have another friend who wants to know all about his boyfriends' pasts. He wants then to describe their exes and what they did in bed. He wants to know everything, from hair color to dick size to favorite position.

I love my friend dearly, but sometimes I wish for bad things to happen to him. "Why shouldn't I know?" he says. "It has nothing to do with me."

"Bah!" I cry when he does this, all of the horror I'm experiencing reduced to this primal sound. "Bah!" I cry, grinding my teeth so hard that I can feel them cracking. *Not have anything to do with him?* How can he think this? It's too well-adjusted, too healthy. I resent having to see it live and in person. I know he's saying it just to annoy me.

I still remember slights perpetuated on me by people in preschool. (Linda Wilkerson, wherever you are, I will have you know that my drawing of a duck did *not* look like a monkey with wings. And David Sears, may you burn in hell for taking the last sheet of purple construction paper and leaving me with orange.) These memories have not faded with age, not one bit. They are still vivid, still ready for poking and prodding when I feel like it.

Confessions of a Don't-Bee

A lot of my early essays were about my childhood. I don't know why, really, except that it was fun to write about. This is one of my favorites. I still like to watch children's television, and I'm really pleased that today's shows are much more inclusive than the ones I used to watch. I still wish Bert and Ernie would come out, though. I have a feeling Elmo will need some gay uncles to confide in.

As a preschooler, one of my great joys was sitting in my parents' big bed each morning and watching *Romper Room.* For those poor souls unacquainted with the joys of this now-defunct '70s-era children's television show, I will explain. *Romper Room* was an idyllic day care center, where an audience of 15 or so lucky 4- and 5-year-olds sang, danced, and experienced sheer joy in the company of the world's perkiest host, Miss Nancy. I understand that different cities had different hosts, but they all seemed to uncannily resemble Miss Nancy, as though some kind of government experiment in genetic cloning had gone horribly awry, resulting in a host of identical children's television personalities with permanent smiles and poor wardrobes. A sort of Kathie Lee for the preschool set, Miss Nancy doled out love to her assembled guests while the rest of us sat at home and watched, wondering what it was we had done to not be allowed to join the rabidly merry kids basking in her glow.

The premise of *Romper Room* was simple indeed. Miss Nancy sang and danced. We watched. In a time when, at least in my neighborhood, many mothers remained at home with their preschool children, it provided an hour of relief for parents who simply wanted to sit and drink their coffee in peace and quiet. Entranced by the fun taking place in Miss Nancy's room, those of us still young enough to find such things thrilling would stop everything to see what new song Miss Nancy would teach us today.

At some point in every *Romper Room* show, Miss Nancy would hold up her Magic Mirror. This clever prop was simply a hand mirror with the glass removed, so that Miss Nancy's buoyant face could peer through. She would stare directly at the camera through the hole in the mirror and pretend to see all of the Friends at Home while she chattered on endlessly about all the fun she and her guests were having. This was supposed to make those of us alone in our rooms feel better about not being able to romp with the more fortunate children.

As much as I loved her, I thought Miss Nancy was full of crap when it came to the Magic Mirror. Even with my rudimentary knowledge of science, I knew she couldn't really see me at home, and I considered myself much more sophisticated than the obviously demented children in the *Romper Room* studio audience who shrieked with glee whenever Miss Nancy peered at them through the Magic Mirror and pretended to be looking across the airwaves. "I see Kathy," she'd say, and Kathy would squeal and clap her hands, in awe of Miss Nancy's mystical powers. Holding Kathy in contempt, I would sit in bed with arms folded, waiting for Miss Nancy to put down the Magic Mirror and move on to something more exciting, like a rousing sing-along of "Row, Row, Row Your Boat."

This all changed, however, the day Miss Nancy was discussing the crucial issue of color. I had always been fond of color, and was pleased that I was going to learn something useful that I could share later on with my parents and friends. I watched carefully as Miss Nancy held up circles of various colors and told us what they were and how they could be put together to form new colors, which impressed me greatly. After going over the relative merits of red, blue, and green, she asked the children in her studio audience what their favorite colors were. "Blue!" they shouted, or "Yellow!"

Then Miss Nancy picked up the Magic Mirror and held it in front of her face. "And what's your favorite color, Friends at Home?" she asked cheerfully.

"Purple!" I screamed back. I knew that, in the greater scheme of things, purple was a sissy color, but what did I care? I was full of Froot Loops and feeling fine. Purple was bold. It was different. And besides, Miss Nancy couldn't hear me anyway. "Purple!" I screamed again, giggling madly.

Suddenly, Miss Nancy's face inside the mirror broke into a wide smile. "I heard a Friend at Home say purple!" she chirped. "That's an *interesting* color to pick, isn't it boys and girls?"

In that instant, my safe childhood world shattered forever. Miss Nancy could hear me. Not only that, but she had announced to the world that a Friend at Home actually preferred purple over blue or yellow. I stared at the television in horror, waiting for all the children in the *Romper Room* world to turn on me and begin laughing derisively.

Then, just as the enormity of what had happened began to sink in, another terrible thought entered my 4-year-old brain. If Miss Nancy could *hear* me, then surely she could *see* me as well. Apparently, my knowledge of how television worked was flawed in a fundamental way, resulting in my horrible admission of being a boy who loved a color I thought only little girls were supposed to favor. Who knew what else Miss Nancy knew about me. She might have seen me engaging in my favorite hobby of thumb sucking. Worse, she might actually be aware that on occasion I not only picked my nose, but actually ate what came out.

Unable to think clearly, I did what any reasonable child would do: I hid under the bed. There, secure among the dust bunnies, I peered out at Miss Nancy, watching anxiously as she put down the Magic Mirror and moved on to the next activity. I breathed a sigh of relief, thinking that maybe she had forgotten about me. The calm was short-lived, however, when there was a knock on the *Romper Room* door and Miss Nancy went to answer it. Throwing wide the door, she turned to the camera and beamed. "Hey, everyone, it's Do-Bee!" she cried.

Do-Bee was the *Romper Room* mascot, and was, in fact, a gigantic yellow and black bee, complete with wings and bouncing antennae. Once every day, Do-Bee would come into the room and greet all of the children. He would buzz around and the kids would go mad, jumping up and down and pawing at Do-Bee's clever costume. Invariably, Do-Bee would cover his mouth with his hands and appear to giggle. Much later, I would realize that Do-Bee was, all along, a Queen Bee. At the time, I simply thought he was fabulous.

The purpose of Do-Bee was to teach us all the things we *should* do or be. "We all want to be good Do-Bees, don't we, boys and girls?" Miss Nancy would say after a lesson on sharing or the importance of neatness, and we would all nod agreeably. The opposite of a Do-Bee was, of course, a Don't-Bee, a title no self-respecting child would claim. Satisfied that we were all normal and properly oriented, Do-Bee would then depart, antennae bouncing merrily, to pollinate the flowers or make honey, whatever he did in his off hours.

Normally, I welcomed the appearance of Do-Bee. I enjoyed his cheerful way of dancing from foot to foot and waving at the camera. But now everything had changed. If Miss Nancy could see me, so, of course, could Do-Bee. Suddenly, in a moment of sheer horror, it all came together in my mind. Do-Bee was Miss Nancy's henchman, the bee who carried out her dirty work. His brief appearance each day gave her the opportunity to point out the Friends at Home whose bad behavior she'd spied in the Magic Mirror. Thus identified as Don't-Bees, those children were then the targets of Do-Bee's wrath.

Clearly, after my declaration of purple-loving, I was now a Don't-Bee.

I scurried out from under the bed and turned the television off, severing the channel between me and Miss Nancy. But I feared it was too late. For the rest of the day, I walked around in terror, waiting for Do-Bee to come for me. I imagined him taking me away to wherever it was that children who didn't like normal colors like blue and yellow were kept. I pictured rows of cages holding children who, like me, had innocently admitted some terrible transgression. Perhaps they'd refused to smile at one of Miss Nancy's little jokes, or been unable to keep up in Duck, Duck, Goose. Maybe they'd sat sullenly while everyone else jumped rope, or, heaven forbid, colored outside the lines. Then, as they went about their days, they were suddenly plucked from their homes by Do-Bee and whisked away.

And if Miss Nancy was capable of such treachery, my feverish mind said, surely Captain Kangaroo was in on it as well. I thought of all the times I'd laughed innocently at Mr.

Greenjeans's jokes, while in all likelihood he was watching my every move and taking notes, and I was filled with terror. By the end of the day, I'd developed a complete conspiracy theory that I was certain involved the core players of all major children's television programs. After gathering their information, Miss Nancy and the Captain would meet with Mr. Rogers, and possibly Bozo, at their secret headquarters. Together they would draw up a list of children who, for one reason or another, just did not fit in. Then, that night, Do-Bee would sweep through their homes like an angel of death, gathering up the wayward kids and taking them, I was certain, to Mr. Rogers's Kingdom of Make Believe, where they would be held captive in Lady Elaine's merry-go-round. Lady Elaine, with her androgynous and slightly creepy appearance, had always frightened me in a vague way. Now I knew why—she was just waiting to get her twisted little puppet hands on me.

For the next week, I slept fitfully, fearful that if I dozed off I'd next wake in some dank prison surrounded by other lovers of purple. My mother wondered why I didn't clamor any longer for my morning dose of *Romper Room*, preferring instead to actually play outdoors, constantly looking over my shoulder. "Don't you want to see *The Magic Toyshop*?" she asked, shaking her head in wonder when I turned pale and retreated to my room to build yet another Lego fortress. I avoided the television studiously, certain that now even Bobby and Cindy Brady weren't to be trusted. Surely they too were under the control of Miss Nancy and the evil children's television cabal.

Things went on in this way for some time. At first I could hardly walk outside my bedroom without fear of being ambushed. I jumped at the slightest sound, and went to pieces at the slightest hint of buzzing. I even tried to ward off Do-Bee by painting lots of pictures in bright, primary colors and hanging them on my bedroom wall. Perhaps, I thought, Miss Nancy would look into her Magic Mirror and see that I had changed. I hid my purple shirt and my purple bathrobe and my purple shorts and wore only blue or green things. I was determined to be normal, even if it made me miserable.

Then one day I was sent to a friend's house to stay while my mother did errands. Andy's mother sat us in the family room and turned on the television to *Sesame Street.* For some reason I cannot now imagine, I had never seen the show before. It was, however, Andy's favorite, and he immediately became engrossed in learning about the number 9 and the letter Q. Terrified, I hid behind a beanbag chair, waiting for the moment when yet another Big Brother figure would appear, pointing an accusing finger at the boy who admitted to a queer fondness for inappropriate shades.

When Big Bird came on, I trembled, watching his enormous, never-closing eyes for signs of spying. Even larger than Do-Bee, his huge feet and sharp beak looked capable of tearing a small boy to bits. I glanced at Andy, laughing at the deceptively affable bird's comic antics, and wondered if I should warn him about the danger he was exposing himself to. Doing so would be risking exposing myself to further danger, especially since, like Miss Nancy, Big Bird had also said hello to the "friends at home." By now wise to the ways of the conspiracy, I knew that was a sign.

Andy was my friend, and I owed it to him to protect him from the clutches of Do-Bee and Big Bird. I had to speak out. But before I could utter a word of warning, Big Bird left and the scene switched to one featuring Bert and Ernie. Momentarily flustered by these new players in the game, I stayed in my hiding place and watched them for a minute to see what diabolic tricks they would try to use against me.

Despite my fears, there was something about the onscreen pair that spoke to me, something I could relate to. Unlike the odd speechless rabbit of *Captain Kangaroo*, or Do-Bee's silent gesturing filled with ominous meanings, they were friendly and nonthreatening. Sure, Bert's single eyebrow was disconcerting, and he did look vaguely menacing. But Ernie's happy smiling face reassured me. His sprightly tuft of hair made me laugh, and his gaily striped sweater looked like one I myself owned.

But more than that, there was something different about the way Bert and Ernie related to one another, something I had never seen before in all my hours of television watching. They joked amiably as they ate cookies together. They talked to each other about the things they liked. They went to sleep in their shared bedroom. They seemed to like each other in a way I could understand. On some deep level I didn't fully understand, I was certain that they too probably liked purple.

Eventually, I came out from behind the beanbag chair, sat down, and watched some more. Soon, I was laughing delightedly as Ernie counted sheep and Bert tossed restlessly beside him, all thoughts of Miss Nancy driven from my mind. While I wasn't entirely convinced that the menacing Do-Bee and his friends weren't still out there, waiting to pounce on children who didn't live up to their expectations, now I knew that I had friends on my side. There were others like me. Others who didn't quite fit in, but who were nonetheless happy. That night, imagining Ernie asleep in a bed next to mine, I slept peacefully for the first time in days.

Fitting In

I get mail—A LOT of mail—from people who say they enjoy my writing because they've always felt a little out of step with gay culture. To be honest, I don't think feeling out of place is all that rare. Most of us do. But somewhere along the line we were sold a bill of goods that made us feel as if we had to act a certain way, be a certain way, and even think a certain way. Well, here's some news: You don't.

I have a confession to make: I'm a bad fag. Seriously. Someone should take away my membership card immediately, because apparently I just don't belong on the team at all. I can't even be the water boy or the rainbow-suited mascot.

I've tried to fit in. I really have. Back when I first came out, I moved immediately to Greenwich Village because it was where gay men were supposed to live. I cut my hair really short, pierced my ear, and attended ACT UP meetings a few times. I went to bars, wore leather motorcycle boots, and even slept with a couple of people, including a UPS delivery guy, which at the time was a mark of true success.

OK, so I never did drag, took Ecstasy, or went to the Saint Black Party and got fisted in a urinal. I didn't go to bars that often, never even thought about joining the Gay Men's

Chorus, and wasn't up on the latest trendy restaurants. I was too busy worrying about how to be really gay to do it all. Still, I did my best.

But it wasn't enough. The longer I stayed in New York, the more I realized I wasn't really cutting it as a queen. I didn't enjoy going out on weekend nights, falling asleep with a book on my chest before my more vigorous gay brothers had even left their apartments to begin partying. I couldn't care less about what Madonna was up to, and didn't even own a cock ring. Worst of all, I found myself completely unable to recognize when I was being cruised. Finally I had to admit to myself that I just wasn't doing it right.

At first this upset me. Why couldn't I fit in with the other gay boys? They all seemed to take to it so easily, as though they'd been born knowing exactly what kind of wine to serve with fish and with a natural inclination to enjoy art openings and benefit performances. Every last one of them seemed perfectly at home in a gym, and their hair always looked freshly cut. But no matter how hard I tried, my carefully rolled-up T-shirt sleeves always slumped by evening's end, I couldn't understand a single painting at MOMA, and no amount of gel would tame the cowlicks that made it impossible for me to have really cool hair. To make everything worse, I didn't see the charm in hanging out all night waiting for the right guy to notice me when I could be at home watching animal documentaries on The Discovery Channel.

Then, just as I was about to give up on ever being fabulous enough, something unexpected happened. Rising up defiantly from the liberal seas, a wave of conservatism swept over our gay land. Almost overnight, the reign of ACT UP was over, and suddenly we weren't supposed to be queer anymore. Now we were supposed to be, in the hypnotic words of the leaders of this new movement, "just like everybody else."

Politically, this disturbed me. I had a vague notion that to be just like everybody else was to not exist anymore. But secretly I was glad that I didn't have to wear my earring any longer. The hole had gotten infected a few too many times, and I was sick of it. So I tossed it out, along with the motorcycle boots and the Queer Nation T-shirt.

I still got to keep my hair short, but now I was free to dress as badly as the straight guys at the office. Now that we (gay people) were just like everybody else, my horrible lack of fashion sense was no longer a disability. In fact, it made my transition into the world of "everybody else" much easier.

So there I was, being just like everyone else. It felt good. I talked about how important it was for "us" to have the same rights that "they" had so that we could indeed be just like them in nearly every way. I decided that gay marriage was a good thing, and even dated one of its principal and most vocal proponents. Over dinner, we talked about how wonderful it would be when we could have the same benefits our legally married straight friends had.

But again, after a couple months of this, something didn't feel quite right. Sure, it was nice to not have to worry about being different, and registering as a domestic partner at City Hall seemed very pioneering. But the truth was, being just like everybody else was, well, sort of boring. More than sort of. I looked around at my straight married friends, pictured years of holidays with in-laws and squabbling over what school the kids should go to, and felt a little queasy.

Deciding that being just like everybody else wasn't for me, I ditched the gay marriage activist and became as gay as possible. But instead of aspiring to the carefree gay life I'd first tried, I focused on being meaningfully gay. Protecting the existence of the unique homo species became a mission. I came out to everyone I could think of, just so they would be aware that someone they knew was queer, a word I began using again now that I wasn't trying to be respectable. I wore gay buttons on my jacket and made sure I took the Monday after every gay pride weekend off so that everyone would see just how hard I'd been out being gay.

In my quest to be the ambassador of all that was gay, I went so far as to appear on the now-defunct *Jane Pratt Show*, talking about how bisexuals and their demand for equal attention were taking precious energy out of the real gay community. The audience applauded my logic, and Jane told me afterward how much more coherent I'd been than the other guests. Even though the producer told us not to mention the fact that at least one of Jane's former boyfriends, rocker Michael Stipe, was admittedly bisexual, it was all very thrilling.

Too exciting. As it turned out, being so gay was really exhausting. It meant paying close attention to the news and knowing absolutely everything about every item even remotely related to gay causes. It meant being ready to lecture my straight friends at the drop of a hat about how their support was necessary to achieve our causes. It meant not just using, but actually understanding, phrases such as "diversity-focused organizational schism" and "intracommunity issue assessment and goal enhancement infrastructure."

But the biggest problem was that it involved being angry. Really angry. All the time. About everything. Each day I would sit down with the paper and scan it for gay-related items. I would dutifully clip them out and read them. Then I would decide how angry to be about each one.

There was a decided hierarchy to gay issues, and the store of anger was meted out appropriately. Anything involving

AIDS—in particular the government's slowness in fighting it or the discrimination against people with it—was given top priority. This was the late '80s. Larry Kramer was everywhere, and we were all busy marching and screaming and generally misbehaving about The Crisis. It was good to be angry, fun even, and there was a lot to be angry about.

After AIDS came gays in the military, followed by adoption rights, the marriage thing, and general gay-bashing. I duly noted each incident and thought long and hard about What Should Be Done About It. I kept bulging file folders filled with gay-related news stories. I was very informed, very angry, and, I thought, very, very gay.

The issue I ended up being the angriest about was the depiction of gays and lesbians in popular media. This was the fault of the Gay and Lesbian Alliance Against Defamation (GLAAD). I attended a meeting of the group with a friend. The topic that fateful night happened to be Rush Limbaugh, the virulently homophobic talk show host who was just coming to power in New York. GLAAD was trying to get Rush fired from his job because he "made us look bad."

After discussing Rush for a while, the conversation turned to how queers were being depicted in movies, in particular the just-released *The Silence of the Lambs.* It was the position of GLAAD that the movie perpetuated a stereotype of gays as psychopathic drag queens who minced around in too much blue eye shadow while talking to poodles. They wanted someone to write a letter about it to that bastion of uppity letter writing, *The Village Voice.* Overcome by my fervor to protect the gay family, I volunteered. Now, I'd seen *The Silence of the Lambs*, and it had never once occurred to me to be offended by the character everyone was getting upset about. But, caught up in the moment, I decided that maybe everyone was right and that this was my chance to do something about it. I wrote a most forceful letter, which appeared the next week in the *Voice* and got a lot of attention from my activist friends. But as I sat in my apartment and read it over and over again, all I could think about was how Jodie Foster would see it and never be my best friend.

I did a few more things with GLAAD, writing letters of protest about Sharon Stone's beaver shot in *Basic Instinct* and about the fact that Doug Savant's gay character on *Melrose Place* never got to kiss anyone. They appeared here and there, always to hearty approval from the people who read them. But my heart just wasn't in it. When the group decided to protest *Sesame Street* because there had never been an openly gay Muppet, I decided it was time to move on.

The trouble was, there was nowhere else to go. I'd done the fabulous thing. I'd done the just-like-everyone-else thing. I'd done the activist thing. The only other thing left was the 12-step thing, which was suddenly hugely popular with a lot of queers. But never having done drugs or overindulged in alcohol, it seemed unlikely that I would find my true calling there. And I'd been so busy trying to fit in that I hadn't had enough sex to qualify for Sexaholics Anonymous. I wasn't even a success at being unhealthily gay.

For a while I went into a depression, saddened by the fact that I just wasn't the queer I should be. Everywhere I looked, people were achieving greatness as the perfect examples of whatever banner they'd chosen to carry, whether it was being the reigning king of the party circuit or the activist with the most arrests under his belt. But there I was, stuck in the middle, neither one thing nor another.

Then, just as I thought my only remaining option was to become straight, one morning I woke up with a realization—I didn't have to be anything. I don't know why I'd never thought of it before. Probably because I was too busy being something I wasn't. But suddenly I started looking at the people around me in a new way. As they scurried off to their meetings and parties, their protests and safer sex orgies, they were so busy being gay that they weren't even living. Being gay was a career choice for them, not a way of life.

That was a decade ago. Since then, I've figured out how to integrate being gay with being me. Yes, I still get angry about things. Yes, I think fighting for causes is important. But so are a lot of other things, things that have nothing to do with being gay. Like enjoying friends because they add something to my life, not because they have Really Deep Thoughts about the existence of a gay gene. Or laughing at Ellen because she's funny, not just because she advanced the gay presence on network television. I might not always know which lawmakers are pro-gay and which ones aren't, but now I understand when to get worked up and when to sit back with a pint of Ben & Jerry's World's Best Vanilla and watch the world go by like one big circus parade.

I may still be a bad fag, but now I'm a happy one. And Jodie, if you're reading this, I really loved you in *The Silence of the Lambs.* Will you ever forgive me?

Could You Hurry Up? I'm Starting to Cramp

I'm often asked if I'm embarrassed about anything I've written. I'm really not. But when it came time to record my audio book, My Queer Life, *this was the only piece I had a hard time getting through without cracking up. This is also the only piece ever to be singled out by a mainstream reviewer as perhaps being a bit "too much" for nongay readers. I've included it here in case any of them missed it the first time.*

I should have known that I would have trouble with sex the day Missy Graham took me back to her house after our fourth-grade class let out for the day and showed me her father's stack of *Playboys*. As we sat on the bed in Missy's room, sucking on lemons sprinkled with salt and looking at Miss November's auburn-colored snatch, all I could think about was that it reminded me of one of the Tribbles from that famous *Star Trek* episode. I imagined Captain Kirk trying to stuff it back inside Miss November before it took over the ship, and I giggled. It was not an auspicious beginning.

I was lucky in one respect—I came of age during the 1970s, and like most kids of that era, I was introduced to sex by Judy Blume. Because I read so much, I knew her books inside and out. And even if I hadn't, our favorite school activity was to sit in the back of the library and read the dirty parts of all the Blume novels to one another.

While *Are You There God? It's Me, Margaret* was the most well-known Blume book, it was for girls, and its depictions of breast development and periods was not especially interesting to me. Her book for boys, *Then Again Maybe I Won't*, did talk about masturbation, and that was a little more exciting. I still remember reading the book while on a picnic with my mother. As she sat in the sun, munching away on her peanut butter sandwich, I read the book as quickly as possible, terrified that she would ask to see it and take it away from me.

While these books were intriguing, I was more fascinated by Blume's later book, *Forever*. This had actual sex in it, and as such was kept on the special reserve shelf in our library, requiring a parent's permission to check it out. But one of my friends, whose parents were very free-thinking, had bought her her very own copy, and she kindly shared it with the rest of us. We sat, spellbound, as Sheila read us the most lurid parts of the book in her best dramatic voice. When the two main characters in the novel finally tried to have sex, we waited breathlessly as Blume, through Sheila, described it for us.

But even this was nothing compared to the scandalous *Endless Love*. None of my friends were old enough to actually see the Brooke Shields movie, but we did manage to get hold of a copy of the book version, and with it we hit pay dirt. It came in the form of anal sex. As I recall, the Brooke Shields character and her boyfriend decide to try it in the back door, and there is quite a good description of it.

We read this passage again and again to one another, beside ourselves with the sordidness of it all. We couldn't imagine anyone sticking anything up a butt except a thermometer. Certainly no boy would want his nice clean willy near one. It was all too much. I couldn't believe that there was really anyone who enjoyed that kind of thing. Surely I myself never would. It was unthinkable.

But then, a few years later, I discovered a *Playgirl* hidden beneath my cousin Sherri's bed. I was in her room, innocently listening to records, and found it when I went looking for the sleeve to the Barry Manilow album I was playing. I pulled the magazine out and flipped through it, staring at all of the naked men standing there with their you-know-whats hanging out for the world to see. Unlike Miss November's muff, these didn't make me giggle.

And then there was John Pellico Jr. I may have misspelled his name slightly, but I recall vividly what he looked like. Dark-haired and mustached, he was wearing a red flannel shirt, open to reveal the hair on his chest. And then there was his impressive...thingy. As I stared at it hanging between his hairy thighs, suddenly that passage in *Endless Love* didn't quite seem so ridiculous after all.

It was a turning point. After that, I was determined to find out all about sex and what people did with one another. The only problem was that I was too shy to actually ask anyone. So I had to find out in other ways, which meant looking for answers in books.

My parents had lots of books, so I started there. After some searching, I came across a battered copy of *The Christian Couple's Guide to Intimacy* found behind some religious titles in my mother's bookcase. It was a rather graphic book, complete with line drawings and diagrams, and it was extremely explicit about exactly how the act of intercourse should be undertaken. I read it over and over again, memorizing the details of what the author described as the perfect wedding night. This entailed the groom lying at his wife's side while he stroked first her nipples and then her labia. When she was ready to proceed, and she was supposed to tell him when the time came, he was to enter her gently. Then—and this is the most baffling part—he was supposed to pause in mid entry for several minutes while he regained his composure, lest he ejaculate from the excitement and ruin things completely.

At the time that I read this, I assumed that the act of Christian intercourse must be the most exciting thing to ever happen to a man. It would not be the only thing about organized religion that I would later find to be highly overrated.

Apart from the step-by-step instructions, the part of the book I remember most vividly is a drawing of the female genitalia, drawn from the perspective of the artist staring directly into the slightly parted lips of some model's Georgia O'Keeffe. Everything was neatly labeled, with arrows pointing to the various parts. It reminded me a bit of the diagram in my history textbook outlining the events at the Battle of Bull Run, only instead of arrows indicating troop movements and Confederate defense strategies, there were lines leading to the clitoris and the labia majora.

While most of it was pretty self-explanatory, I was very confused by the notion that there were two openings in the vagina, one for urination and one for—presumably—the penis to enter during sex. I returned to the book over and over, trying very hard to remember which hole was which. While I was beginning to suspect that I would never find myself needing to use such knowledge, I very much wanted to make sure I knew which hole to concentrate on should I ever be required to do so. Little did I know that should have been paying more attention to the drawing of the rectum on page 73.

The cumulative effect of the book, the diagrams, and my own vivid imagination was that the idea of heterosexual relations was not one I cared to dwell on for long. And since there were no discussions of what two men could possibly do together on *their* wedding night, I was forced to make up my own scenarios.

In general, these involved the men from *Adam 12* rescuing me from a robbery attempt. From time to time, I would cast John Pellico Jr. as the robber, and then I was always torn between being saved or remaining captive for an indefinite period while John tried to extract an exorbitant ransom and my parents haggled over my price. Other than that, I wasn't sure what we would all do together. I think I had some vague notion that it would involve having a cookout and maybe playing some badminton, but the details were sketchy.

I have friends who tell me wild stories about all of the sex they had as adolescents with other neighborhood boys, friends at summer camp, and even various distant relations during family reunions. Apparently these men lived in very different neighborhoods from mine. Apart from one awkward sleepover when my friend Steve pretended to roll over and accidentally put his hand on my dick, nothing of interest happened to me.

High school and college were no better. In fact, during college I somehow found myself dating a headstrong Italian girl named Michelle. I don't know how it happened exactly. All I can remember is that one day we were sharing a biology class and the next she was making out with me in the little room we used to store frozen cat corpses for anatomy class. We remained boyfriend and girlfriend for the better part of my sophomore year, and the only reason I was spared actually having to sleep with her was that she felt very strongly about our Christian college's edict against engaging in sexual intercourse. While the idea of sex with Michelle was not entirely unpleasant, I was glad to be spared the encounter, primarily because I had long forgotten the diagram from my mother's book showing which hole was which, and feared making a mistake.

Thus I entered adulthood still wildly unprepared for what was to come. As a result, on the night that I decided it was time to dive headfirst into the world of gay sex, I had no idea what I was in for. But I had an apartment, I had the will, and I was in the heart of gay New York. I headed out that June night ready for action.

I found it at the only bar I knew of. After standing around for an hour and trying to figure out just how it was all done, I was relieved when a man approached me and started talking to me. His pickup line was, "What's your favorite movie?"

Deciding that this was a trick question, and being too flustered to actually think of a movie I'd seen recently, I blurted out, "*Escape From Witch Mountain.* How about you?"

Either I caught him off guard, or he was too horny to care about my apparent Disney obsession. Whatever the reason, he smiled and told me that his personal favorite was *The Philadelphia Story*. Not having yet seen that movie at that point in my life, I nodded vaguely in agreement. This seemed to be enough for him, and a few minutes later he asked me home.

We went to my place because it was closest. Once inside, it all went very quickly, and before I knew it I was in bed with a naked man for the very first time in my life. Trying to remember everything I could from *The Christian Couple's Guide to Intimacy*, I went through the wedding night steps in order, simply switching the pronouns from "she" to "he" and the word "bride" to "trick." It worked perfectly well at first. I managed to get through the kissing, the breast fondling, and the stroking with ease. I even threw in a few things the author of the *Guide* had failed to include, proud of myself for being so bold my first time out.

Then I got to the intercourse part, and suddenly things got dicey. Even though I couldn't recall the exact layout of the vagina diagram, I knew roughly how a woman worked. But even though I'd imagined anal sex with a man, I hadn't been confronted with the actual plumbing or the physical details of how it was done. There I was, lying on my partner's left side, stroking him. His moaning made it clear to me that he was ready to proceed. But I didn't know where to go from there.

"Are you a top or a bottom?" he asked, sensing a pause in the action.

I looked at him blankly. I had no idea what he meant. As far as I knew, tops and bottoms were fashion terms or directional signals printed on refrigerator cartons. No one had ever asked me this before. Once again, I tried a neutral approach.

"What do you want me to be?" I asked, hoping that putting the ball in his court would give me a tactical advantage.

"Fuck me," he answered breathlessly.

I couldn't imagine many Christian women saying that to their Christian husbands on their honeymoon nights, but I got the message loud and clear. Now that the whole top and bottom thing was sorted out, we could continue. Only I couldn't tell this man that he was my first time, that I had zero experience in the fucking department.

Once again helping me out, he reached over and took a condom from the bedside table. I'd had enough sense to put some out before I left the house, having seen enough safer sex materials to know that they might come in handy at some point. I watched as he opened it deftly with his teeth, removed the rubber, and slid it over my dick. Then he pulled his knees back and looked at me expectantly.

"Got any lube?" he asked.

Lube. I hadn't thought about lube. I didn't know I might need it. I'd assumed the condoms came ready to use. But apparently this was one more thing I'd gotten confused about.

"I'll be right back," I said, as if somewhere in the apartment there was a whole vat of lube I'd simply forgotten to wheel out and place beside the bed.

I ran into the bathroom and threw open the medicine cabinet. The only thing in there was a tube of Crest. It might leave everything minty fresh, but I had my doubts about its lubricating qualities. I paused briefly at the Vicks, noting its resemblance to Vaseline, but I remembered from childhood experience that it really didn't feel very nice on the skin.

Finding nothing in the bathroom, I tried the kitchen, frantically looking for olive oil, butter, or even a can of cooking spray. But there was nothing that might be useful. I could hear my beau in the bedroom, calling me back, and I knew I had to find something soon or risk having my debut fuck turn into a complete disaster.

Finally, I looked at the sink and saw the dispenser of Yardley's of London Lavender Hand Wash that someone had given me for Christmas months earlier. I'd never used it, finding the scent a little bit cloying, but now it shone before me like the Holy Grail at the end of a long and dangerous journey. Snatching it up triumphantly, I raced back to the bedroom.

My intended was still on his back on the bed, legs spread and eyes willing. Kneeling confidently on the bed, I flipped open the Yardley's and squeezed some onto my hand. By that point I'd figured out exactly what needed lubricating, and I diligently set about making sure everything that needed to be was good and slippery.

"That smells great," my soon-to-be first time said.

"Um, yeah," I responded. "It's new. I think it's organic or something."

The hand wash did indeed do the trick. A moment later, I was in like a thief through a wide-open window. Remembering what the book had said, I paused a moment to prevent an abrupt ending to the experience, and then continued on. Like a Labrador discovering water for the first time, I found that everything came quite naturally, and was both thrilled and relieved to finally be finding out what the big fuss was all about.

And then the bubbles started. They began as foam, really, but as the friction continued they grew in size. A few minutes later, tiny bubbles began to detach from my paramour's sudsy nether parts and float into the room. I stared in horror as they drifted through the air and settled gently on his stomach.

"Hey, what's that?" he asked, his steady stream of grunts and groans interrupted as he poked at the bubble on his chest hair.

I thought maybe he'd ignore the bubble if I thrust a little harder, so I tried that. Unfortunately, the additional effort merely increased the size and frequency of the bubbles, and it wasn't long before his backside had turned into a veritable bubble machine, filling the air with a cascade of shimmery orbs. They landed and popped on our skin, covering us with their lavender scent.

My foray into the wonderful world of homosex had turned into *The Lawrence Welk Show*. I imagined my grandmother sitting on the couch, watching us rut as smiling dancers twirled around the bed and she clapped along merrily. It was all too much to take. I continued with the production for a while longer, but in the end I had to give up before the finale.

You would think that after that I would have given up on sex altogether. But it was only the beginning. As hard as I tried to, I couldn't resist the call of the wild forever, and eventually I found myself once more on the search for fun and adventure.

One of the problems with gay sex is that we have very bad role models in the form of gay porn movies and gay porn fiction. From watching such movies, or reading such books, it's easy to get the impression that sex between men is always incredibly hot, incredibly clean, and incredibly fulfilling.

The truth is almost always the complete opposite. More often than not, sex with men involves a lot of fumbling with the button flies of 501s, trying to figure out which way the condom rolls, and enduring prolonged coughing fits when stray hairs slide down our throats. It is seldom the smooth operation pornographers would have us believe it is.

Take, for example, the issue of big dicks. I confess that I have something of a fondness for them, and for some time fantasized about finding a man who had one that would defy description. Well, you should always be careful what you wish for. My fantasy materialized one evening in the form of a very tall, very large, very handsome German man. When he undid his jeans and I saw what lay beneath, I had to be revived by a splash of cold water to the face.

But alas, Gunther had one small problem. Or rather, one very large problem. For while his dick was indeed of Teutonic proportions, getting it filled to capacity with the blood necessary to make it hard meant that other areas of his body had to do without. Unfortunately, the result of an erection was that his brain was unable to function fully, making sex with him about as exciting as the *Dr. Who* reruns he insisted on watching during lovemaking.

And when he was erect, there was the tiny matter of what to do with something so large. While it was kind of fun to play with him, it was a little like swinging a Wiffle bat around. Getting my mouth around the whole thing would have required installing hinges, and just the thought of him trying to put it anywhere else made me feel faint. While I tried valiantly to make the most of his natural gifts, in the end I had to abandon Gunther to someone with more relaxed throat muscles and no fear of a future marred by the inconvenience of incontinence.

Then there's the whole problem of expectations. Again, pornographers would have us believe that every sexual encounter is a roller coaster ride of earthshaking moments of pure ecstasy from beginning to end. But it doesn't work that way. While I would truly like to believe that there are men who spend each moment of their escapades in bed shouting out things like, "Oh, yeah, do me harder, you big stud," and "Just like that, baby. Do it. Do it. Do it," I think the reality is somewhat different for most of us.

I, for example, am more likely to be thinking about the fact that I am missing the second half of the miniseries that began the previous night, or worrying that perhaps having Indian food for dinner was not as good an idea as it had seemed a few hours before. Rather than staying in the moment and contemplating my partner's handsome face or our impending orgasms, I tend to wander in and out. One second I'll be wondering what I might get my friend Katherine for her upcoming birthday, and the next I'll be noticing that the walls need painting again. I may throw in a few half-hearted groans from time to time, but rarely can

I bring myself to actually say something along the lines of "Take that big dick" or "Give it to me harder." Even when the action is, in fact, hot and heavy, things are not nearly as thrilling as they are in the fictional word. While one or the other of us does his best to bring things to a boil, I can generally be counted on to be thinking, "Could you hurry up? I'm starting to cramp."

Maybe it's the fault of *The Christian Couple's Guide to Intimacy.* Maybe I should blame it on watching too many Falcon Video releases. Maybe somewhere out there there are men who have amazing sex all the time, and they're just keeping it a secret from the rest of us. All I know is that somewhere along the line I got sold a bill of goods, and no one has delivered on it yet. When I lie in bed after another go at launching my own sexual revolution, I feel less like a sated stud from a Gordon Merrick novel and more like the protagonist from *Forever* who, after her first attempt at sex with her boyfriend ends with his premature ejaculation, lies on the oriental carpet in her bedroom listening to her overeager lover washing up in the bathroom and wonders if it ever gets any better. I hate to break it to her, but it doesn't.

Fame

It's always nice when you can turn your failings into something fun. This piece was written on a day when things were not going very well at all. I think I'd received unpleasant calls from just about every agent, editor, and publisher I have. I turned the phone off and wrote this. It made me feel better.

I ought to be famous. I say this because my name has appeared in an issue of *Entertainment Weekly.* Harrison Ford is on the cover, and I am on page 118. I have the clipping to prove it.

Never mind that not one of my many friends who eagerly devour the magazine each week even noticed my mention, and that I only found out about it when one of the guys at the gym said, "Someone with the same name as yours is in the new *Entertainment Weekly.* Isn't that weird?" Forget for a moment that there is only one sentence about me. Ignore the fact that the only reason I'm there at all is because I put Alec Baldwin's name in the title of one of my books and someone thought it would be amusing to point this out. These things are not important. What's important is that I am in *Entertainment Weekly*, right there in the same paragraph with Al Franken. I think that entitles me to something.

Fame

I have always loved those stories in which some small incident starts a chain of events that results in fantastic good luck for someone. You know, like when you hear an actor talking about how only six months ago he was living in squalor and licking the stains on the couch because he couldn't afford food, but then some director happened to catch a commercial he made for shaving cream and decided to cast him in the biggest movie of the summer, launching him into superstardom. Or when some television mogul on a cross-country flight needs something to pass the time and reads a really great book by this writer he's never heard of but whose book he picked up because it was the first thing he saw at the newsstand, then likes it so much he calls the writer to see if maybe he'd like to try writing a sitcom, ending that writer's worries about paying rent.

These are very nice stories. Unfortunately, they do not happen nearly as often as one would like, especially if you are one of the struggling actors or writers waiting for one of these life-changing phone calls. It is all well and good to believe that just when you are on the brink of running out of money and becoming homeless that the manuscript you sent out a year ago and forgot about will be bought for $1 million by someone who has just plucked it from the pile on his desk. In my experience, however, what is more likely to happen is that while you're waiting for the phone call that will change your life, your agent will send you an E-mail informing you that she has just returned from a meeting at which it was decided that no one likes you and you should die.

Still, I try to remain optimistic. So when I discovered my name in *Entertainment Weekly*, I was fully prepared for the phone to start ringing off the hook with offers from people in Hollywood. I didn't know what kind of offers, exactly, but I had ideas. I thought surely they would find the title of my book so hysterical that they would beg me to turn my talents to the screen, big or small; I didn't care which one. After all, I'd always been told that agents and executives scan the pages of such magazines looking for previously unknown talent to exploit. Surely at least one would see my mention and decide he had to have me.

Well, this did not happen. During the first couple of days after the issue hit the stands, I barely left the house. I knew that if I did I would miss a call from Steven Spielberg or the producers of *Will & Grace* begging me to lend my talents to their latest endeavors. I blamed their silence on the fact that I was on page 118 and they probably hadn't gotten that far yet, being busy with other matters like deciding where to take me to lunch once they found me. I fantasized about what I would do with all the money they were certain to offer (get the dog a new hip and me a haircut), and I checked the phone often to make sure it was working properly.

When the next week rolled around and the Harrison Ford issue was replaced with the Jennifer Lopez issue, I started to worry. Everyone knows that last week's news is ancient history in Tinseltown, and now I was competing with a whole new crop of would-be stars. I opened the magazine and flipped through it anxiously to see what I was up against. Then I saw it. There on page 34, a whole 84 pages before my mention had appeared, I found an article about some 19-year-old college student who had been paid nearly $1 million for his first novel, which some studio exec on a cross-country flight happened to read and decide to make into a movie for that oh-so-desirable 18–24 market.

I handled this as well as could be expected. I took out the clipping with my name in it and stared at it while stifling the wracking sobs that longed to break forth from my throat. Maybe, I tried to convince myself, it was enough just to be mentioned. Isn't that what the people who lose at the Oscars always say while they smile and reach for the Prozac in their handbags? But in my heart I knew it wasn't. I'd gotten so close. I was in the same issue with Harrison Ford. But it was the wrong Ford on the cover. I wanted it to be me up front and him on page 118.

Maybe I wouldn't want fame so badly if I hadn't already had a little taste of it. A few years ago I wrote a number of young adult novels based on a sort-of successful television series. There happen to be quite a lot of children on my block, and some of them read these books and realized I was the person who wrote them. From that moment on I became the Writer Guy. Every time I took my dog, Roger, for a walk, a little group of 10-year-olds would cluster around and ask if they could pet him. Afterward, they'd run off looking at their hands as if they'd never wash them again. Sometimes they would drag their little friends home with them and point me out when I walked past. "There goes the Writer Guy," they'd say, and their friends would stare at me with the same awe they reserved for the Backstreet Boys. I found out later that one enterprising little girl was giving her schoolmates tours of my front porch for a quarter a head.

I know, groupies who don't come up to your waist and have no disposable income are hardly something to get excited about. But it was fun being the Writer Guy for a while, at least until the kids started asking why my books weren't as popular as the Goosebumps and Animorphs series, at which point I started walking the dog on a different route.

And at least the kids were excited about seeing a real live writer. Adults couldn't care less. Only twice have I ever been recognized in public because of my books for adults or from my newspaper columns. Once was at a bookstore, where a man charged over to me and said, "I know you. You're that guy who signed my book." It took a minute for him to remember *which* guy and *which* book, but eventually he did, at which point he smiled and said, "You have a nice signature." Just what every writer in search of fame wants to hear.

The second time my writing brought me a fleeting moment of celebrity was at the gym, where I was standing in the locker room after having just run five miles on the treadmill. I was contemplating the thrill of a post-workout shower when I had the strange sensation that someone behind me was staring at me—very hard. I turned around and discovered a man gazing with great concentration at my butt.

"You're the guy who wrote that column about your ass, aren't you?" he said.

I had, in fact, recently written a newspaper column about this very subject. However, this is a very disconcerting question to be asked when one is standing, holding nothing but a sweaty jockstrap, in front of a stranger. All I could do was nod.

"I thought I recognized you," he said, and walked out without saying another word.

You'd think I would be excited over finally being noticed. But having someone recognize me because of my ass was not really what I had in mind when I dreamed about fame. Besides, now I was convinced that every single man in my gym was secretly looking at my butt and forming opinions about it. Probably they all talked about it when I wasn't there and smiled meaningfully at one another when I passed by. This was not reassuring in the least.

I suppose it's better than what I usually get, though. Many times I've walked into bookstores where I'm scheduled to do a reading, only to have the salespeople look at me blankly when I walk up to the counter. "You don't look like you," is the usual response when I finally tell them who I am. I'm not sure what this means, but it unnerves me, like I'm running around impersonating myself and pretty soon someone is going to get me for it.

My friends think this is funny. Once, while standing in line at a local gay bookstore to pay for our purchases, my friend Mark David noticed that my book *That's Mr. Faggot to You* was right next to the cash register with a big #1 BESTSELLER sign on it. When he reached the counter, he picked up a copy of the book—which has my picture right on the front cover—and turned to the very bored-looking clerk. "Is this any good?" he asked.

The young man looked at the book, looked right at me, and said, "Everyone seems to love it, but I don't see what the big deal is. I didn't think it was that good."

Luckily for everyone involved, I was too tired to be horrified. Instead, when it was my turn to pay I handed the clerk my credit card. He looked at the name on it, then looked at me, then looked at my picture on the cover of the book. He turned an interesting shade of red and said, "Oh, these are on the house, Mr. Ford." I left wishing I'd bought more. But it's always nice to get porn magazines for free, so I'm not complaining.

I guess the whole fame thing is relative. Several times reporters and readers have said to me, "It must be so nice to be at the height of your career." I'm sure these people all have the best of intentions, but I can't help but wonder what they think my life is like. To me, fame means not having to clean my own house and not worrying about things like buying food and paying rent. That and being best friends with Cher.

But I have none of these things. Instead I'm still walking around picking up the dog's poop myself and wondering if anyone will buy one of my kidneys for a lot of money. And the only way I'll ever get to see Cher is if I pay for it. Even then I can only afford the cheap seats, so all I'll really get to see is a kind of blurry miniature Cher waving from a distant stage. But at least everyone in the stadium would *know* that it was Cher. What's even sadder is that while one person recognized my ass, millions recognize hers. Even her butt is more famous than I am.

I do have friends who are truly famous, people who seldom if ever leave their houses because they can't go anywhere without being noticed and asked for autographs. They complain a lot about how annoying this is. Oh, boo-hoo. I feel so bad for them. It must be just awful to have people paying you gobs of money for your work because they think you're fabulous. I stay in the house most of the time too, but it's because I'm still waiting for the phone to ring.

Heart Failure

This piece is very sweet in its way. The irony is that when Valentine's Day did roll around, Patrick was out of town on business and I forgot all about it. Still, it's the thought that counts.

With Valentine's Day coming up, my thoughts turn, naturally, to romance. More specifically, I can't help thinking how bad gay men are at it. I know I've complained about this before, but this time of year I'm reminded of it even more because odd as it seems, most of the guys I know face February 14th with a sense of doom.

There are a number of reasons for this, but I think we can trace the origins back to one specific moment in every queer boys' life: Valentine's Day in the third grade.

You remember this day. Most likely a week or so before, the teacher had you decorate a box of some kind with hearts and flowers and cupids. This was your very own Valentine card box. Trimmed with lace and sparkling with glitter, it was perfect for all of the Valentines your classmates were going to stuff inside it.

As for the Valentines themselves, you were supposed to have made or bought one for each person in the class. Maybe your mom went out and bought a package of cards with the Peanuts gang on them, or perhaps Garfield or Bugs Bunny or some other popular character. Maybe you made your own from red construction paper. Then, armed with a list of your fellow students' names, you were expected to make sure everyone had a card from you, preferably all of the same size and type.

But this was never how it worked. There were always people in the class who you liked more than others. For these people you saved the best cards, the ones with the cutest pictures and wittiest inscriptions. Everyone else could have the Peppermint Patty and Lucy cards, but there were those for whom the Woodstocks and Snoopys were reserved.

Inevitably, one of these people was the object of a first crush, usually some boy who, for whatever reason, you wanted to have as your special friend. Maybe you dreamed about him, or had fantasies of holding his hand on the swings. Probably you didn't have any real understanding of what attracted you to him. You just knew that thinking about him made you feel funny. But you saved the best Valentine for him, making sure your printing was neat and your message meaningful. No generic, "Happy Valentine's Day" for his card. Oh, no. Something along the lines of "Knowing you makes every day special," was better or, if you were feeling particularly daring, the suggestive "Be mine."

On the big day, after far too many sugar cookies had been eaten and cups of red Kool-Aid drunk, it was time to go around the room stuffing your Valentines into one another's boxes. This ritual was accompanied by much giggling and nervousness. It was, after all, your first taste of romance, however innocent. You tried to avoid looking at your own box while you went about your business, but as soon as you were finished delivering your own cards it was a mad dash back to your seat to see what was waiting for you.

Heart Failure

Cards from friends were nice, but they weren't what you were after. You wanted to find that one card that would make the day really special. Tearing open envelopes with a vengeance, you quickly noted the sender's name and went on to the next. Then, if you were lucky, you'd come to the one you were waiting for, a card from the object of your affection. Holding your breath, you opened it to see what it was.

And then, you were crushed. There was no special card with a secret message. No "Be mine" or "My heart belongs to you." Probably it was a generic Mickey Mouse card, or maybe one with racing cars on it. Inside was a hastily scribbled signature and nothing more. Looking around, you saw that everyone else had received exactly the same card.

Even worse, the boy you liked didn't seem to even notice all the work you put into his card. It was jumbled in a pile with all the rest as he went in search of another cookie. Or, the most crushing blow of all, you saw it lying on the floor where he had carelessly dropped it, someone's dusty footprint spoiling the message you'd so carefully written.

For most of us, this was the last time we let ourselves have romantic thoughts. Seeing our hearts—both figurative and literal—trampled by the uncaring feet of a rejecting suitor, we gave up. The disappointment was simply too much. And now when Valentine's Day comes along we play it safe, waiting to see what the other guy is going to do first before we start making our own plans.

A couple of weeks ago, I asked my boyfriend what he wanted to do for Valentine's Day. "I don't know," he said warily. "What do *you* want to do?

I understand his caution. This will be our first Valentine's Day together. In some ways, it's a test of the relationship. If one of us does something more extravagant than the other, it could be a disaster. I have a friend who went to Valentine's Day dinner with his boyfriend armed with what he thought was the perfect gift—tickets to a show they both wanted to see. But before he could present them to his lover, he found himself being handed a small box. Inside was a wedding band. Dessert was a bitter affair.

I'm not sure what I'm going to get my boyfriend. But I do know that I'm saving the Snoopy Valentine for him. This time, I don't think he'll step on it.

My Life as a Dwarf, Part 6: Doc

I've never liked going to doctors. There are the obvious reasons for this: Having to go usually means something is wrong, I don't enjoy being poked or touched with cold instruments, paper gowns flatter no one's ass. Then too there are my own peculiar aversions. I dislike authority in any form. I resent having to ask for help. I have inherited my father's attitude that if you can still walk and there's no visible blood, you're fine.

A little more than a year ago, however, I found myself in need of a doctor. The situation was made even more irritating by the fact that it wasn't to deal with a suspicious lump or nagging cough, something physical and easily diagnosed; it was because I really, really, really could not leave the house.

I'm exaggerating a little. I could leave the house. I just didn't want to. Every time I did, or at least every time I went farther afield than the few blocks that comprised the dog's daily walk routes, I became completely and spectacularly mentally unwell. I imagined all kinds of horrors, all of them totally unreasonable and unlikely. But they were real enough to force me back to the house, to the safety of rooms I knew and away from the dangers of the outside world.

The situation might have been even more disturbing had I not dealt with it in lesser forms over the years. I've always been more comfortable at home. I've never enjoyed parties or "going out." I've bought tickets for concerts I never made it to and signed up for classes I never attended. Even necessary trips to the grocery store have frequently been so overwhelming as to ruin entire days.

My first self-diagnosis, unsurprisingly, was agoraphobia. The fear of leaving the house (more precisely, the fear of being in crowds or in public places), I discovered, is more common than you might think. Essentially it stems from a fear of social situations, of having to interact with unfamiliar people and deal with potentially embarrassing moments. Those suffering from it prefer the familiarity of home where few, if any, surprises await them.

This sounded reasonable to me. The problem was that I really wasn't afraid of meeting new people or dealing with new situations. I'm actually a very relaxed traveler, having been all over the world without incident. A veteran of book tours, speaking engagements, and the other responsibilities that accompany the writing life, I'd never felt the least bit of anxiety anticipating such occasions.

No, this was something deeper. Much deeper. I just didn't want to be involved with the world outside my own house. Like most writers and other "artsy" types I know, I've wrestled with depression over the years. Most of us come to see it as something we're handed along with the ability to move words or paint or musical notes around. It comes and goes, sometimes just popping in for a quick hello and other times camping out on the couch for days or weeks as we try to find a polite way of asking it to leave so we can get on with our lives.

This time, however, it seemed determined to move into

the spare room, perhaps even take over the entire attic and set up a home office. The usual tricks of getting it to move on weren't working, and as the days passed and I grew more and more weary of trying to keep my head above water, it dawned on me that it was time to call in the cavalry.

I found Dr. Craye through my friend Roy. "So," I said when I called Roy, whose displays of depression rival anything staged by the New York Ballet or the Royal Shakespeare Company. "This depression thing. Who is it you talk to about that?"

Even after getting Dr. Craye's phone number I put off calling him for several weeks. I was feeling better, I told myself. The clouds were passing. I didn't need to talk to anyone after all.

Then one night I had to rush home after dinner with friends because I was sure I was going to die. Right there. In the restaurant. Only getting home would save me. When I arrived, I picked up the phone and left Dr. Craye a message. "You don't know me," I said. "But I think I'm going crazy."

Three days later I was sitting in his waiting room. It was raining, a thunderstorm of virtually unheard of proportions. The rain drummed on the roof, and every so often lightning split the sky and rattled the windows. I felt calmer and happier than I had in months. Storms have always had this effect on me, perhaps because when they arrive the outside world finally mirrors my inner one.

While I waited for my appointment I surveyed the room. More a living room than a waiting room, it was filled with comfortable furniture and soft lighting. A white noise machine purred contentedly beside the couch, undoubtedly to drown out any traces of the conversation going on behind the closed door to the doctor's inner sanctum. One wall was taken up by a long, low bookcase.

The books a person chooses to keep, and especially to display publicly, are always a reflection of his or her life. What, I wondered, did Dr. Craye's book selection say about him? I scanned the shelves. Jack Kerouac's *On the Road* stood beside a compendium of Greek drama and *Halliwell's Film Guide.* There were several different "Let's Go" travel books, including ones for Spain and France. I opened them and read the publication dates: 1995. Did he actually go there, or were these just for show?

Other titles were more interesting. In particular I was drawn to *On Kissing, Tickling, and Being Bored: Psychoanalytic Essays on the Unexamined Life* and *Guns, Germs, and Steel: The Fates of Human Societies*, not just because of the titles but because they were incongruously sandwiched between *Christmas Time with Martha Stewart Living* and *The Scrabble Dictionary.* The latter had affixed to its spine a library numbering sticker, which thrilled me. Did Dr. Craye take it from the library and never return it? Was he secretly a kleptomaniac? And why, of all things, would he take something like a *Scrabble Dictionary*? "This guy is nuts," I thought.

My browsing was interrupted by the opening of the door and the appearance of two men, one of whom I assumed to be Dr. Craye and the other his patient. They shook hands, and then the one I'd taken for a fellow lunatic said "So, I'll see you next Tuesday. Same time. Call me if you need anything."

As the gentleman I'd thought was my new shrink left, I faced Dr. Craye and smiled nervously. He looked at me kindly, the way you'd look at a dog you've just encountered on the street and whose disposition is as yet unknown. "Shall we?" he said.

I don't remember a lot about that first conversation. It was, really, pretty unremarkable. I do remember Dr. Craye stared at me a lot, which made me keep talking. I was convinced somehow that if I stopped talking he would cease to exist, that his heart continued to beat only because I was telling him stories. (It would be several more visits before I realized that the whole staring thing is a standard shrink trick. Then I started staring at *him*, which made him draw little circles on his yellow notepad and which was much more fun for me.)

I talked and talked and talked, and much too quickly Dr. Craye informed me that our session was over. I balked. I didn't want to leave, at least not without something to show for my efforts. Perhaps, I suggested gently, a prescription might be in order? I'd been thinking, despite my usual aversion to drugs, that this might be the way to go. I'd even gone so far as to look up the various kinds of medications for mood disorders and settled on one or two I would consider taking. I thought this was a generous concession on my part, and I waited patiently to be rewarded.

No, Dr. Craye said, I would not be leaving with happiness in a bottle. We had some more work to do before he could determine whether or not that would be helpful to me. In the meantime, he asked, how would I feel about coming to see him again?

I did go to see him again. Several times. I didn't want to, really, but at the same time it felt good to unload on someone besides myself. And after a few more visits I did get that prescription I'd been hinting at. It was for Zoloft.

Now it says something about the state of mind I was in at the time that I was actually disappointed to be given Zoloft as my particular medication. Zoloft is the most commonly prescribed of the antianxiety drugs. I'd secretly decided I needed to be on something more exotic, something only select mentally ill people were allowed to take.

Being lumped with all of those other depressed people made me feel like I'd been passed over for AP English, or scored in the lower percentiles on the SATs. I did not feel special.

Still, I had my medication. This, I thought with some strange sense of pride, was proof that my brain was just a little bit fucked up. The chemical wiring was out of code and needed some adjustment. Perhaps I wasn't special, but at least I was not normal.

When I got the actual pills from the pharmacy I took them home and opened them. Holding one of the little yellow tablets in my hand I sniffed it. It smelled like Elmer's glue. I imagined taking it. What would it do? How would I feel? I'd been told by Dr. Craye not to expect anything dramatic, at least not at first.

He was right. At first the only thing I noticed was that my stomach hurt a little bit and that I had the worst case of cottonmouth I'd ever had. The more dramatic results took a little longer, and came on more slowly. The first indication that the Zoloft was doing something was when Patrick and I went to dinner in the Castro and for the first time I didn't count the minutes until I could get back on the subway to come home. Then I began noticing I no longer wanted to kill people who drove badly. This was a novelty, and I decided things were improving.

The brain is a wonderful thing, both magical in its capacity for creation and exploration and terrifying in its ability to turn on you and plunge you into total despair. Now that I had Zoloft surfing my neural oceans I decided to read everything I could about what was actually going on in my head. The discoveries I made were fascinating. I found my brain had a whole other life apart from the one it had been letting me in on, that my bouts of depression were almost like little holidays my neurons were taking from their work days.

My Life as a Dwarf, Part 6: Doc

Like someone who acquires a new dog and has to talk to everyone else who also has that same breed, I found myself discussing mental illness with anyone who would listen. Over dinner with another author friend one night we discovered we both were taking the same med. Afterward, driving home, Patrick remarked with some surprise how easily we'd revealed our depression to one another.

"It's like a club," I said cheerfully. "We just don't get merit badges for being in it."

Every morning now I take my little yellow pill. *Zoloft and water*, I think as I swallow. *The breakfast of champions.* And every so often I go back to Dr. Craye to talk some more. Things have changed dramatically since that day I first walked through his door. I no longer see him as something to fear, but as someone who can help me understand the delicate balance that exists in my mind. One of these days I may even ask him about that *Scrabble Dictionary*. But not quite yet.

Just One of the Girls

This essay brings back all kinds of memories. I had just moved to New York. I was just starting to explore the gay community. Everything was new. Even though a lot of the time it was disappointing, it was still special. The dance at the center of this piece was especially meaningful to me. I wish I still had that T-shirt.

My first summer living in New York, I couldn't wait for the annual pride weekend to come. I moved there in the spring, and as the days became warmer, I started counting down to the last weekend in June. After years of having no contact with a gay community, suddenly I was going to have a whole weekend devoted to all things queer. I scanned the Pride Guide carefully, making lists of things I thought would be fun to do. Parades. Rallies. Performances. Dances. They all went onto the list, and I was carefully to balance the gratuitously decadent happenings with the more socially responsible events.

My guide that first summer was a lesbian friend from work named, appropriately enough, Mary. I knew very few gay men at that point, and Mary was hooked into the gay world in a way that I wasn't. She shepherded me around to the various events and made sure I saw everything. On Sunday, she announced that we were going to what was supposed to be the crown jewel in the pride weekend crown—the annual dance on the Christopher Street pier. Mary was very much into dancing and the club scene. I was intrigued by the idea of mostly naked men, and she thought the pier dance would be a great way to indulge both or interests and allow us an opportunity to enjoy a couple of hours with our shared community.

Well, she was wrong. When we arrived at the dance, we discovered that Mary was one of only a handful of women present. Because the music sounded bearable, and because we had laid out 20 bucks apiece, we stayed. During the two or three hours we were there, my friend was treated to a continuous stream of hostile looks and sometimes outright abuse. More than once a dancing beauty would take a break from posing and come ask Mary if she was a "real" girl. Instead of feeling part of a community, she felt like an intruder. The only "pride" that seemed to be going around was in showing off the results of hours spent at the gym and under tanning lamps. The experience was ruined for both of us, and I vowed never to attend another dance again.

The next year when pride rolled around, I wasn't too enthusiastic. By then I'd had my fill of bars and clubs, one-night stands and handsome men with empty minds. With just one rotation of the seasons I'd decided that gay New York was a sorry place indeed. I decided that I'd sit pride out and do something really fun, like sleep.

Then some friends invited me to join them at a women's dance that was being held as part of the pride festivities. Now, it's a long-standing joke among my friends that I make a better lesbian than I do a gay man. I haven't seen *The Wizard of Oz* since I was four. I own every k.d. lang, Indigo Girls, and Melissa Ferrick album ever made. I even (and this frightens even my dykiest friends) know all of the words and accompanying hand motions to "Waterfall." I don't understand why John F. Kennedy

Jr. is a sex symbol. I think Ann Richards should be Pope.

Sitting at Henrietta Hudson's and looking at all of their expectant faces peering at me over mugs of Guinness, I was torn. I wanted very much to spend what amounts to the equivalent of Queer Christmas with my chosen family. But I still hadn't quite gotten rid of the bad aftertaste left by the miserable experience of the year before. Besides, I am also painfully aware that, compared to the number of men's spaces, there are very few places where women can go to be alone with other women. Reading *Our Bodies, Ourselves* in college will do that to a man.

But they worked on me the rest of the afternoon, and after three or four pints and an endless stream of pleading on their part, I found myself standing in Judith's Room in line to buy a ticket. I was, of course, the only man there, and I was convinced that everyone was looking at me with grim thoughts in their hearts. I sang along with the Ferron tape that was playing, just to let them know I was harmless. I heard whispering behind me. I sang louder and leafed through a copy of *Radical Chick*, hoping the newsprint wouldn't come off on my sweaty palms.

After what seemed like days, I finally made it to the counter and asked for a ticket. The woman, who sported a Thelma & Louise for President T-shirt, glanced at me, then looked back again. "Is this for you?" she demanded. Eyeing the wicked-looking labrys around her neck, I briefly considered lying and telling her it was for my friend whose double shift at the co-op/women's shelter prevented her from being there herself.

"Yes?" I finally said doubtfully, fully expecting her to send me packing.

To my surprise, she actually smiled. "Good," she said emphatically, handing me a ticket. "See you there."

Relieved to have passed the first test, I went home and

got ready. As the time for the dance approached, I began to have second thoughts about the whole thing. The more I thought about it, the more it seemed what Pooh would call a Very Bad Idea. I called my friends several times, trying to get out of it with a variety of excuses.

"Look," Anne said firmly. "I know for a fact that you do not have to go to a 12-step meeting for codependent pet owners tonight. Blaine is in that group, and she's all distraught because it was cancelled for pride. Apparently Gertrude and Simone have hidden under the bed and refuse to come out, even for liver snaps."

"Oh, please," said Katherine. "They are *not* going to make you recite Dorothy Allison poetry as proof of sisterhood. Besides, you know it all anyway. I saw that autographed copy on your shelf."

"You are not coming down with a temperature," said Emma, sighing. "Now get dressed and get your ass over there. We'll meet you at nine."

Finally, they all stopped answering their phones.

Knowing that what awaited me if I didn't show up was infinitely worse than anything that could happen at the dance, I dutifully walked over to the college where it was being held. Especially for the occasion I wore a T-shirt I had found that read LESBIAN TRAPPED IN A MAN'S BODY. It had seemed fun and carefree when I'd purchased it, but now I felt as though I was just asking for trouble. When I arrived at the school, I began to panic in earnest. There were about 2,000 women thronging the walkway. And me. I tried to be inconspicuous. But nothing could change the fact that I stand 6 foot 2 in my boots and am quite a bit hairier than most women. In short, I did not blend.

I half expected the women at the door to send me right home. But they took my ticket, stamped my hand, and let me in. I vaguely wondered if I had been given a blue ink stamp on purpose, but decided not to worry about it. Even if I'd wanted to, there was no turning back against the incoming tide of bodies anyway. Once inside, my anxiety grew when I couldn't immediately find my friends and thought that they'd abandoned me to a horrible fate. But after a few minutes of frantic searching, I discovered that they had very kindly situated themselves at the back of the room, forcing me to wade through swarms of dancing women to get to them. They thought it was funny.

"See any hot prospects?" one of them asked evilly.

"Just one," I shot back. "But it turns out she only likes butches."

We talked for a while, then hit the dance floor. I was so preoccupied with trying not to knock over anyone smaller than myself that I forgot about my shirt. Then just as I was finally relaxing, I noticed a woman pointing at me and laughing.

That's it, I thought. *They've figured it out and they're going to make an example of me.*

The pointer worked her way over to me. In her 50s, she had a crewcut and wore a leather jacket with a skull painted on it. She reminded me of all the old-guard dykes I saw playing pool at the bar near my apartment, the kind who spoke fondly of the days when femmes were femmes. The Grim Reaper had come for me, and she was one butch number.

She stopped in front of me and looked me up and down, as though confirming that she would have no problem taking me down. I glanced around and saw that all of my friends had backed away. So much for family.

"I just want you to know," the Reaper said in a gravelly voice, "that I'm glad that you're here. Thanks for coming, it means a lot." She gripped my hand in a viselike shake. Then she kissed me and disappeared back into the crowd.

I stood there for a minute, stunned, not knowing what to think. I wasn't sure if I was more surprised that I was still alive or that I'd just been kissed by a woman more masculine than any of my dates had ever been. Now that the tension I had been feeling was broken, I started to look around me. On the dance floor there were women of all shapes, colors, and sizes. Their ages ranged from young teens to women well into their golden years. Women in Chanel suits danced alongside women in combat boots and flannel. I noticed five or six women in wheelchairs.

In some ways, it was a complete parody of every lesbian stereotype. But it was also very real, and it suddenly occurred to me why everything felt different. It wasn't just that I was the only man around. I had attended dances before, but they had all been sponsored by and for men. At those dances, the groups were hardly what could be called mixed. The less-than-beautiful never belonged. Likewise the old, the disabled, women, or, for the most part, minorities. Sometimes someone from another group would manage to sneak in, but he usually spent his evening alone and ignored.

During the course of the evening, over 100 women (I stopped counting at 136) came up and said something to me about my shirt. Countless others smiled or laughed without saying a word. It got to the point where I suddenly noticed my friends were being suspiciously silent.

"What's wrong?" I asked Anne, who was leaning against the wall sullenly.

She gave me a black look. "You're talking to more women than we are," she wailed.

"Yeah," said Katherine. "I thought that cute woman in the leather mini and the Wonderbra was coming over to flirt with me, but all she wanted to do was hug you."

At one point, someone grabbed my arm. "Hey," she demanded loudly, "Are you a real girl?"

For a brief, horrible moment I was transported back to that first horrible pier dance, when my friend had been asked that same question. Only this time the question was meant in fun, posed by someone with no malice in her voice. Instead of questioning my right to be there, she asked me to slow dance. She led.

I suppose there were some women at the dance that night who objected to my being there. But if there were, they were kind enough not to let me know. Unlike other "community" events I have been to, the criteria for belonging were not physical beauty, political correctness, or a well-honed ability to make other people feel less than acceptable. Rather, the people at this dance were all there because we wanted to celebrate together what we spend so much of our time fighting for—the ability to be lesbian and gay people without having to live up to other people's standards.

Camille Paglia says that the lesbian and gay community will not advance until we learn to stop thinking in terms of gay and straight. I would add that we also must stop thinking in terms of women and men and start thinking in terms of people. We have enough other battles to fight with outside enemies; it's time to end the ones within our own family.

In the past, I've noticed the relative invisibility of women at a lot of community events I have attended. But I never really thought about why it is that lesbians and gay men do so few things together. Now I know. Just like in junior high, when they suddenly grew six inches and developed breasts way before we needed to shave or wear jockstraps, the girls are still waiting for the boys to catch up with them.

Runaway Train

One of the inherent dangers about using your life as source material is that, on occasion, you're going to reveal things that will later come back to haunt you. Like ex-boyfriends. The fellow mentioned in this piece and I broke up before the book in which this essay appeared even came out. (Not, I should point out, for any of the reasons mentioned in this piece.) While I was tempted to leave the essay out, it's one that sums up what a lot of us go through when dating, so I decided to leave it in.

There is an inherent danger in dating writers that stems from the fact that we are people who are used to dealing with an infinite range of possibilities. In our work we have to be able to imagine many outcomes for any problem our characters might face. Consequently, our minds, either through training or natural inclination, can generate a shocking number of ways to deal with any situation we might find ourselves in. This can be a positive trait. Sometimes. For example, writers are more willing that most to hold romantic notions about finding true love and living happily ever after, if only because we have read far too many fairytales.

But this ability to consider a range of options for any given situation can also lead to trouble, especially if, as I tend to be, the writer in question is drawn to the grimmest and most dramatic of options. In this case, an overactive imagination can turn a perfectly reasonable situation into an emotional meltdown. This is especially true when it comes to relationships, which tend to be touchy areas for writers anyway because we spend far too much time thinking about such things while avoiding deadlines.

Case in point: On Tuesday, my boyfriend did not call me all day. For most people, this would probably not be a huge deal. Some people might not even *notice* if their boyfriends didn't call them for 24 hours. But I'm used to hearing from mine at some point during the day, so I started to wonder. I tried not to wonder too much—I know how I can get—but by late afternoon I couldn't help but have a couple of passing thoughts as I pretended to distract myself by working halfheartedly on a manuscript.

I started small. *Maybe,* I thought breezily, *he's busy working on something himself and just hasn't had time to pick up the phone.* That made me a feel a little better. For two seconds.

Of course, I couldn't leave well enough alone. That would be too easy. And emotionally healthy. Instead, I went for the more familiar option: I fretted. There is a scene in one of the Winnie the Pooh books in which the perpetually bitter donkey, Eeyore, is annoyed at the perpetually optimistic Piglet and Pooh for assuming that a tenuous situation they are all involved in will come out just fine in the end. "Think of all the possibilities before you settle down to enjoy yourselves," Eeyore says gloomily. And this is what I did. I did it all evening while I waited for the phone to ring.

After it became clear to me that the BF and I had absolutely no psychic link whatsoever because if we did, he would have felt me staring sorrowfully at the phone and picked it up to call me immediately, I decided to go to bed. Sleep is a great way for me to avoid this kind of mind game, as I can channel the extra worry into my dreams and pretend it's all just some healthy process of filtering out my neuroses. Besides, he frequently calls late at night so we can talk without interruption, and this way I could be unconscious while waiting.

This turned out to be a fine idea. I was so tired from all the fretting that I passed out quickly and went into a deep sleep—until I woke up for no reason whatsoever, rolled over, and saw that it was 1:37 in the morning. And, of course, the first thing that popped into my head was that I still hadn't received a call. Fumbling in the dark, I picked up the phone and checked for the telltale beeping that indicates a waiting message, hoping maybe I'd been so tired that I just hadn't heard the phone (located two inches from my head) ringing. Hearing only the ugly, flat drone of a dial tone, I put it down, closed my eyes, and tried to go back to sleep quickly, before my brain started functioning fully and ruined things utterly.

Too late. My imagination had already kicked in. And as every first-rate worrier knows, stewing in the middle of the night takes on a life of its own. Suddenly I found myself writing a screenplay all about the reasons for my guy's silence. It went something like this:

He's out on a date with someone else. He didn't call all day because he knew I would be able to tell that he was up to something. He's tired of our relationship, and he's decided to sow his oats elsewhere, or at least have a fling. Fine. Let him do that. I don't care. Oh, who am I kidding? Of course I care. But who might he be out with? Does he look like me? Is he better in bed? Who can I go out with to get even?

Or, worse, he's lying in a hospital bed. A careless driver has crashed into him. The car was totaled. Jaws of Life were involved. There were many paramedics, all shouting, just like in E.R. He's in a coma, and no one knows to call me because he hasn't remembered to give my number to any of his friends, as I've asked him to many times. And I don't know any of their numbers either so I can't even call them to ask which hospital he's in. I wonder if the operator would connect me to all the emergency rooms in town? But what if I don't find him? It could be weeks, months, before I know what happened. And what if he's dead? I'll be a widow. How long do I have to wait until I date again, and will that hot guy who smiled at me at the gym want to go out with me if he knows my last lover died tragically? Or would it be more satisfying to grieve for a really long time and never love again?

Or, he's merely fallen asleep while watching television and forgotten to call me. He is sleeping peacefully, snoring in that way of his that I usually find so adorable but now resent more than anything I can think of while I lie in bed and worry myself sick. How could he? Doesn't he know I'm waiting to talk to him? Doesn't he understand that when you say "I'll call you later tonight" to a writer, what the writer hears is "I will call you before midnight because at one minute after midnight it is tomorrow and therefore no longer 'later tonight'"? Doesn't he need me as much as I need him? Is he doing it just to make me mad?

I hoped he was having nightmares.

I looked at the clock again. It was 1:39. In the span of two minutes I had gone from being horribly jealous to horribly concerned to horribly vexed—a new world record in anxiety. But still the phone didn't ring, even when I counted backwards from 300, telling myself if everything was all right he would call before I got to zero. I dawdled on three, two, and one, drawing them out as long as possible, but nothing happened. Finally, I turned on the light, picked up a book, and read until I fell asleep again a few hours later. Then, only moments after I dozed off, it was time to wake up and walk the dog.

You might be wondering why I didn't just pick up the phone and *call him*. Well, that's easy. It would take all the fun out of everything. Plus, if I'd done that, he would have known I was worrying, and I couldn't have that. It's one thing to be mentally unwell; it's quite another to prove it to those who suspect it might be true.

He did finally call, the next afternoon. And, of course, as soon as I heard his voice I was fine. It turned out he hadn't called because he'd gone to a late movie with a friend and didn't want to wake me when he got home. Never mind that 12 hours before I would have given anything for him to have woken me up. It was suddenly as if the entire previous day had never happened and I was right back where I'd started, blissfully in love with the most wonderful man in the world. I couldn't believe I'd let myself get so worked up about nothing.

"I'll call you later," he said before we hung up, "and I love you." It doesn't get much better than that, and it was just what I wanted to hear from him. I hung up and went back to work, laughing at how silly I'd been. Then, about half an hour later, I looked up from where I was happily pecking away at my keyboard and found myself thinking, "I wonder if he meant he loves me like he loves his favorite shirt or he loves me so much he can't possibly live without me?"

The Crown of Heaven

This essay is a companion of sorts to "Packing for the Second Coming." I like to call them my Baptist Bookends. Like most kids, I never thought my upbringing was particularly odd. At least not until I started telling friends about things like trying to save the souls of the neighbors. I guess it was a little strange. Then again, I also once spent a summer as a missionary in France. I can still say "Without Jesus you will burn in hell" with a perfect French accent.

The clearest memory I have from my eighth summer is of kneeling behind a station wagon in Mickey Whitlow's driveway and saving the soul of a girl named Susan. I have forgotten Susan's last name—or likely never knew it at all—but I do remember that she had a pinched face, startling green eyes, and frizzy red hair. We were frequent playmates, and usually spent the long July afternoons racing our Big Wheels up and down the street in mad delight.

That summer, I was spending several mornings a week attending Vacation Bible School at our church. Vacation Bible School is the Baptist version of summer camp, but without the fun or the mosquitoes. It consisted of sitting on the scratchy-carpeted floor of the basement of the Immanuel Baptist Church and listening to our teacher,

Nancy Higgins, tell us about Jesus. Nancy Higgins was a college student home on break for the summer. Before assuming the role of teacher, she had been known to the neighborhood kids simply as Fat Nancy, an unkind but completely appropriate appellation. Now, placed in a position of authority, she was determined to get her revenge for our years of torture.

On the first day of Vacation Bible School, Fat Nancy suggested that we each pledge to win over a soul to Christ by summer's end. Should we fail to accomplish this goal, we would disappoint Jesus in some fundamental way that, she implied, would result in his not liking us very much. She did not quite say that we wouldn't be allowed into heaven, but somehow we were nevertheless left with this impression.

Deciding that I might as well get it over with as quickly as possible, I decided that the most logical choice for my conversion subject was Susan. On the day in question, I took it upon myself to take her down not the road upon which our Big Wheels raced, but the much more exciting road to heaven. Fat Nancy had been very explicit in her instructions for soul-saving, and I had memorized the required steps thoroughly.

"You have to pray to Jesus," I told Susan as we knelt on the scratchy asphalt, the tar warm under my bare knees. She looked at me and blinked. "Like this," I said. I folded my hands and tried to appear as earnest as possible. "Dear Jesus," I intoned solemnly, "Please forgive me for all of my sins and come into my heart."

Susan repeated my plea in a quiet voice. When she was done, she frowned. "I don't feel any different," she said. "If he's in my heart, shouldn't I feel it or something?"

I nodded. "You won't for a while," I reassured her. "But he's there. Now, no matter what you do, you won't go to hell."

We had spent a long time on Hell before getting to the actual moment of salvation. I had described it for Susan in the fullest and grimmest of terms—all fire and burning and endless centuries of torment. I assured her that without Jesus she was headed there immediately, should she suddenly be struck down by a car while riding her bike, or choke to death while downing the contents of a Jumbo Pixi Stik from the 7-11. That, in fact, was what finally sold her on the Son of God and all he had to offer. That and the fact that I told her that her dog would be waiting for her in heaven when she got there.

"Is that it?" she asked, picking absentmindedly at a scab on her elbow. She seemed to be expecting some big finale, like a musical number or something.

I thought for a minute, staring at our distorted reflections in the slightly rusted chrome of the station wagon's bumper. I didn't want her to go away thinking she'd been cheated. "Now we sing," I offered.

Her face brightened. "What do we sing?"

I chose at random a song I had heard my sisters playing on the stereo. "Don't stop, thinking about tomorrow," I warbled. Susan joined in, her thin voice mingling with mine as we chanted the familiar chorus together. "Don't stop, it will soon be here." Thus sanctifying our act with the words of Christine McVie and Lindsey Buckingham, I declared her Born Again.

That night, over dinner, I told my mother what I'd done. She beamed at me over her meat loaf. "You'll get a jewel in your crown for that," she said, as she spooned peas onto my plate.

This was the first I'd heard about jewels, or crowns. All Fat Nancy ever talked about was making Jesus happy. "What kind of jewel?" I asked. I had visions of something vaguely tiara-like, similar to what Miss America wore on her runway walk, or perhaps something more reminiscent of the crown the Burger King wore in the television commercials for his restaurant.

"Was Susan Catholic?" my mother asked.

I looked at her blankly. I really had no idea.

"Was she Jewish, then?" my mother suggested hopefully.

"I don't know," I said finally.

My mother sighed. "You really must find out," she said. "It's important."

"Why?" I asked. Quite honestly, I didn't really know there was a difference. I'd just assumed there were Baptists, like us, and then a general multitude of sinners. Until her salvation by my forceful message of grace, Susan, I had believed, was simply one of the latter. Now, if I was hearing correctly, there were actually categories of the unsaved. Secretly, the thought delighted me no end.

"It's important," my mother explained, "because when you get to heaven, you will get a crown covered with jewels, one for each soul you've saved while you're here as God's messenger. You get different kinds of jewels for different kinds of souls. For Catholics, you get sapphires. For Lutherans, you get emeralds. For all of those eastern types like Buddhists and Hindus and whatnot you get rubies. And for Jews," she said triumphantly, "you get diamonds, which are the best of all. That's because the Jews killed Jesus, and winning one back is very special."

"I think she was Catholic before," I said doubtfully. Although Jews were clearly the bigger prize, to my mind sapphires seemed somehow much more festive than diamonds.

My mother smiled. "That's fine," she said, seemingly satisfied with my achievement. "There are so many of them; it's good when we can show one of them the right way."

I sat through the remainder of dinner contemplating this

new information. If my mother was right—and I had no reason to believe that she was not—the choice of which souls to lead to salvation held far greater importance than merely swelling the ranks of Christ's army. Where once I had thought it enough simply to snatch my peers away from Satan's fiery grasp, now I understood more clearly what was really at stake in the cosmic battle between good and evil.

As I thoughtfully consumed my meat loaf, I envisioned the crown I would one day wear in glory, the construction of which would be my life's work from that moment on. Now that I knew the rules, I feverishly designed in my mind the exact pattern of jewels I would work toward. Not to be satisfied with any old hodgepodge of gems, I was determined to meet my Lord dressed in a smartly encrusted crown of diamonds and sapphires, with perhaps a hint or two of emerald, if I could scare up a few Lutherans.

Later that night, alone in my room, I took a piece of yellow construction paper and cut it into two strips, which I taped together to form a crown. Using the blue crayon from my Crayola 48 set, I drew a sapphire onto the paper. Placing the crown on my head, I looked in the mirror over my dresser and gazed at myself. Although admittedly only a poor copy of the real crown I was sure was being forged for me up in heaven, it looked very nice indeed, if a bit bare. It was time to get started on filling up the empty space with jewels.

I took out the school annual and found the picture of my class. I ran my finger down the list of names, counting the numbers of souls waiting for the deliverance I, with the helping hand of Christ, could offer them. With a red felt tip pen, I carefully wrote in C's next to those students I felt must surely be Catholic, and J's next to the ones who seemed, by whatever vague criteria I was using, to be Jewish. Those I was unsure of, such as Annie Chang, received question marks. When I was finished, I had a list of nine Catholics, five Jews, and four question marks. Folding it neatly, I stuck it into my notebook, where I could easily find it when the appropriate time came. Putting my crown on top of my bedside table, I went to sleep.

I dreamed that night of Jesus. He came to me in a long white robe, His face rosy with celestial delight. I approached, and He beamed, His mouth curling into a beatific smile. In His hands He held a crown—my crown—only now it was glittering with blue and white, the accumulated reward of a life spent in faithful service. As I stood before Him, holding my breath, He placed it on my head. I felt its weight settle around me, and looked up into my Lord's adoring eyes. As the heavenly host broke forth in song around us, He leaned down, bathing me in all His glory.

"Fabulous," He whispered in my ear. "Absolutely fabulous."

The next day, my salvation campaign began in earnest. No longer motivated simply by the fear of Fat Nancy's veiled threats, I now had a real reason to spread the word of God throughout my neighborhood. Armed with my notebook and list of names, and fueled by my dream of the night before, I marched straight over to the house of the first kid on my list—Wayne Lerner.

I knew Wayne was Jewish, because the previous Christmas our teacher had given us a brief description of Hanukkah in order to explain that not everyone sang carols and waited for Santa to come down their chimneys. At the time, I had felt sorry for Wayne because he didn't get to have Christmas. Now that I knew that Jesus was also absent from his life, I considered it my duty to attend to his salvation as quickly as possible. Besides, I remembered what my mother had said about Jews being worth diamonds. Winning them over to the Lord might be tough, but I was experienced.

With my easy conquest of Susan under my belt, I felt no need to warm up by practicing on a few Lutherans first. Ringing the Lerner's bell, I waited patiently until Wayne appeared.

"Hi, Wayne," I said cheerfully.

"Hi," he said. "I'm watching cartoons. What do you want?"

"Want to hear about Jesus?" I asked hopefully, visions of sparkling diamonds floating through my head.

"Jesus?" he said, his face wrinkling into a bewildered look. "There's no such thing as Jesus."

I stared at him, my mouth hanging open. No such thing as Jesus? I couldn't believe what I was hearing. Perhaps, I thought, this wasn't going to be so easy after all.

"But Jesus died for you," I said. "He died for your sins. You have to believe in him, or you'll go to hell." Hell had worked wonders on Susan; I hoped it would do the same for Wayne.

"There's no such thing as hell either," Wayne said. This time he seemed very pleased with himself, as though he knew something I didn't.

"There is too a hell!" I yelled, determined to make my point. "And there is too Jesus! You take that back."

Wayne held his ground. "No, there isn't. Jesus is all made up. So is hell. My dad said so."

He had me there. He had his father's word behind him. The only authority I had to back up my claims was Fat Nancy and my mother, and I knew their names carried no weight with Wayne. Frustrated, I resorted to the only weapon I had left in my arsenal. Recalling what my mother had said about Jews, I gave him a menacing look.

"Killer!" I said forcefully, pointing at him. "Murderer! You killed Jesus!"

The next thing I knew, Wayne was flying down the steps.

He tackled me, and we fell to the ground, shouting, punching, and kicking. We rolled around in the grass for a minute, both of us yelling our heads off. Then Wayne's mother appeared and managed to pull us apart.

"What's going on here?" she demanded.

Wayne and I scowled at one another. "I was trying to save him from hell," I explained, sure that any intelligent adult would see the reasonableness of this. "I was *trying* to tell him about Jesus."

"He said I killed Jesus," Wayne said sullenly. "He said I *killed* him."

With Wayne and I in tow, Wayne's mother marched over to our house, where she told my mother what had happened. "He said that Wayne killed Jesus," she said. I hung back, silent, knowing that my mother would side with me. I waited for her to come to my defense.

Instead, she grabbed me by the arm. "Apologize," she said, thrusting me toward Wayne. "Go on—tell Wayne you're sorry."

"No," I said. "I won't. He killed Jesus." Fat Nancy had told us several grim stories about missionaries being persecuted by the very people they were trying to save, and she assured us that suffering for Jesus was just as good as actually saving souls. "Besides, you said...," I began.

My mother pinched me hard. "*Say* you're *sorry*," she hissed through clenched teeth. Then she leaned down and whispered in my ear, "If you do, you can watch an extra hour of television tonight."

I was confused. My mother was actually encouraging me to lie. It didn't make any sense. Why didn't she want me to stand up for Jesus? Just last night she had told me that the Jews killed Jesus. Now here she was making me apologize for saying so. Wayne and his mother were both staring at me, waiting for me to say something. My mind raced as I tried to decide what to do. I weighed the possibility of an extra hour of television against the reward I might get for standing my ground for Jesus. Then I remembered that *The Love Boat* was on that night. I'd never been allowed to see it before because it was on past my bedtime. I caved in.

"I'm sorry," I said sweetly.

Wayne's mother smiled. Wayne made a face at me. My mother said, "Honestly, I don't know where he comes up with these things." Then the two of them left. Afraid that my mother would revoke her promise if questioned too heavily about it, I left her to her gardening and spent the rest of the day in my room.

That night, after a blissful hour spent watching Gopher and Isaac laugh it up with Charo and Robert Wagner, I went to bed. Again I had a dream where I was wearing a jewel-studded crown. Just as before, I saw Jesus approach me, and I waited to feel his forgiving hand on my shoulder. I knew he would understand why I had done what I'd done. Who could stand firm against the temptation of Charo?

Just before he reached me, Jesus was transformed into the glowering figure of Fat Nancy. She stood over me, her terrible eyes flashing, as she snatched the crown from my head.

"You've disappointed Jesus," she said venomously. "And you lied. He's taking back your crown, and you're going to hell!" The ground beneath my feet opened up, and I felt myself falling into a pit of flames. Above me, Fat Nancy held up my crown and cackled triumphantly as I screamed, "I'm sorry!" and plunged to my doom.

Just before I hit the flames, I woke up. I looked around my dark room for the horrible spectre of Fat Nancy as my heart raced wildly. Finding myself alone, I turned on my light. The crown was still on my bedside table. Picking it up,

I tentatively placed it on my head. I knew that the dream was a warning. I'd been forgiven once, but I couldn't fail a second time. I had to make it up to Jesus.

Opening my notebook, I looked at the next name on my list—So Yung Kwan. Afraid to go back to sleep and encounter Fat Nancy again, I leaned back against the pillows and went over and over in my head exactly what I would say to So Yung the next day when I rang her bell.

That's *Mr.* Faggot to You

I did not enjoy my high school years, and I know very few people who did. Whenever I hear people talk about their upcoming reunions, I tense up. I can't even imagine wanting to see the people who knew you when you were 17.

In 1996, a young man named Jamie Nabozny successfully sued the Ashland School District in his home state of Wisconsin. What made the court victory so interesting was that Nabozny wasn't suing because he'd received an inadequate education or because an overbearing gym teacher forced him to do too many squat thrusts. He sued the school because as a student there he'd been physically and mentally abused for being queer and the administration did nothing to stop it.

The details of Nabozny's case are disturbing. Over a period of years, he was repeatedly taunted and roughed up. At the most extreme, he was urinated on, and once, punched in the stomach so hard that he required hospitalization for internal bleeding. Much of this abuse went on with the knowledge of the school faculty, and despite repeated requests by Nabozny and his parents, the school refused to do anything about the harassment. When Nabozny's mother requested a transfer for her son, she was told that there was no school in Wisconsin where an openly gay boy would be safe and that Jamie should just get used to it.

At the trial the school administrators denied any knowledge of Nabozny or his troubles. Many said they didn't even know who he was. But testimony from former students told a much different story, and ultimately the Ashland School District was found negligent in protecting the civil rights of Jamie Nabozny. An out-of-court settlement was reached for a sum just under $1 million.

I find the Nabozny case interesting because I had a somewhat similar, although nowhere near as severe, experience in school. It started when I was about to enter the fifth grade, and my father retired from his government job and moved us to the small town in upstate New York where he'd grown up himself. He had happy memories of the place, and he wanted me to grow up somewhere safe and pleasant as he had.

But the reality was much different for me than it had been for him 40 years earlier. He'd been a hotshot athlete, captain of several teams, and holder of many school records. I couldn't make a free throw if someone held me over the basket. He'd been very outgoing and had a lot of friends. I was introverted to the extreme. The idea of speaking to other human beings made me feel queasy, and anyway, I didn't see the point.

In short, I did not have a good time. Dropped into the middle of an insular farming town where everyone had grown up together, I did not blend. Within 10 minutes of my first day there, I became the school queer. Granted, it originally had more to do with being an outsider than with any actual knowledge of my sexuality, but it was a label that stuck with me for the next seven years, until I refused to go back after the 11th grade.

Michael Thomas Ford

To tell the truth, I hadn't thought a lot about life at Poland Central School until I read about the Nabozny case. Then, like a bad dream, it all came rushing back. Suddenly I recalled vividly what it felt like to one morning look at the class roster taped to my homeroom teacher's desk and see the word "faggot" written next to my name in red pen. She hadn't bothered to cross it out. Or the day my best friend, the school's other misfit because of his bad haircut and weight problem, told me his mother (an alcoholic welfare cheat with a string of abusive boyfriends) didn't want him talking to me anymore because she'd heard I might try to make him "that way."

Unlike Nabozny, I was never physically abused. No one ever hit me. No one pushed my head in the toilet. But it was just as bad for different reasons, mostly emotional. When Ray Donaldson grabbed his dick in the shower room after I'd spent a miserable 45 minutes trying to just not screw up in gym class, and told me to get on my knees and suck him off, I never feared that he would actually make me do it. What I feared more was that I actually *wanted* to do it. Later, as I lay on my bed jerking off and obeying Ray's order in my mind, I came despite my hatred for him.

When I remember those years—day after day of dreading getting on the bus and week after week of waiting for 3 o'clock to come so it would be over—I know something of what Nabozny's life must have been like. So when I think of him depositing that million-dollar check, I smile to myself and hope he spends it on something he's always wanted. He certainly deserves it.

But there's another victory that Nabozny will have to wait a few more years to feel the effects of. See, no matter how much money he gets, it doesn't change the reasons he was picked on. It doesn't give him a chance to kick his tormentors where it counts. No amount of money in the world can make the kids who beat him up understand why they're the losers and make him see that he's come out on top after all. But time just might.

Eight years after I left high school, I received a phone call from someone I'd gone to high school with. A transfer student like I was, Charles Canterbury was a smart kid with a wicked sense of humor. He and I became friends, at least until he realized that he could finally gain some small amount of prestige with the rest of the school crowd by picking on me and another kid, John, who was also suspected of being queer.

I solved the problem by leaving school and going to college a year early. John remained and endured the torture of Charles and his friends, which included repeated calls to John's parents informing them that their son was a "cocksucker" and frequent burnings of gasoline on their front lawn.

Charles said he'd called me because he was thinking about how great things were back in high school and he wanted to see what I was up to because we'd been such good friends. Then he brought up John's name. "I called him the other day to say hello," Charles said. "He said I'd ruined his life back then and he had nothing to say to me. Then he hung up. Can you believe what an asshole he is?"

I made up some excuse to get off the phone and hung up myself. I was shaking, not from fear, but from anger. Back in school, I had wanted to kill Charles Canterbury for the way he'd treated me, John, and other people just to save himself. I'd even plotted various ways to do it. Now, eight years later, I couldn't even tell him that we'd never really been friends at all. And to make things worse, he didn't even seem to remember any of it.

Periodically over the next two years I would think about that telephone call and be filled with rage. Then one day I opened my mail to find an invitation to my 10-year reunion.

Never mind that I'd never actually graduated or gotten a diploma, I was being invited back to see everyone who had made my life miserable a decade earlier.

The letter was filled with buoyant paragraphs about how high school had been "the best times of our lives" and how the reunion was a chance to catch up with "the friends who provided our fondest memories." At the bottom was a handwritten note from the reunion organizer, a girl who had said maybe two words (and not kind ones) to me during our entire seven years attending the same school. "Dear Mike," it said. "I really hope you come. We had such good times together!"

Attached to the invitation was a questionnaire asking us to write an update of our lives to be included in the reunion souvenir program. I wrote the following in the space provided:

> Michael Thomas Ford is very proud to announce that he is still queer, despite the best attempts of his schoolmates to convince him that it is an unacceptable lifestyle. He would also like to take this opportunity to tell everyone he went to school with that he is happier, more successful, and a great deal more attractive than they are.

My entry did not appear in the program (I had my sister get one and check), but writing it made me let go of a lot of feelings I discovered I'd been carrying around. And looking through the pages of pictures of my balding, bloated classmates with their dreary lives and stained memories of a time when they'd once felt important, I realized that everything I'd written was indeed true. I hope one day Jamie Nabozny gets to do the same.

The F Word

This piece was my attempt to put into words some of my thoughts about a subject that's bothered me my whole life: fun people versus nonfun people (a.k.a. the rest of us). Partly it was also meant as a warning to my boyfriend. After reading it, he looked at me and said sadly, "You poor thing." While his condescension is annoying, he has not suggested a trip to an amusement park since, so the way I look at it, I win.

I am not a fun person. This may surprise some of you, particularly those of you who find what I write to be, well, funny. And I'm truly sorry to disappoint you. But it's true. I'm not fun.

My friends are frequently asked, usually by those who have read my books and found them to be amusing, what it's like to be friends with me. (Strangely, people who ask this question generally seem to think that it must be something like spending a drunken evening with Dorothy Parker, or perhaps one of the more sarcastic characters from children's literature, say Eeyore or Paddington after he's just eaten too many sweets.) Usually my friends snort and respond with something like, "It's not a lot of *fun*, I can tell you that."

I think this is a bit unkind of them, particularly when, it

could be argued, I usually have the grace not to point out the fact that many of *them* have just the tiniest flaws—mood swings of roller coaster proportions, say, or obsessive compulsive disorders that cause them to wash their hands 786 times a day—that make knowing them challenging. But I admit they're not far off the mark. I have issues with fun. You might even say, without correction on my part, that I don't know what fun is.

It is true that many funny people are not very much fun to be around in real life. This is because a great many of us are not the most mentally well people you've ever come across. Probably this is genetic, or the result of childhoods spent in forced labor camps. Whatever the cause, most funny people are funny because we're trying to fight something else, something more sinister that lurks in the back of our consciousness, waiting to get us if we let up for even a moment. The humor keeps the monsters at bay, much like the little night lights many of us insisted on having beside our beds as children.

Most funny people I know are terrified on a daily basis that one day we will no longer find amusement when we look up at the dark cloud we tend to live beneath and that, in an odd way, renews us whenever it opens up and rains on us. It's like we're some kind of freakish reverse Sleeping Beauties: The Good Fairies gave us something special at our christenings—the ability to find humor in lives that might otherwise be too much to look at straight on—and we're afraid that we might use it all up if we aren't careful. Or, as my friend Ed once said, "It's like God gave you just the tiniest little serving of fun, and you're afraid to eat it in case there isn't any more in the refrigerator." This is clearly not a man who grew up fighting with his siblings over the last piece of cheesecake.

The F Word

At any rate, the fact remains that I am not fun, nor do I particularly recognize fun when it's happening. When someone says to me, "Oh, you should try [fill in the blank with any chosen activity/restaurant/recreational drug]. It's a lot of fun," I am immediately doubtful. *What is fun?* I think. The concept eludes me.

I am not alone in this. My friend Gretchen has a similar problem. A philosophy professor, she spends a great deal of time worrying about things like whether we really exist, and if we do, why. She thinks this is fun. She's wrong, of course, because nothing is actually fun. But that's neither here nor there. The point is that Gretchen, like myself, doesn't understand the concept of fun when it's applied to normal people (i.e. people who aren't philosophy professors or writers). Once, when a potential date asked her what she liked to do for fun, Gretchen replied truthfully and instantly, "I like to think." You can imagine how such a person might be regarded by others. You'd be right.

This would not be such a terrible problem except that Gretchen has two poodles, Blaise and Zoe. Blaise and Zoe, being dogs, like to have fun. Dog fun. This is different, I believe, from people fun, but it is fun nonetheless. The problem is that Gretchen doesn't understand dog fun. She takes Blaise and Zoe to the park and stands there helplessly while they bark at her expectantly.

"They want to have fun," she says grimly, looking at me for help.

Now, dog fun I understand. It is a simple, defined thing chiefly characterized by lots of running about aimlessly. So I pick up a ball or a stick and I throw it. Blaise and Zoe chase madly after it, tails wagging. This goes on for some time, until they or I tire of it.

"Was that fun?" Gretchen asks timidly.

"Not for me," I tell her. "But the dogs are happy."

People fun is an entirely different thing. Most people I know are quite adept at having fun. Yet none of them can really explain to me *why* certain things are fun. "I love going out dancing," my friend Sophia said the other night. "It's so much fun."

"Why?" I asked her, completely unable to imagine that going out, let alone dancing, could in any way resemble fun.

"I don't know," she said. "I just feel good when I do it. It's *fun*, you know?"

No, I don't know. I do not like to go out. I do not like to dance. And this disturbs my friends, all of whom are desperate for me to have fun. Sometimes, they tell me, I approach *almost* having fun. But I never quite get there. "It's like there's this switch in your head," my friend Dan said the other day. "You'll be almost having fun, and suddenly it goes off. You can actually see it in your face. It's weird."

I suppose it is. Dan thinks it's my Baptist upbringing. He says that there's this gigantic reservoir of guilt in my brain, and whenever I start to have fun the dam opens and I'm drenched with an overwhelming sense of doing something wrong. Perhaps. But I honestly think it's just that I don't get it.

Now, I feel the need to explain that it's not like I don't *enjoy* things. I like going to baseball and hockey games. I like going camping. I like napping. Yet whenever I do these things with people (except the napping, which is generally a solitary undertaking) I inevitably get hit with, "Why aren't you having fun?"

"Why do you think I'm not having fun?" I ask wearily, because until that moment I was enjoying myself.

"You just don't seem to be having fun," comes the standard answer.

At this point I sometimes feel the need to do something demonstrative, something to prove without question that I really am having a good time. "More defense!" I might bellow at the fellows on the ice, or perhaps, "Wow, those rapids were *fast*." If pushed, I might even resort to doing a little dance with a team mascot or waving my hands in the air and screaming.

"Now you're being hostile," is generally the response I get from whomever I'm with.

"Was I a fun child?" I asked my sister recently. She's 10 years older and therefore had the opportunity to observe my behavior fairly closely.

"Not really," she said. "You always looked like you were waiting for bad news."

Maybe that's it. Maybe I'm convinced that if I actually experience fun, it will all be downhill from there. It's like when you spend all those years thinking about what your first time having sex will be like, and then it happens and all you can think is, "Is that *it*?"

Also, I am a writer. Writers, in general, *observe* things. But we don't necessarily experience them in the way that normal people do. Several weeks ago I was taken, against my will, to an amusement park by my boyfriend. Patrick is a fun person. He understands fun. He likes it. He's good at it. This is one of the things I love about him. It's like living with someone who can dance beautifully; I watch him doing it and I'm filled with a wonder that it comes so effortlessly to him when my own attempts at it resemble a profoundly retarded child attempting to sing opera.

Now, for the fun-deficient, amusement parks are just below eye surgery on the pleasure scale. But I went, because I knew Patrick would enjoy it and because I knew I would enjoy being with him, even if I wasn't too thrilled about the idea of things like rides and crowds and the potential for vomiting. And not five seconds after we entered the park I found myself strapped into a chair that was attached to a tower. A very tall tower. I looked over at Patrick, who was strapped into the chair next to me, and asked innocently, "What does this do?"

Before he could answer I found myself being hurled into the air at a very high rate of speed. I looked up and saw that we were, as far as I could tell, being launched into the sun. And then, just as suddenly, we stopped going up, hung in the air for a second, and plunged back to earth. We bounced a few times, gently, and then I was released from my chair.

As we walked away from the ride Patrick turned to me and said, with some concern, "I watched your face as we went up. Your expression didn't change, not even once. You may as well have been sitting on the couch in front of the television."

This doesn't surprise me. Because I wasn't really experiencing the ride as a ride. I do recall, as we lifted off, thinking, *So this is what it feels like to be shot into the sky.* But it didn't really occur to me that it was happening to *me*, and that I was supposed to *react* to it by screaming (like everyone else did) or wetting my pants (as one little boy did). I was simply observing it, storing the memory for future use; for example, if one of the characters in one of my novels is ever involved in a training mission for a voyage to Venus.

I tried explaining this to Patrick, but I don't think I did a very good job. For the rest of the day, as we went on one ride after another, I often caught him sneaking glances at me. I know he was wondering what kind of man he'd taken up with, and perhaps was even thinking of ways to gently break it to me that he might prefer to be with someone who had, say, a soul. Several times he took my hand and said soothingly, "You poor thing," as if I was clearly having the worst time since Joan of Arc was invited to her own barbeque.

I *wasn't* having a bad time, but I knew there was little use in trying to convince him of this. People who are good at fun don't really understand those of us who aren't. And for some reason, amusement parks are always a battleground for those of us on opposite sides of the fun issue. "I *despise* amusement parks," my friend Robrt said when I talked to him later in the week. "Every time Todd and I go to one and I refuse to go on the rides he says, 'Honey, it's OK if you're afraid. You can admit it.' I'm not afraid. I just think rides are stupid. But he thinks I'm lying, and then I feel I have to prove to him that I'm not afraid, so I go on them and want to push him off just when we reach the highest point of whatever idiotic thing we're on."

Perhaps I'm being too cynical. Maybe all I need to do is give it a try. But I'm not even sure how to go about it. Maybe going out dancing *would* be…interesting. But I can't imagine why. Early on in our relationship, Patrick casually remarked as we were walking by a bar near my house, "That place is really fun to hang out in."

When I didn't respond he said, "What's wrong?"

"Nothing," I told him. The fact was, I was trying to figure out how to explain to him that he was dating someone for whom fun was not an option. Because, frankly, just the idea of being in a gay bar at all is absolutely horrifying to me. The idea of it being *fun* is something I am not even willing to consider, even on my most upbeat days.

The older I get, the more I resent the pressure to have fun. "What do you do for fun out there in California?" my mother asks when she calls, making me grind my teeth. "Drink heavily and wait to die," I feel like saying. "What can we do this weekend that would be fun?" my friends ask, and immediately I feel pressured to come up with something, and fast.

Recently Patrick announced that we will be taking a trip to Las Vegas in the near future. "It will be fun," he said decidedly.

"Will it?" I asked neutrally.

He narrowed his eyes. I knew he was thinking about the amusement park incident. "You're going to have fun on this trip if it kills you."

"Just remember," I told him. "You can't remarry for two years, and you have to wear black."

According to my dictionary, the word *fun* is derived from the Middle English word *fonnen*, which means "to dupe." This, it seems to me, is exactly the problem. We're told that we *have* to have fun, otherwise we must be depressed, or angry, or dead. Not content to just let us sit quietly enjoying the moment, the Fun Cheerleaders come by to ruin everything, waving their pom-poms in our faces and attempting to get us to stand up and do the wave with them. Well, I've had enough of it. I say down with fun and those who promote it shamelessly. Let's hear it for plain old contentedness, or even mild satisfaction. Are they so bad?

The next time someone asks me if I'm having fun, I think I'll smile pleasantly and say, "Yes, I'm contemplating setting you on fire." Now *that* would be fun.

My Life as a Dwarf, Part 7: Happy

When I was 13 my mother gave me a book called *How to Be Happy Though Young.* It was, as you can imagine, a well-intentioned advice guide meant to cheer up adolescents who, plunged into the depths of despair and humiliation by our changing voices, shaky sense of self, and frightening primal urges, needed a good pep talk.

What strikes me most about the book is the title, and particularly the use of the word *though.* Why not *How to Be Happy While Young* or *How to Be Young and Happy?* Sticking *though* in there implies that the normal condition of being young is misery, or at the very least that happiness is a privilege reserved only for those who are *not* young, like driving or being old enough to purchase cigarettes. It doesn't leave a lot of room for interpretation.

I certainly *wasn't* happy when I was young, so I really can't fight the book's premise too strongly. Still, I wonder how successful a book called *How to Be Happy Though Black* would have been, or *How to Be Happy Though Female.* And for all of the book's enthusiastic promise, I don't believe reading it had the implied effect.

I thought about *How to Be Happy Though Young* recently

when I was discussing books with an editor friend of mine. "Why," he asked "are the top-selling books for gay readers always porn-star biographies and books about how to find true love?"

It's true. If you ever look at year-end lists of the best-selling books, they really *are* almost always about either sex or love, and in particular how to find those things. Not that there's anything wrong with either of these topics, but the dichotomy is hard to ignore. As a group, we seem overly preoccupied with needing to get off and get hitched. And I don't think that's coincidence. I think it's what happens when people are trying really, really hard to be happy.

The answer, it seems to me, is *How to Be Happy Though Gay*. No, it's not a perfect title, suggesting (much as *How to Be Happy Though Young* did in regard to young people) that gayness is inherently an unpleasant state. This, after all, is one of the fallacies about homosexuality that we've worked so diligently to prove incorrect. But let's just go with it for the moment. What would such a book be like? What kind of advice would it contain?

How about 12 steps to happiness? No, that sounds too much like an AA program, and the notion of gayness as addiction is not something we want to promote. Besides, it's too may steps. Readers would get weary of the effort. So maybe seven, as in *Seven Days to Being Happy Though Gay*. Seven is a nice number, a magic number. But I don't know. It might be a little too easy to do it all in a week. We want people to get their money's worth, after all. How else will we justify the $24.95 cover price?

I say we go with 10. Everyone likes 10. Top 10 lists are perennial favorites. Ten is a good, solid number, round and healthy looking, like a prize steer. So 10 it is. But 10 what? Steps are out, and so are days. I know, how about keys? *Ten*

My Life as a Dwarf, Part 7: Happy

Keys to Being Happy Though Gay. I like that. It sounds practical yet not too self-helpy. Besides, keys suggest mystery and surprise, a book that will help you unlock hidden doors. I think we have a winner.

Now what are we going to put inside this fabulous book? Having promised 10 keys, we need to come up with them. Why don't we start with:

KEY 1: LIVE IN THE PRESENT

This is an excellent way to kick things off. After all, how many of us waste a good portion of our time and energy worrying about things people did to us in the past and stewing over what might happen to us in the future? While we're doing all of that worrying, we're forgetting to live, and then by the time we think about it the present has become the past and we're right back where we started. So before we go any further, let's resolve to just focus on what's happening right now. Forget about "when I lose 20 pounds," "after I find the perfect job," and "as soon as I marry Ben Affleck." Abandon too "those awful things he said to me," "that time you slept with my boyfriend," and what Father Mahoney made you do after CCD class. That's over. Done with. Life is about what's happening to you at this very moment, not about what did or what might happen. Get out there and have fun. But while you do, keep in mind Key 2.

KEY 2: RESPECT YOURSELF

Hey, a Madonna reference. That should get people's attention. But really, I think the Material Girl was on to something here. If you respect yourself, you're going to be less likely to do any of those, well, potentially embarrassing things like overindulge in the booze and happy dust. Sex too, at least the kind that can leave you with little nasties in your blood. If you keep in mind that *you* are the most important person in your world, it might also help you make the correct decisions on those occasions when you're presented with the choice of either, say, getting a good night's sleep or sitting by the phone at 3 in the morning waiting for that call your supposed boyfriend said he'd make when he left "to have dinner with an old college friend."

KEY 3: AGE GRACEFULLY

Not to point any fingers or anything, but there are some of you out there who think you're Peter Pan. It's all well and good to want to look your best, but come on. If you're over 30 and wearing *anything* that says Abercrombie & Fitch on it, it's time to reassess your priorities. It's not that you don't look good in those things, it's just that you don't need someone's name emblazoned across your chest to give you an identity. You should have your own by now. The same goes for that CD collection of yours. Dance music might be fun on a Saturday night, but have you ever heard of jazz? And those magazines on your coffee table—they should have more articles in them than fashion spreads, more ideas than just how to get the perfect tan. Never Never Land may be all twinkly and fun-filled, but being a Lost Boy quickly gets tiresome.

KEY 4: CULTIVATE FRIENDSHIPS

OK, this is important news: Fuck buddies and guys you only see at the bars or the gym are *not* friends. Neither are the queens who give you advice at the Clinique counter. We're talking real friends here, the kind of people who know more about you than what dirty name you like to be called in bed, how much you can bench press, or what your preferred moisturizer is. Friends can be (and usually are) even more important than lovers, so you want as many around as you can get. Even the Spice Girls figured this one out when they said, "Love won't last forever, but friendship never ends." Of course, they hate each other now, but whatever. It's true. Look at the pictures you have around your home. Do the same faces show up time after time, looking slightly older as the pictures become more recent? If so, good for you. But if your frames hold mostly images of men you slept with for a while who then disappeared, you might want to think about hanging out with a different crowd.

KEY 5: MAKE A DIFFERENCE

We're always told to take as much as we can get, but how about giving as much as we can give? There's a novel idea. This may come as a shock, but life isn't all about you. Go out and volunteer, and not just your money. Anyone can do that. Give your time and attention to something you think is important. I don't care what it is: an animal shelter, a outdoor group, an AIDS hospice. Just get out there and involve yourself in something other than your job. And don't do it hoping to meet a boyfriend (remember the part where I said this isn't about you?) Do it because it needs to be done and because you enjoy helping out. Most of the truly interesting things that happen in this world happen because somebody decided it was time for a change. Be one of those people.

KEY 6: TAKE CHANCES

Remember that time you saw the really hot guy at the bar, the one you were afraid to talk to? And remember how finally you *did* talk to him and you ended up having really hot sex on the beach? Life can be like that all the time. Well, perhaps not with the sex part, but there are always chances to be taken, and the more of them you go for the more adventures you'll have. Don't be afraid to fall down or make a fool of yourself. If everyone sat around being safe and predictable, the world would just keep spinning around with nothing much happening, kind of like *Friends* in the sixth season. Inject some excitement into your life from time to time, just to see what happens. If people didn't take chances, we wouldn't have things like airplanes, or Ben & Jerry's, or gay rights. Just imagine what could happen if instead of thinking about it, you actually signed up for that dance class, or took a trip to Amsterdam, or started writing that screenplay you've been talking about for 16 years.

KEY 7: DON'T FALL IN LOVE

Huh? Why wouldn't you want to be in love? Well, you do, but not until *after* you're already happy. Falling in love won't make you happy. In fact, until you're happy with yourself and your life you can't really be happy with someone else. So stop looking for love to change everything. Make the changes first, and love will follow. I know you've heard this before, but love comes around when you're not expecting it. Yes, I hear you saying defiantly, but trying not to think about love is like trying not to think about the word *catawampus*. Now that it's in my head it's all I *can* think about. Well, distract yourself. Take those chances we talked about. Explore your own life. And I swear, just when you're all wrapped up in something else—*bam*—love will knock you upside the head. If it doesn't, I'll buy you an ice cream cone.

KEY 8: STOP BLAMING EVERYONE ELSE

We've all had shitty boyfriends, tiresome friends, and asshole bosses. We've all had a bastard of a father, a mother who said terrible things, or siblings who generally made life miserable. Maybe you've really lucked out and had (or have) all of these. Well, guess what, you don't have to have them anymore. It's time to stop blaming those people for everything you don't like about yourself and your life. Drop the bitchy friend. Tell the boyfriend to pack his bags. Irritating family members are harder to ditch, I admit, but it can be done. Don't answer those phone calls from Mom where she tells you everything you're doing wrong. Stop visiting your perfect sister (who probably, for the record, has just the merest hint of a drinking problem) for the holidays. People can only drag you down if you let them do it. Sure, there are certain people who have to be in our lives, at least temporarily, and we learn to deal with it. But if you find yourself blaming your lack of happiness on someone else, it's time to think about moving on, moving out, or moving up.

KEY 9: LEARN TO SAY NO

Oh, boy, this is a big one. You don't think so? OK, when was the last time you went to a party for someone you didn't even really like, just because you felt guilty about not going? When's the last time you had sex with someone even though you weren't really in to him? How'd you feel afterward? Now imagine if you'd just said no, just stayed home and watched your favorite movie instead of going to that party, or said good night to that so-so date instead of wondering how long it would take him to come and praying he wouldn't ask to stay over. Take a look at your calendar. Is it filled with commitments you wish you could get out of, covered in appointments and dates and events you really have no interest in? You need to learn that when you don't want to do something, in most cases you don't have to. This is one of the absolute best things about being a grown-up. Your time, with some exceptions, is your own. You can do with it what you want. So don't waste it doing what other people want you to do.

KEY 10: EXPECT JOY

Did you wake up this morning thinking *I wonder what really great thing is going to happen to me today?* Probably not. What would happen if you did? Try it. You might just be surprised. If you're always thinking about what awful thing could happen, it most likely will. "Expect the worst and you'll never be disappointed" is not a philosophy designed to promote well-being. But if you go around expecting things to go well, expecting your life to unfold in interesting and exciting ways, you're already halfway there. Remember, they started calling us "gay" because we seemed happier than most people, more carefree and full of life. Why not live up to the name?

Well, it wasn't so difficult coming up with 10 keys after all. Probably we could have gotten twice that, or maybe even three, four, or five times that many. Those people trying to be happy though young have nothing on us. Maybe there *is* a book here, although I'm still not wild about that title. How about *How to Be a Happy Homo*, or maybe *Happy Gays*? No, you're right. But once we come up with a good one, Oprah, here we come.

The Perils of P.E.

I used to dread gym class the way most kids dread going to the dentist and taking tests. I believe I hold the world record for "forgetting" my gym clothes on P.E. days. And frankly, I think most of the gay guys who spend hours working out as adults are just trying to make up for the moment when they *dropped the ball or missed the free throw.*

Summer is here, and I should be in shape. I even promised myself that this year I'd go to the gym and just do it. But once again I'm not ready. My stomach is still too big, my shoulders too small. Blame it on Wally Shufelt.

Wally Shufelt—Mr. Shufelt—was my fifth grade gym teacher. One of those aging ex-jocks who failed to make it to the majors, he told us at least once a month how the Dodgers almost signed him right out of high school but a knee accident sidelined him before the start of spring training. Instead, he spent his years taking his frustrations out on the boys he used to be, dedicating his life to making men out of us. And he took to it with a fervor generally found only in missionaries and defenders of the spotted owl.

I think for most gay men, gym class was a black or white thing. For those of us who could actually do things like tackle, hit balls, and sink free throws, it was a junior version of nirvana, complete with sweaty bodies and blossoming hormones. For those of us completely bereft of any coordination whatsoever, it was a different story altogether.

While today I can enjoy physical activity and have even been known to watch sporting events from time to time, back in my school days I was decidedly in the second camp. Although my father had been the star athlete at the same school 25 years earlier, I inherited none of his talent. And in a backwoods school where excelling in academics was nothing compared to being able to score 42 points in the first half of whatever game one was playing, this was a decided disadvantage.

How I dreaded those alternating days when fourth period came and I had to enter that cavernous, wooden-floored palace of misery with its stench of varnish and unwashed adolescence. Many were the mornings when I would stand waiting for the bus in the morning and pray as hard as I could to God to bring about the Second Coming before 11 o'clock rolled around and I was forced to see what new ordeal Mr. Shufelt had prepared especially for me.

You see, while we engaged in the usual seasonal gym class cycle of soccer-basketball-baseball, Mr. Shufelt was happiest when putting us through the paces of some activity of his own design. He was of the firm opinion that athletics must involve (1) the hurling of some kind of solid object at a target, (2) winners and losers, and (3) pain. His favorite activities featured all three of his sports criteria, and the crowning jewel in his jockstrap was bombardment.

This clever game involved first dividing the class into two teams. Placed at opposite sides of the gym, we would wait, twitching with terror or anticipation depending upon our natures, as Mr. Shufelt walked into the center of the gym holding seven hard rubber balls. When he dropped them and blew his whistle, we would run as quickly as possible to snatch them up.

Then the slaughter began.

The object of bombardment was, essentially, to kill one another by throwing the balls with terrific force at your opponents. If you hit or were hit, you were out. If you caught the ball thrown at you, whoever threw it was out. Eventually, only two people would be left to face off against each other like gladiators in a ring.

In theory, this game could be amusing. However, in reality it was a total bloodbath, especially for the small and uncoordinated. Since having your ball caught would disqualify you, the larger boys avoided this potential embarrassment by pitching them with such force as to knock any reasonably sized target unconscious.

The obvious solution to the problem was to get hit as quickly as possible. I usually managed to do this within minutes of the game beginning, taking a whack to the arm or chest and then dashing for the safety of the bleachers. On occasion, I even managed to feign being struck by emitting a loud groan and limping slightly.

But one fateful day, things didn't go my way. I tried my best, but some evil angel seemed to be delivering me from shot after shot, even when I threw myself directly in the way of oncoming balls. Before I knew it, I was the last person on my team left on the floor. And I was face to face with Andy Peerson. Andy was the biggest kid in class. Rumored to be 23, he'd been left back so many times his name filled up every line of the "This book belongs to:" section of his English text.

I stood looking at Andy and at the ball gripped tightly in his massive hand. Somehow, I also had a ball in my hands. I had no idea how it had come to be there, or of what to do with it. I'd never gotten to hold one before.

"Hit him!" someone yelled from the sidelines. I wasn't sure if he was yelling at me or Andy.

Andy narrowed his eyes. I saw his huge arm rise up in the air, the ball held aloft. He let out a growl.

I closed my eyes and waited to die. Then I had an idea. In the split second before Andy threw, I could throw my ball and hit him in the legs. It wasn't the bravest way to end the standoff, but it would do, and I'd be a hero for once. On my deathbed, it would be the shining gym class moment I'd recall before passing on.

I opened my eyes and let fly my ball. I watched as it sped toward Andy. My heart filled with joy.

Then he stepped aside. Just like that. My ball whizzed past him and smacked impotently against the wall with a sad little plop.

Andy sneered and threw. As if in slow motion, I watched as the ball sailed toward me. It hit me square in the head and I fell down, my ears ringing and my eyes filled with stars. When I looked up. Mr. Shufelt was standing over me.

"Nice catch, Ford," he said mockingly. "Your team gets 50 push-ups for losing."

Nearly 20 years later, I still see Mr. Shufelt in my mind whenever I think about going to the gym. But confronted with the idea of spending yet another summer indoors because I haven't managed to get into swimsuit shape is enough to scare me out of my desk chair and into the nearest temple of body worship. I decide to overcome my fears once and for all.

I am fully aware that I am a lazy son of a bitch, and I know that I won't do so much as change into my shorts and sneakers without being forced to do so by someone else. I decide that my best course of action is to hire a personal trainer. It's hideously expensive, but I remind myself that since quitting therapy I have more disposable income. Besides, I like the idea of dropping the phrase "my personal trainer" into conversations, much as I used to think saying "my agent thinks I should try scripts" was a real kick.

I begin by looking through the local gay newspaper for a suitable candidate. There are two ads for personal trainers. One features a photo of a well-muscled man wearing a sleeveless flannel shirt and jeans unbuttoned at the crotch. The other ad has no photo. I stare at the first ad. I imagine staring at this man's crotch while he yells at me to "pump it." While this concept is not unappealing, I decide I need a trainer, not a porn star, and call the second ad.

My trainer's name is Paul. He does not wear flannel shirts or jeans open at the crotch, at least not when I meet him at the gym. He is very lively and encouraging, and although I find this disturbing at 7 in the morning, I try not to let it get to me. I'm having a hard enough time being in an actual gym wearing actual gym clothes. I find myself worrying that, like Mr. Shufelt, Paul will demand to know if I am wearing appropriate support gear. I decide to start off our conversation by informing him that I am.

Paul takes this in stride, and tells me that we will begin our session by seeing just how fit or unfit I am. I chuckle at this, and tell him that I don't need any help knowing how unfit I am. But he perseveres, and minutes later I am standing in front of a rack of weights while Paul tells me the correct way to lift them.

"Aren't we going to just use those machines?" I ask, waving vaguely at the shiny rows of equipment that fill the gym.

"Those?" says Paul with disgust. "Those are for sissies. Real men use free weights."

Already I am feeling depressed. I have issues about weights, having been given a set for Christmas the year I was

10. I had been hoping for a giant stuffed lion, and was more than a little dismayed when I raced downstairs and found a barbell wrapped with a red bow sitting under the tree.

I feel the same way now as Paul has me lift the bar to get used to the heft of it. I manage to hoist it up to my waist, and then to my chest, as Paul keeps up a steady stream of encouragement. Then down it goes again, dropping into the receiving brackets with a clink.

"Good," says Paul. "Now we'll put some weight on it."

I watch, terrified, as he pulls two weights off the rack and slips them onto the ends of the bar. I was hoping we'd just stick with the empty steel rod for the first time. But Paul has other ideas. He puts two more weights on the bar, then tells me to lift it. I wrap my hands around the bar and pull up on it, tentatively testing the weight.

"Lift!" Paul bellows in my ear.

Caught off guard, I propel the barbell up and over my head without even thinking. Then I stand there, swaying slightly from side to side, not knowing what to do.

"Good man," says Paul, slapping me on the back. "Now you can put it back. But make sure you do it slowly. We don't want you to hurt yourself."

I think it's probably too late for that, but I lower the bar slowly until it's safely in its original position and I can let go.

I look at Paul, and he's writing something in a little notebook.

"This is your workout record," he says, noticing my quizzical look. "I'm writing down how much you can lift. This way we'll know how you progress."

"So what was that?" I ask. "A hundred? A hundred and twenty?"

Paul smiles. "A little less," he tells me, shutting the notebook with a slap. "Why don't we move on to some other things?"

For the next hour, Paul has me lifting and pulling on a variety of weights. I have no idea what any of them are doing, but I duly lift and press and put the weights back again, making sure never to drop them. By the time we end, I am feeling slightly better about this whole workout thing.

"Great," Paul tells me when we finish the last exercise. "Now let's try some cardio."

Trying some cardio, I come to find out, is Paul's way of saying he's going to make me run on a treadmill for 20 minutes. He wants to see if I can do it without fainting. At the five minute mark, he asks how I'm doing.

"Am I supposed to taste blood in my throat?" I ask.

Paul turns off the treadmill and we're finished for the day. He hands me the little notebook he has been scribbling in and pats me on the back again.

"Good work," he says cheerfully. "We'll have you in shape in no time."

I go home feeling proud of myself. I have survived an actual training session with an actual personal trainer. Surely I can't be all that hopeless. After all, I was able to lift the weights Paul asked me to without too much trouble. I feel very butch as I swing my gym bag and head for the subway. I imagine running into Mr. Shufelt on the street and kicking his ass, and I laugh.

Later that night, before going to bed, I empty my bag and discover the little notebook. Curious to see just how much I was lifting, I open it and take a peek at what Paul has written there. Almost instantly my good mood vanishes.

Next to the first exercise he's written in 60 pounds. Here I thought I'd been heaving a respectable 100 pounds over my head. But 60? That's the weight of a medium-size Labrador. Why, my dog weighs 110, and I've picked him up before. But there it is in blue ballpoint. Sixty pathetic pounds. The rest of the numbers are equally depressing. I can't even look at them. I close the notebook and shove it into the bag where I won't have to look at it. Then I crawl into bed.

I fall asleep and immediate start to dream. I am walking toward the front door of the gym. As I open it and begin to step inside, I see all of the men turn from their treadmills and weight machines and pick up the rubber balls thrown into the middle of the gym. Stepping out of the shadows, Mr. Shufelt blows his whistle and I cover my head and scream as the sound of rushing air fills my ears.

When the alarm rings at 6 the next morning, every muscle in my body hurts. Crawling out of bed, I call Paul. I've decided that the gym thing just isn't for me. Luckily, I get his answering machine. I leave a message saying that I have decided to enter a monastery after all and won't be needing his services. Then I stumble back to bed, pull the blankets over my head, and go back to sleep. This time, I dream of nothing.

Over the Hill

I've received a lot of mail about this piece from readers chastising me for whining about growing older. I guess I didn't do a very good job with the essay, because I thought what I was doing was gently mocking those of us who do obsess about it. But maybe I really was indulging in some self-pity. Oh, well. At least now that 40 is only a handful of years away I really *have something to whine about.*

I'll be turning 30 this year. That's 79 in gay years. And I'm not taking it well.

The odd thing is, I've always wanted to be 30. Since about the age of 5, I've looked forward to the day when I would hit that milestone. People who were 30 seemed so grown-up to me, so sophisticated and together. I had this idea in my head that on your 30th birthday a delegation arrived at your door and presented you with all the trappings of adulthood, including a car, a fulfilling career, a nurturing relationship, the keys to your own home, and a fully funded IRA.

But here I am only months away, and now I see that I was sadly mistaken. Unless something truly unexpected happens, I will wake up on my big three-oh with no car, no relationship, a far-too-expensive rented apartment, and no financial future whatsoever. OK, so I have something of a career, and on some days it is fulfilling. But I was hoping for more.

I don't know what it is about turning 30 that seems like such a big deal. In fact, when an editor recently rejected a book proposal of mine saying I was too young to be writing it, I stormed around the house for days furious at her for not recognizing my maturity. "I've written 27 books!" I bellowed at the dog, who yawned (he's only 4 and has no worries) and went back to sleep.

Maybe that's the problem. When I was 25 and had written a handful of books, people were impressed. Editors would phone me and say, "This is amazing for someone your age." My agent couldn't wait to see what I would do next.

But now it's old hat. Why, mere children have written novels these days. Every time I open *The New York Times Book Review* there's another article about some 20-year-old Columbia student who's published a stunning book about how terrible it is to be young and beautiful. I used to read these pieces and think, "Wait until *my* novel comes out. I'll show them all."

And I would have shown them—if I'd ever written it. Now it's too late. Now the ideas that would have seemed so smart, so witty, so mature coming from the pen of an undergraduate are merely dull coming from my almost-30 self. Now when I tell people at parties that I'm a writer, they simply yawn and slap another nacho into the ranch dressing when they discover that none of my books have been made into films starring pale boys and English models with hyphenated names.

What's most disturbing to me is that there no longer seem to be gradations of aging. Now you're either in your 20s or you're not. The threshold is getting lower and lower. Where once upon a time people in their 30s looked ahead at the 40-something elders and rejoiced that there were a few more plateaus to reach before death, nowadays anyone over 30 is simply, well, not 29 anymore. There is the MTV generation, and then there's the rest of us.

I *used* to be a member of the MTV generation. I remember it well. Finally there was a television station that was all about me and the music I listened to. I tuned in and watched as Cyndi Lauper she-bopped across the screen and Billy Idol sneered at the 30-year-olds who dared try to invade his wild territory. Now Billy is well over 30. Cyndi is into her 40s and has a baby. Why, even Madonna is about to hit her 40th. And I can remember when she writhed across the road in "Burning Up" like an eel pulled from the water and flung upon the deck. Now I bet she'd break her hip if she tried it.

I don't know when it happened, but at some point I was sitting in bed watching TV and realized that I had the channel on VH1. I did some quick calculations and discovered that I hadn't seen MTV in weeks, probably months. I was watching a Stevie Nicks video. They used to show Stevie on MTV. Not anymore. Now everyone I used to watch on that channel has been pushed over to VH1, the channel for "older" viewers.

In defiance, I flipped back to MTV. I didn't recognize any of the VJs. When I was younger, they'd all had names like Martha, Nina, and J.J. Now the place was crawling with kids named things like Kennedy and Carson. They were all pierced and tattooed and surly. Not that I have anything against piercings and tattoos, but back in the old days, that role was reserved for Ricky Rachtman, who hosted *The Headbangers Ball* at midnight on Saturdays. Now they're everywhere.

Then there was the music. Now, I'm a big music fan, and I used to pride myself on knowing every singer and band out there. I loved them all, from AC/DC to Laura Branigan,

Heart to Ozzy Osbourne. I could watch MTV all day and know every word to every song they played. It made my mother crazy. As I sang along with the car radio, she would sigh wearily and wonder out loud why no one liked The New Christy Minstrels these days.

Ha-ha. Now the joke's on me. Now I recognize maybe one out of every 20 artists they show. Janet Jackson is easy. But these other ones confuse me. For one, they all look the same. For another, they all sound the same. I can't tell a Matchbox 20 from a Smash Mouth, or a Chumbawumba from a Squirrel Nut Zipper. And who's this Puffy person that keeps stealing other people's songs? In my day anyone called Puffy would have had his ass kicked by Ann and Nancy Wilson from Heart. But now even they're over on VH1, relegated to crooning during the Sunday Brunch segment. Brunch. No one in their 20s has brunch. Only we old folks do.

It's strange—one day you're the new kids on the block, and the next day you're nothing. Just ask the New Kids on the Block. When they started out, they were the same age I am. We thought they would save the world. Now they're all pushing 30 as well, and who gives a damn about any of them? Now it's all about Hanson.

When I was in high school and everyone was talking about what my generation would accomplish, we felt very good indeed. We were the Live Aid generation. We were the space shuttle generation. We were the Rubik's Cube generation. OK, so we didn't actually have anything to do with creating those things, but they represented our youthful vigor and enthusiasm, our cutting-edge possibilities. Now nobody cares. Now it's all about Generation X and what they're up to. And even they're getting nudged aside by their younger siblings. Well, don't look to me for sympathy.

Over the Hill

More and more often, I find the phrase "I remember when" creeping into my conversations. This terrifies me. When I was a kid, I cringed whenever one of my parents would start with the "I remember when" stories. They were always things like, "I remember when we had to walk 15 miles to school," or, "I remember when only hookers wore shoes like that." They were things old people said. Tired old people. Not young vibrant people.

Now I'm one of them. I made a list the other day of things that didn't exist when I was a kid. ATMs. The Internet. Alanis Morissette. Why, I can still recall when VCRs were hardly household items. It was a special treat when my father would go to the store and rent one for the weekend. Even then, there were probably only 20 movies to choose from. I recall also the first time I received a bank card. Until then, we'd had passbooks. Nobody ever conceived of having machines all over the place that would spit money at you just because you punched in a secret code. As for compact discs, I insisted they were just a fad. And now just a few days ago I heard a 15-year-old say, "Why do they call these record stores? Didn't records disappear, like, years ago?"

My other elderly friends and I now try to outdo one another in this game. "I remember when lunch box thermoses were made of glass," my friend Diane will say. "Yeah, well I remember when *Saturday Night Live* was funny," our buddy Brian will retort. On and on it goes, with each of us trying to outdo the other in the aging department. I once tried to get them all with, "I remember when we didn't have fire," but their faculties aren't that far gone that they would buy it. Maybe next year.

This whole gay thing doesn't help matters either. If I were straight, I'd worry about not yet having made partner, or my first million, or any number of ridiculous things. But being a queer man, all of those failures pale in comparison to the biggest one of all—I can no longer be the boy of the moment.

Once upon a time, I looked forward to being the object of lust of men everywhere, at least men older than myself, men who would do things like fly me to Paris for the weekend and use me as a decorative object near their swimming pools. Never mind that it would be shallow and empty; it would be fun. When I turned 30, I could at least sigh and remember fondly the year I was 23 and the Count threw me a party at his palace where we all danced naked in the fountain and fed one another grapes.

Somehow, though, it all passed me by. Maybe I was too busy writing all those books. Maybe I was just too tired. Whatever the reason, I've quietly slipped past the point where anyone is going to call me "that handsome young man" and pine longingly for me. Now I find myself futilely eyeing the 19-year-old stock boys at Stop 'N' Shop as I pile frozen burritos into my cart and hope the night will bring a Discovery Channel documentary about the feeding habits of sharks.

I know in my heart that 30 is really just the beginning. But not everyone seems to agree with me, and that makes it hard. I opened a book a couple of months ago, a gay novel that was being touted as a masterfully crafted look at gay middle age. The opening scene has the protagonist watching a group of men dancing in a bar. He has his eye on one of them, but fears the boy won't have any interest in him because of his advanced age. A few pages later, we discover that the narrator is something like 32. Thirty-two! Only three years older than myself.

When I was first coming out, I always dated "older" men. Now I've become one of those men. I realized this one night when a visiting friend of mine invited me out to meet up with some of his other friends. When we arrived at the appointed restaurant, I found myself sitting at a table with a group of other men around my age. One of the men had with him a young man he had recently started dating. The boy was 21 and recently out himself.

As the evening progressed, I watched this young man. He stayed silent as he listened to what we were talking about. When dinner arrived—sushi—his companion had to explain to him what sushi was, and how it is eaten. As I watched him fumbling with his chopsticks and taking his first tentative bite from a piece of maguro, I had the sudden realization that he was looking at all of us the way I had looked at the older men who took me under their wings when I was his age. He was watching our faces and, I could tell, wondering what his life would be like when he was as old as we were. I had to resist the urge to tell him.

At least I can take heart in the fact that I am not the only gay man to feel the effects of the big Three-Oh. A few days ago I was complaining to my friend Tom, newly thirtied, about my dismal romantic possibilities. "Don't even start," he said. "Last week I had my first sexual experience where someone called me 'daddy.' I pictured my father and immediately lost my erection."

"Just be glad he didn't call you 'ma'am,' " I told him wearily.

At our age, you have to count your blessings.

Rite of Passage

I have a real fondness for this piece, which makes the fact that there's really nothing to say about it sort of unusual. I think I enjoyed writing it so much because there was nothing overly serious about it. I like to think of it as my "summer song," sort of like the Go-Gos' "Vacation" or Katrina and the Waves' "Walking On Sunshine." With barbeque sauce.

Yesterday I became a man. It happened in the checkout line of Home Depot. I was standing there, waiting to pay for the brand-new 18-inch Weber grill that sat in its box in my cart, when a voice behind me said, "That's a fine grill you've got there."

I turned around. The speaker was a man in his 60s. He was wearing plaid shorts, a Red Sox T-shirt, and white socks. He appraised my grill and nodded approvingly.

"I've had my Weber for 30 years," he said. "You'll get a lot of use out of that baby if you treat her well."

Clearly this was a man who knew his stuff when it came to outdoor cooking. I patted the box, pleased that I'd made a good choice. "Yep," I said. " I can't wait to fire her up."

Something about that sentence struck me as familiar. Then it hit me: My father had uttered the exact same words 25 years earlier. I was 5. We were standing in line at Dart

Drug. It was summer. And he'd just purchased a new grill.

I still remember that grill. As soon as we got home, my father set it up in the back yard. He loaded it up with charcoal, ordered us all to stand back, and set a match to it. We oohed and aahed appreciatively as the flames leapt up, burned brightly for a few minutes, and then settled down to a dull glow.

From that moment on, the grill was the center of my dad's universe. Every night that summer we waited expectantly as he stood over the fiery embers, turning the hot dogs, flipping the burgers, and moving the pieces of chicken to just the right spot to get the skin crispy while the inside stayed juicy. Like some kind of strange suburban alchemist, he mixed secret barbeque sauces and developed his own peculiar basting rituals for getting the various items just so.

My sisters and I were the beneficiaries of his mastery of the grill, and in those three months during the summer of 1973, we consumed more meat than an entire herd of wild dogs, falling upon his creations ravenously night after night. Bellies full to bursting, we would sleep contentedly, our mouths watering as we dreamed of steaks, rare and tasting faintly of ash.

The grill was my father's domain. The rest of us were forbidden to touch it, or even to go near it. "Get away from that!" my father would shriek as one of my sisters attempted to take another hot dog on her own. Racing over, he would snatch the tongs from her hand. "You have to do it a certain way," he'd explain patiently, carefully lifting the frank and setting it on her plate like an angel descending from heaven. The message was clear—we were not worthy to attempt grilling ourselves.

I was not, of course, the only boy whose father knew the magic of the grill. All across my neighborhood were men who stood on patios at dusk, filling the skies with the thin smoke of roasting food. Their eyes all held the same faraway look, a pleasure bordering on madness, as they presided over their round, fiery kingdoms. For those of us who stood nearby and watched, the grills became holy grails, things we could spend a lifetime studying but never fully understand.

Sometimes during the day, while our fathers were at work, the boys of the neighborhood would congregate in a back yard. Unlocking the shed or garage where the grill of the house was kept, we would stand around it, looking at this symbol of manhood whose secrets were as yet unknown to us. Even empty of glowing coals, they fascinated us. Their steel bowls held the promise of adulthood. The tools that hung from their specially designed racks—spatulas and tongs and extra-long forks—gleamed seductively. We dreamed of the day when they would be ours to wield.

Various cultures have their own special ways of marking the passing from childhood to adulthood. Some send the young person into the forest for a few days to fend for himself, armed only with his wits and maybe a length of twine. When he returns, carrying a slaughtered wild pig on his back, he is welcomed as a man. Others mark the transition with dancing, drumming, and the ritual scarring of delicate body parts.

In our society, the celebrations are usually less dramatic. Graduation parties. Trips to the mall for training bras or athletic supporters. The securing of the all-important driver's permit. Living rooms across America are filled with photos of children, long since grown, hoisting swimming medals in triumph, or standing next to prom dates whose ill-fitting tuxedos or broad swipes of blue eye shadow are the plumage of burgeoning maturity.

Although they might not be as splashy as the traditions

of other cultures, these moments are nonetheless highlights of a person's life. Looking back, we can see each step we took as we grew closer to the time when we were no longer children. I have friends who remember the exact date and hour of their first pimple. My sister, now in her 40s, still talks nostalgically of the first time she used a tampon. Standing in the bathroom with one foot resting on the edge of the bathtub, she inserted the plastic wand with trembling fingers and marveled at the mysteries of flowering womanhood.

Gay men, of course, are not exempt from these rites of passage. But for many of us these modern-day manhood rituals are at least somewhat traumatic. The purchasing of a jockstrap, for example, may coincide with the discovery that one is not at all skilled in dribbling a ball from one end of a court to another. The first school social, carrying with it the necessity of asking a girl to attend, might bring terrors of enormous proportion. Rather than feeling the first stirrings of adult freedom, many gay men realize that they quickly need to develop a repertoire of excuses to explain why they prefer to stay home watching *Now, Voyager* to dancing the night away with their peers.

My own transition to adulthood went largely unnoticed. I stayed far away from school social functions and left high school before graduation. My first shave occurred while I was at camp, without my parents to take note of it. Not that I would have wanted them to. Because we lived in farming country, I was driving our truck long before I was legally allowed to, and it was years before I got a proper license—and then only because I needed one for identification purposes.

For me, becoming an adult was a journey with murky road marks. One day I was playing with blocks; the next I was paying my own rent on a studio apartment in New York.

It all happened very quickly, and my parents, not being particularly sentimental, have never offered any stirring memories of my change from boy to man. It just sort of happened. And somewhere along the line I forgot all about the grill. After all, gay men don't grill. We broil.

At least until yesterday. Warmed by the summer sun, I suddenly had a longing for a nicely grilled steak. Sure, using the oven would be easier. But I pictured myself standing by my grill, tongs in hand, and I liked what I saw. So off I trundled to Home Depot. It wasn't until I was in line and found myself discussing the merits of my new purchase that I thought of my father. When I did, I smiled to myself as I realized that finally, on the cusp of turning 30, I felt like a grown-up. And it had nothing to do with the IRAs I'd dutifully contributed to, the books I'd written, or the many other little trappings of adulthood that decorate my life. It was because I had my own grill.

I decided to invite my friend Jackie over to celebrate my manhood. A veteran of hundreds of post–softball game cookouts, Jackie is my one friend whom I knew would truly appreciate the symbolic meaning of my first time overseeing the grill. After setting up the Weber, I filled it with charcoal and lit it, just as my father had before me. I waited patiently until the coals were glowing warmly, then brought out the platter of steaks. Lifting one gently with my new tongs, I set it onto the grill and heard the beautiful sizzle that heralded my newfound status. I felt like howling at the sky in some primal way.

My euphoria lasted approximately 30 seconds. Then Jackie came over and snatched the tongs from my hand. "Get out of the way," she said, setting her sights on my steak. "You're doing it all wrong."

Once Upon a Time

Looking at the opening line of this piece, I am not unaware of the irony that it follows my essay "The F Word," and that some readers will have doubts about my ability to discuss the nature of something "being fun." Be that as it may, I stand by the sentiments expressed here. There was a time when being gay was fun. And I hope that day comes again. Indeed, I think we're taking tiny steps in that direction. I chose to end this best-of collection with this piece because, if nothing else, I hope my work reminds readers that what we are, and who we are, is worth celebrating. My writing comes out of my experiences of being a gay man, and is fueled by my belief that remembering what makes us unique will also make us stronger, both as individuals and as a larger, often fractious, community that still needs to work together to achieve common goals. We've come a long way, but it's not over yet. Let's try to keep our sense of humor about it all.

Remember when being gay was fun?

When I was growing up in the '70s, I thought gay people were the coolest. My best friend, Stephanie, had a gay uncle named Fred. Fred had a mustache, wore jeans and T-shirts with work boots, and frequently drove us to Dairy Queen for hot fudge sundaes. On Friday nights, Stephanie and I would beg Fred to take us roller-skating. As the Bee Gees and Alicia Bridges sang to us, we would circle the rink hand in hand, watching the gay men who swarmed around us and wishing we could be just like them. We weren't exactly sure what being gay was, but from the little we'd seen and heard on shows like *Three's Company*, we figured it must be thrilling beyond words.

As I got older I realized that I was, in fact, one of those men like Fred. While the prospect was a little bit scary, the idea pleased me to no end. In my room decorated with Shaun Cassidy posters and littered with copies of *Tiger Beat*, I listened to the Village People and imagined a life where men walked around in fabulous costumes and did exciting, if not entirely explicit, things with one another. I imagined myself in my T-shirts and work boots like Fred's and wondered how I'd look with a mustache.

Things changed slightly when I entered junior high and my family moved from an urban area to a small town in the New York countryside. It was the '80s. AIDS had just begun to appear in the news. The other students in my small-town school talked about "fags" and "lezzies" and how awful they were, even as they danced the night away to bands like Wham! and Culture Club. For a number of reasons I was singled out as the school queer, and life was not particularly pleasant. Still, I knew being gay was something special, and I couldn't wait to get out of there and jump headlong into the queer world. I read Gordon Merrick novels and was both horrified and aroused by them. I watched *Making Love* and fantasized about kissing Harry Hamlin. I secretly snuck downstairs to watch the documentaries on gay life shown by the local public television station each June, counting the years until I could be part of it myself.

Once Upon a Time

After high school, I ended up in a college run by fundamentalist Christians. Homosexuality was not particularly encouraged there, and as a result what little gay life existed was kept deeply underground. The queer student body consisted primarily of the women's basketball and softball teams and a handful of repressed men who dated women but snuck into one another's rooms at night for the action they really longed for.

Oddly, I loved the clandestine nature of gay life there. I liked being subversive (even if I was also invisible), and I liked knowing I was doing things (or at least thinking about things) the rest of the school would find appalling. I read books about gay history and was fascinated by the stories of bars with red lights over the doors to warn of police raids. The idea of belonging to a group of people who moved below the surface of society appealed to me greatly, despite the dangers associated with it.

When I graduated and was let out into the real world, I ended up in New York City, smack in the middle of Greenwich Village. Finally, I was surrounded by the culture I'd been waiting my whole life for. Gay bars. Gay bookstores. Gay restaurants. All around me there were queer women and men living their queer lives. It was what I'd dreamed of as Stephanie and I whirled around beneath the glitter ball all those years ago. The first night I stood on a dance floor surrounded by sweaty men moving to the sounds of Janet Jackson, I remembered how Donna Summer had sounded when I was 12, and I felt as though I'd come home.

But there was something else going on in those days. As I read the magazines and newspapers I found all around me, I saw that more and more the articles were about making demands. Queer people were demanding to be allowed to march in other people's parades. We were demanding that people listen to what we had to say. We were demanding that they pay attention to our writing and our art. We were demanding that people stop pointing at us and calling us names.

That's when I realized—being queer was no longer about having our own little corner of the world. Now it was about making everyone be nice to us. It had become about fitting in.

We never used to care. We used to like being different. We thought it was really great to have our own music, our own books, our own style. It was our secret world. OK, so a lot of people didn't think very much of us. And a lot of times people were mean to us and did things like beat us up, take our children away, and fire us. They even blamed things like AIDS on us. So we fought back. We marched in the streets and carried signs into churches. We threw rocks. We stormed city halls across the nation. We took back the night, although the women of the Seven Sisters schools admittedly had the idea first.

And things did change. People started talking about us and what we were demanding. They stopped ignoring us. They stopped saying we were psychotic (officially). They stopped firing us (at least for being gay) and stopped taking our children away (some of the time). They put us on magazine covers and invited us to speak at their conventions. They admitted (reluctantly) that we'd done some really cool things for them. They even gave some of us (the least offensive ones) things like Tony Awards and Grammys.

But they haven't stopped hating us. Not really. They haven't stopped blaming us for things like AIDS. They haven't stopped beating us up or telling their children that if they turn out like us, they'll make Jesus throw up. They might have cut down a little on calling us names to our faces, but when we aren't around, they still talk about what a pain in the ass we are and wish we would just shut up already. They've added us to their list of endangered species, but they still don't care if we survive. They pretend to invite us to their parties, but they hope we won't really come.

So was it worth it? In our bid for respectability, what have we given up? We used to have things like disco and John Waters. Now we have gay marriage and Andrew Sullivan. We used to have our own neighborhoods and our own style. Now even in the Village you can't always tell the queers from the straight wanna-bes who think it's fun to look like us. Straight culture has co-opted everything from our music to our kitsch. Even U2 thinks they're the Village People now, and last night I saw a commercial for Kraft Macaroni and Cheese featuring a contented housewife stirring her pot to the tune of Donna Summer's "Love to Love You Baby."

And what do we have to show for it? We've turned into a serious bunch of people who want to see our queerness as just another part of who we are, rather than as an essentially defining part. Instead of relishing what makes us unique, we want to see it as an accessory we can take off or put on depending upon how we want to appear to the outside world. If showing too much means getting disapproving glances, we tone it down a little. We gather sympathetic straight celebrities around us and ask them to be our friends, so that everyone will see that we're really OK. We watch what we say and what we do because we don't want to give anyone "the wrong impression" about what queers are really like. We want to be just like everyone else, because it makes us feel better.

I'm not saying that fighting for our rights isn't important. I'm not saying that there isn't important work to be done around homophobia and equality and making this a better place for queer youth. I'm not saying I'm not thankful for straight people who stick up for us once in a while.

But why do we have to achieve those things by pushing who we are into the background? Why do we have to be so thrilled when they give us a pat on the back after they've decided that maybe drag queens and inoffensive gay characters are OK because they play well in suburban multiplexes after all? Why do we have to pretend that the men in leather and the dykes on bikes in our pride parades are embarrassing, when secretly most of us wish we could be more like them, if only for a night? Why do we want everyone to like us so much?

Maybe I'm just cranky. But more and more I feel like a kid at story hour. When I talk to gay men a decade older than myself, the conversation is peppered with phrases like "Remember when" and "Back in the old days." Those days are far from ancient history, and they were certainly far from perfect, but in many ways they might as well have belonged to the time of the Brothers Grimm. In this era of political correctness, avalanches of ribbons and causes, and debates over what's right for our community, the past has become something of a fairytale. Increasingly, our gay pride festivities are more about lobbying and planning than they are about partying and letting loose, more dogged sign-waving than celebration.

At one of my first pride rallies in New York, I sat with thousands of other queers as speaker after speaker got up and spoke about our rights and what we'd accomplished during the year in our campaign for respectability. The audience dutifully applauded after each one and shook their fists at appropriate times. So did I, all the time feeling guilty that what I was really feeling was boredom. I could have been at any rally for any group. I didn't feel special or different. I didn't care if Madonna and Tom Hanks liked me.

Then somewhere someone turned on some music. All of a sudden, the sounds of Gloria Gaynor's "I Will Survive" swept over the park. A great roar went up as a group of men, most of whom had probably heard the song when it was first played in a disco, stood up and started to dance. These were men who had been gay before AIDS, before we decided that getting married would make us respectable, before Madonna ever thought we were cool. They'd seen the wonderful highs and the awful lows. And they were dancing because it was fun and because it didn't have to mean anything.

At first, people stared at them as they would a child who had just blurted out some horrible family secret in the middle of a dinner party. They'd broken the solemnity of the speeches and the earnestness of the moment. Then, slowly, throughout the park men and women jumped to their feet and began to join in, hands over their heads as they clapped and sang along. For a few minutes, it was as though I was back in that roller rink. Only this time I was one of the men speeding by, happy to be different. It was a moment that could only happen when 7,000 queers stood up and reminded themselves that to be just like everyone else might be comforting, but it's a lot more fun to be different, even if it costs us something.

I hope we don't ever forget that.